Palca and Pucara

A Study of the Effects of Revolution on Two Bolivian Haciendas

Palca and Pucara

A Study of the Effects of Revolution on Two Bolivian Haciendas

By

ROGER A. SIMMONS

UNIVERSITY OF CALIFORNIA PRESS

BERKELEY·LOS ANGELES·LONDON

University of California Publications in Anthropology
Advisory Editors: J. B. Birdsell, Eugene Hammel, Robert Heizer,
  Roger Keesing, Clement Meighan, H. P. Phillips,
  Albert Spaulding

Volume 9
Approved for publication November 19, 1971

University of California Press
Berkeley and Los Angeles, California

University of California Press, Ltd.
London, England

ISBN: 0-520-09440-9
Library of Congress Catalog Card No.: 78-187742

CONTENTS

ACKNOWLEDGMENTS

This work has many collaborators. First among them is my wife Cynthia Schofield Simmons, who endured eighteen months' separation while I was in the field and whose intelligent influence may be detected on many pages. I am greatly indebted to my advisors, Professor May Díaz, Jack Potter, and William McGreevey for funds and encouragement that made the work possible, and to Professors Kenneth Bock, Gerald Berreman, and Nelson H. H. Graburn for numerous helpful comments. In Bolivia, only the members of the University of Wisconsin Land Tenure Center team, Drs. Ronald J. Clark, Katherine Barnes, Carlos Camacho, and Marcelo Peinado, know how much I owe them. Most deeply, I am indebted to Dr. Jorge Dandler-Hanhart, who worked near me in the field, and to Father Javier Albó, S.J..

I must thank my field assistant, Eusebio Solíz, who also alone knows how much I owe him; Mrs. Esther Lucero, who accomplished the long and tedious task of typing the manuscript; and Laurens Denison, who made all the pen-and-ink drawings.

Finally, I acknowledge the assistance—amounting at times to rescue—of the late Professor T. D. McCown.

CHAPTER I

INTRODUCTION

THE PROBLEM of change, or modernization, in the underdeveloped areas of the world is crucial in our time. For «underdeveloped» Staley's (1961:13) definition may serve: a nation falls into this category if it is marked by chronic mass poverty, not the result of some temporary condition, but caused by methods of production which could be changed to make increased use of available human and natural resources. Underdevelopment usually implies high illiteracy and poor communications, a large percentage of the population engaged in agriculture or living in misery in cities, diffuse or intermittent political structures and a fragmented political culture,[1] which results, in part, from the number of enclaves in the society. The result is not only stagnation, but also potential conflict as the submerged peoples become aware of better conditions elsewhere and begin to demand a share in such benefits.

According to these criteria much of Latin America is underdeveloped, marked by the persistence, from the days under the Spanish, of backwaters filled with «internal colonies» (González Casanova, 1965: 27); of Indians of the countryside, mines and latifundio, whose economic relationship to the city is decidedly asymmetrical; of reflected subcultures; and of politico-military entrepreneurship (caudillismo) (Kling, 1956; Wolf, 1965: 93).

The condition of agriculture defines a crucial dimension of backwardness. Latin American agriculture shows considerable lag relative both to its potential and to industrial development,[2] and it is poorly articulated with the national money economy (Anderson, 1967: 53, 43). Particularly important here is the latifundio, an unbalanced structure of land tenure dating from colonial times. For this reason, I focus in this work on problems of the interior (campo) and of the latifundio.

---

[1] «Political culture» is here defined as the «patterns of individual attitudes and orientations, cognitive, affective, evaluative, toward politics in a political system» (Almond and Powell, 1966, ch. III).

[2] Between 1951 and 1960, industrial production for Latin America as a whole increased 97 percent, while agriculture rose only 47 percent. Given the swift population growth of the area, this left Latin America, after this decade, with a per head industrial advance of 54 percent, while agricultural production grew only 11 percent per head. Though over 50 percent of the economically active population for the region as a whole is engaged in agriculture, this sector accounted for only 20 percent of the total production of the region. Cf. Anderson, 1967: 62.

In particular, I study the results in a localized area of the efforts of one populist party, the Movimiento Nacionalista Revolucionario of Bolivia, to abolish the latifundio. This was part of its overall program to effect agrarian reform, industrial development, economic growth, and social justice in a revolution.

In spite of its violent history (Morse, 1964), Latin America has seen few revolutions in the modern meaning of the word—genuine efforts to transform the social order by violence. Mexico, Bolivia, and Cuba provide the only cases so far. Agrarian reform—the attempt to alter lopsided landholding arrangements on latifundia—has been a crucial aim of all three. I focus here on the effects of the Bolivian agrarian reform on two classic latifundia in the Cochabamba highlands, aiming to assess the changes they brought about on the local level, their significance in the context of social, economic, and political change in Bolivia as a whole, and their general implications for a view of Latin American development, agrarian reform, and modernization.

AGRARIAN REFORM, BOLIVIA

Students agree that the system of latifundia—large, labor-intensive, relatively undercultivated and poorly productive farms, which are still common in Latin America—must change if economic progress and greater prosperity are to be attained by the masses. This need for change arises in part from demographic factors—the rapidly burgeoning population; in part from political and economic factors; and in part from considerations of culture and personality. If the population keeps expanding at its present rate, people will simply need more food than latifundia can provide. Industrialization has not been able to create enough jobs to absorb the population growth (Chonchol, 1965: 75-79), and the fast flow of labor from the land to the cities —itself a sign of stagnation and lack of prospects in the campo— has resulted in a proliferation of urban slums. Frustration here provides a source of instability and violence, especially as the masses grow more aware of better conditions in the developed countries. There is evidence that the latifundio has a close functional link with its apparent opposite, the *minifundio,* or very small farm (Carroll, 1965:175), and that peonage produces people who are shy, apathetic, inward-facing and dependent[3] —hardly the best material for dynamic innovation or nation-building (Vellard, 1963:221).

---

[3] Also illiterate. Weeks (1947) suggests that, in Bolivia, the greatest barrier to social mobility and participation from which the peons suffered was lack of education; also, that this ignorance was the result of policy consciously enforced by the patrones as the strongest chain by which they bound peons to the hacienda.

The hacienda or latifundio[4] tends to constitute at least a partially closed system (Tannenbaum, 1962:80-89; Anderson, 1967:21-22, 62). Although it produces for market and may be considered open to this extent, within itself it tends to be autarchic, producing most or all of what it needs. This acts to curb economic activity in small towns, since the hacienda buys little and sells what it has to sell usually in the city (Tannenbaum, 1962:88). The hacienda economy is poorly articulated with the national exchange economy (Anderson, 1967:62).

Reinforced by the fantastic geographic variation of Latin America and by poor communications, the latifundista has been able to act as a law to himself on his estate, setting up nothing less than a way of life for his peons. Through kinship, marriage, and *compadrazgo,* landowners have frequently been able to dominate whole regions as *caciques* (bosses) (Tannenbaum, 1962:87). In such a situation, entrepreneurial incentives are small; indeed, it is often to the owner's interest to stifle innovation on the part of tenant or peon, since such behavior might help him become independent (Anderson, 1967:50). Further, looking abroad as he often does, living well, the latifundista tends to spend income on imported goods and not to invest in local commerce or industry.

To sum up, we may say with Carroll (1965:175) that «*latifundia* exercise an influence far beyond their boundaries.» And they are still very real. Worked by *colono* or peon labor with, in some regions, tenant and share-cropping arrangements (ILO, 1957), they are typical of the most underveloped areas, and they existed in Bolivia before 1952.

Indeed, if one wanted to choose an extreme case —an almost ideal type which would portray important features of Latin American underdevelopment,— Bolivia would serve as well as any. It was, and is, a poor country. Its political history is a fantasy, a nightmare of strife and terror played out against a landscape D'Orbigny called a «microcosm of the planet», so extreme is its variation. Bolivia's economy has been traditionally dual: extractive mining and agriculture, with some modern industry developing only after World War I (Alexander, 1958:xiv).[5] the economy was markedly skewed; the gulf between the poverty-stricken, illiterate, disenfranchised rural masses and elite was as great as that between the *altiplano* and the steaming Oriente. Typical of the campo were the haciendas, which proliferated after laws were passed during the nineteenth century making each Indian the owner of the land he then held in his possession (Alexander, 1958:13). Unaccusto-

---

[4] Conceived broadly, almost as an ideal type. A full typology of haciendas in Latin America still needs to be written.

[5] Railways were built and the tin industry developed during the period of relative stability from 1880 to 1930 (Patch, 1963:103-105). Bolivia was «half a nation fascinated with the possibilities of Western technology, half a nation ... living in the sixteenth century» (Patch, 1963:105).

med to entrepreneurship or the principles of private property according to Manchester liberalism, the Indian proved easy prey to whites
and mestizos who gobbled up his land at a cheap price.

The prerevolutionary hacienda in Bolivia was, in some ways, from
a social point of view, feudal. The colono[6] was granted a portion of land
on which to build his hut and grow his crops and animals. In return for
this right of usufruct, the Indian had to work on the rest of the estate
in the service of his absentee patrón and in addition render the latter
personal services in his house (a custom known as *pongueaje*), and care
for his animals, and transport his produce to market. Conditions could
be hard indeed for the peon, sometimes running up to as much as six
days of work per week in the service of the patrón. In some areas a
small cash wage was paid (Erasmus, 1964; Vellard, 1963:207). Though
the hacienda produced for the market and sold its goods for cash, such
produce as the peasants raised on their own plots they largely consumed
themselves—a subsistence or subsistence-oriented agriculture—and
their relations with their overlords were personal. Finally, it is perhaps
not quite correct to call the hacienda «feudal» even from a social point
of view since, according to Pirenne (1967:422, 429), serfs during the
Middle Ages in Europe were both exploited *and* protected. He stresses
that there was a familial-protective aspect to lord-serf relations. My
work will suggest that, no matter with what rhetoric the hacienda-
owner in Bolivia surrounded his activities, for some of them noblesse
oblige hardly existed. It was exploitation, no less.

The MNR[7] revolution of 1952 ended this system in Bolivia. In
many cases the peasants themselves, by means of their newly formed
unions, or sindicatos (Patch, 1960:110-111; Heath, 1959), seized land,
houses, vehicles and machinery. The government set up a formal
agrarian reform council. Studies were made and a law drafted and
signed by President Paz Estenssoro at Ucureña in the Cochabamba
Valley on August 2, 1952.

But the Bolivian revolution aimed at more than mere changes in
land tenure. It sought incorporation of the Indian masses into national
life, with a significant raising of their living standards, and creation

---

[6] A significant word. Peonage in Bolivia was often called *colonato*, and González Casanova (1965), Johnson (1969) and Stavenhagen (1965) use the concept
of «internal colony» to describe the condition of people in mines and on haciendas,
i.e., «those populations who produce primary commodities for markets in cities,
who constitute a source of cheap labor for enterprises controlled from the metro-
politan centers, excluded from participation in the political, cultural and other
institutions in the dominant society, a society within a society...» (Johnson,
1969:9). As Stavenhagen (1965:27), among others, points out, independence for
such people simply meant substitution of domination by the Spaniards by that of
the creoles. Exploitation of the Indians continued «having the same characteristics
as before.» I find the concept of «internal colony» useful because it links attitudes and behavior as described for the colonial past (Reyeros, 1949:30-42) with
phenomena I observed in the field. Cf. Chapter V.

[7] Movimiento Nacionalista Revolucionario.

of a unified society and nation. Policies included nationalization of the mines, educational reform, and reform of the franchise (Patch, 1963: 110). An effort was made to teach the Indians to speak Spanish and to make them literate, although they were given the vote regardless of literacy.

It is hard to tell at this point fully to what extent the Bolivian revolutionary counter-elite has succeeded in its avowed modernizing aims. It must be kept in mind that of the three nations in Latin America which have attempted genuine revolutionary change, Bolivia started from by far the lowest base in terms of national integration, infrastructural development and standard of living (Anderson, 1967:305). The entire country might be viewed in a sense as marginal, a backwater or «area of weakened action» (Lambert, 1967:132). Without massive injections of United States aid (which many Bolivians resent as «colonialism» and interference in the internal affairs of their country), it is possible the revolutionaries would have accomplished nothing and discredited right-wing parties would already have resurged to power (Anderson, 1967:110). Moreover, the MNR leaders were by and large moderates—Malloy (1968:445) has called them «reluctant revolutionaries», working within Western liberal traditions.[8] The result has been a «simple» or «restrained» revolution (Johnson, 1966; Patch, 1961), relatively lacking in chiliasm.

That is indeed the precise special interest of Bolivia. What happens when a truly «backward» nation of Latin America, exhibiting certain typical Latin American problems to an extreme degree, attempts a relatively humanistic revolution? In general, indications are that the MNR was not able to contain and satisfy all the demands generated by the upheaval; that numerous and conflicting demands and expectations—in the face of scarce resources—led nearly to chaos, and this was contained only by the resurgence of militarism (Veliz, 1965-1967). If the period 1952 to the present may be viewed as a case of institutional breakdown and reintegration (Patch, 1963:113-114; Malloy, 1968), such reintegration has taken a preeminently traditional course under the present (1964-1969) military guardian regime. It appears that only such a regime has been able to hold things together in the face of fragmentation on every level possible, including the loose coalition of the modernizing elite itself (Malloy, 1968:ch. 13).

This is not to say that the rosca (literally «screw,» colloquial name for the old oligarchy) has managed to return to power and turn the

---

[8] Malloy (1968:254-246, 263; ch. 14) shows that the MNR made no radical break with the past but preserved the institutional structure of the time, seeking only to broaden it. He goes so far as to suggest that the MNR leaders, many of them, were really only middle-class «outs» who wanted in; hence the scramble for patronage which marked the years 1953-1964 and which is still going on. Also, the discredited right wing,, the Falange, still holds power in the cities, in professions, etc. How, in this context, any regime can mobilize resources for development seems a question for research.

clock back (Hennessey, 1964:53). The military regime (at least up until 1969) remained committed to ideals of the revolution. But it is questionable to what extent those ideals can be realized» in an atmosphere of continued instability and interest politics.

As far as events in the countryside go, there is a proliferating literature on the agrarian reform (Carter, 1963; 1964; Erasmus, Heath, and Buechler, 1964; Ferragut, 1963; García, 1964; Heath, 1959; Patch, 1956; 1960; 1963; Smith, 1965). In general, these works conclude that the reform, which aimed broadly at both social justice and economic betterment,[9] has had overall greater success with the former than with the latter. The abolition of peonage, of gratuitous services on the latifundio, meant the Indian no longer was a true social pariah. He could no longer legally be denied certain basic human considerations. An informant told Ferragut (1963:81):

The greatest benefit we have received from the reform is not exactly that they have made us masters of a piece of land, but that now feel ourselves to be men. Before the reform when a *campesino* went to the city they didn't let him into public parks, nor was he received or attended by anybody. Now the *campesino* is received everywhere.

Some thinkers, notably Antezana (quoted in Heath, 1969:207; cf. also Alexander, 1958:76), feel that a «profound psychological transformation» has occurred in the peasant:

when the announcement of the reform was made, they began to walk on their own land and to feel free, as if they were standing on top of a mountain. They learned to speak in a loud voice, with pride and without fear....
The worker of the countryside had been dignified by being given land and liberty in all of its aspects.... Today the *campesino* is the equal of anyone.... The peasant is a human being capable of receiving instruction, of reaching the University, of being owner of the land he works and making it produce, since the land belongs to him who works it.

My central working hypothesis goes counter to this line of thinking, as well as to the assumption on the part of certain writers (Powelson, 1964:53-54; Smith, 1965:16-17) that setting up of family farming on a large scale leads to greater incentive and «pride of achieve-

---

[9] See Urquidi (1953), Malloy (1968:305-307). The ultimate aim of the revolution was socialism, but it was believed this could only be attained by passing through a stage of state capitalism. As Malloy writes, «The aim of the reform was to provide a rational basis for agrarian economic development.» Second, the reform should aim at making the peasant a «motor» force and protector of the revolution. The first aim would be achieved by bringing capitalist forms of production to the campo, the second by meeting the peasants' demand for land and organizing them into unions and militias attached to the revolutionary party.

«The reform was to realize its economic aim by destroying the *latifundia*. The basis of the feudal structure would be shattered, freeing both land and people for more rational ... relationships. The Indian would achieve mobility while at the same time, by grace of becoming a landowner, be enabled to become both a producer and consumer» (Malloy, 1968:306, 307).

ment.» Equally dubious is the related assumption on the part of the reformers themselves that abolition of the latifundio—making the peasant both producer and consumer—would release a drive toward capitalism in the campo. Rather, as Ferragut (1963:138-139) puts it, if the reform solved some problems it helped create others, notably land fragmentation in many areas as a result of population increase and the break-up of great estates; see Erasmus, 1964, 1967; Ferragut, 1963:13; García, 1964:431-432). Certainly these writers are not sure that the formal legal change effected by the reform has been sufficient to create the «transformation» invoked by MNR partisans, like Antezana. They hold that the influence of the latifundio. «beyond its boundaries» extends vertically as well as horizontally, lasting through time in the survival to this day of interactional patterns and attitudes learned during the longstanding patrón-peón relationship. This is to be expected: such patterns and orientations, deeply rooted in family relationships and early learning, are slow to change. I therefore posited that on the level of informal daily interaction, *encogido* (literally «shy,» see Erasmus, 1967, 1968) dependent patterns (for example, toward the patrón or his surrogates) would persist, although displaced or disguised. One might expect also a crisis of leadership or drift among peasants with so little training for leadership. In addition, the granting of plots of land to such peons, far from turning them into innovators or entrepreneurs, would have a conservative effect.[10] Political socialization would probably be rudimentary and lead to a «subject competence» (Almond and Powell, 1966:59, 305). In short, my assumption was that people—the basic building blocks—are important factors in change; that Bolivian peasants would show many vestiges of interactional patterns, learned attitudes and behavior poorly adapted for economic innovation or political incorporation, and that these factors might cause the structural changes occasioned by the agrarian reform to function in unexpected ways. Moreover, my hypothesis was that *these vestiges would appear most strongly where prereform conditions had been most severe.*

Another problem, finally, which became an object of investigation, was the nature of the structural changes brought about by the reform. To what degree did the formal-legal change correlate with the total structural changes, institutional and other, impinging on the peasants' daily lives? Might there not be levels of structural change and stability which needed to be identified and their interrelationships analyzed? What of the effects of scarce economic and educational resources,

---

[10] There was already, at the time I went into the field, some evidence for this. For example, Vellard (1963:chs. 14, 15) documents the reform's failure up to that point to implement a program of cooperatives by which it was hoped to improve production. He shows that most peasants, having received their land, continued on in individualistic subsistence farming and became, if anything, even more hostile to the outside. Cf. Vellard, 1963: 221.

stressed by writers like García and Vellard in connection with Bolivia,[11] which might be expected to perpetuate patterns of political entrepreneurship and illegality in a bureaucracy (Kling, 1956; Moore, 1966: 57-58) or at best result in paralysis. In other words, I suspected that Antezana and other optimists, like Juárez earlier in Mexico, placed too much faith in law, ultimately in ideology, and in theory, as impelling factors in change, and that even the fact of land expropriation might not be sufficient to achieve the results they desired.

My work was accordingly carried out on two former haciendas in the Cochabamba highlands: one a huge ex-hacienda, Palca, where the land is fertile, production traditionally high, but where prereform conditions had been nearly subhuman,[12] and the second, Pucara, a neighboring hacienda of medium size, where conditions had been less severe. Due to limitations of time and resources, Palca received much more intensive study than Pucara, which is not treated below until Chapter IX. Significantly, in view of the above hypothesis, although Palca produces several times the amount of cash crops of the smaller hacienda, and contains within itself peasants who are considerably richer, this is not reflected in innovation; indeed Pucara has made important innovations, notably in connection with its school, not found on the richer place. The area appeared a promising locality to test my hypothesis, as well as differing theories (Erasmus, 1967; Foster, 1965) concerning blocks to innovation among peasantry. I lived among the ex-colonos of these haciendas for a total of thirteen months from June

---

[11] I borrow this idea from Barrington Moore, Jr. (1966:57-58) who suggests that it is impossible for the central government in nonindustrial societies to pay its bureaucracy enough to insure its primary loyalty to the system, to eliminate the demobilizative effects of the diffusion of wealth according to privatistic or family patterns, i.e., «corruption.» Kling (1956) has further shown that mobility in static colonial economies tends to be channelled into the military or politics.

Scarcity of resources, furthermore, is relative. The Bolivian government, in cooperation with organizations such as the Inter-American Development Bank and USAID, has apparently been able to mobilize considerable resources to promote colonization and commercial agriculture in the lowlands to the east. As Malloy (1968:466, 469) shows, the developmental policy of Paz Estenssoro between 1960 and 1964 was mainly to promote a «new Bolivia» in the east based on commercial agriculture and oil at the expense of the «old Bolivia» based on tin. Malloy shows how this was done at the cost of restricting the demands of labor, particularly the miners. I think it can be shown that peasants in the highly populated, subsistence-oriented areas of the altiplano and valleys paid a price also in that they have been courted politically, told they were the «future of Bolivia» etc. (Malloy, 1968:473), and brought into town in trucks with their rifles every time La Paz got nervous; and yet they have been left to their own devices until, hypothetically, other economic alternatives have been created elsewhere in the society.

[12] Nuclear Palca, where this study was carried out, has a present population of 383, with 86 family heads. Professor Ronald Clark of the Land Tenure Center of the University of Wisconsin, who has spent four years studying land problems in all parts of Bolivia, assures me that conditions in Palca are the worst he knows. In general, large farms had more severe prereform conditions for the peasant than medium and small farms.

1967 to November 1968. Working with the help of an interpreter, since the peasants of this region are virtually monolingual in Quechua, I participated in the people's lives as fully as possible, eating and drinking with them, sharing their fiestas, funerals, weddings and labor. Methods used were those of traditional ethnography: observation, participant observation, formal and informal interviews. What I felt to be strategic life histories were gathered. In addition, I had access to production data for Palca and social questionnaires from that hacienda gathered by Sr. Marcelo Peinado of the Land Tenure Center of the University of Wisconsin in whose company I visited the area for the first time in June 1967. I had occasion, even, to attempt two small innovations at Palca myself and observe the peasants' attitudes toward these. Finally, I had the advantage of consultation with Bolivian agronomists located on an experimental farm *(granja)* run by the Alliance for Progress at Ucuchi Kancha above nuclear Palca.

Persistence and change in all aspects of culture were the focus of attention. In particular, I was concerned with the history of the haciendas and how this was reflected in the present daily life of the peasants: what are the present economic correlates, for example, of encogido attitudes and details of behavior inherited from the past? How does the past influence the present in terms of patterns of leadership, marketing, labor, political and ceremonial behavior? In a sense it was necessary to live on two levels—to be an historian of the traditional type gathering narrative, and to observe as carefully as possible comminuted details of everyday life. In this way I tried to see how structural, historical and attitudinal factors interact to influence events in the present time.

To accomplish this it was necessary to study behavior not only within the hacienda, but in every context the peasant enters: in provincial towns, at weddings and fairs, at political rallies and fiestas. The hacienda in my opinion cannot be understood if conceptualized as a closed system; one must also study the «hinge groups» or «cultural» brokers by means of which it articulates with the larger society. The revolution (at least nominally) substituted «modernizing» brokers for those of a «traditional» type, in Wolf's terminology (1965:97-98). It was an important subject for research to discover just how the new linkages which have resulted from the agrarian reform actually function on the grassroots level.

There are as yet few intensive, qualitative studies of haciendas (Holmberg, 1960; Stein, 1961; see also Cotler, 1970a; 1970b). The proliferating literature on the Bolivian agrarian reform, cited above, consists of summary works in the main. Carter's (1964, 1963) study of an indigenous community and seven ex-haciendas near La Paz is a groundbreaking work, a type of controlled comparison in some ways similar to that which I attempted. However, Carter documented mainly structural changes within the communities induced by the reform; he has not dealt in great detail with the structure and function of the new «cultural brokers» which have sprung up since then. Further, the results of my study qualify his, notably in regard to the effects of education and changes in access to land. There is still plenty of room for the kind of studies in depth Nelson (1964: 77) called for, focusing on values: what does the hacienda *campesino* want? What are his aims in life? Can certain assumptions, such as the «revolution of rising expectations,» be applied to him and if so, to what degree? Haciendas are still largely—at least in their development since 1810—unstudied (Wolf, 1955: 468; Mörner, 1973: 215).

The names of places and individuals have been changed for obvious reasons.

CHAPTER II

THE GENERAL SETTING

THE EX-HACIENDAS of Palca and Pucara lie side by side in the highlands 64 kilometers east of the city of Cochabamba within easy access of the Cochabamba-Santa Cruz Highway. They form part of the canton of Tiraque, the nearest small town about 7 kilometers distant; the canton of Tiraque lies in the province of Arani, which in turn belongs to the Department of Cochabamba. The area is a vast upland plain of great beauty about 9,000 feet above sea level, like a deep dusty sea in the dry season, lush and green during the rains. Mountains rise on every side: jagged peaks every shade of black and brown often streaked with snow. When it snows on the heights, as it often does during the winter in June, it can get cold in Palca; frosts and hailstorms pose hazards for the crops, but on the whole temperature is moderate, (annual average 50° F) only slightly colder than the city of Cocha-bamba itself.. There is, however, considerable variation in rainfall from year to year, a factor which influences production particularly of pota-toes, the main crop, and prices and income of the campesinos are accord-ingly affected. Thus, average rainfall for the city of Cochabamba for the past ten years is 580.9 mm.[13] More detailed, though incomplete data [14] indicate that total rainfall in a given year can be as low as 250 mm. (e.g. in 1958) and as high as 810 mm. (1960). As important perhaps from the point of view of the peasant is the fact that rainfall in a given month can vary considerably, from, for example, 20 mm. in February of 1958 to 219 mm. in February of 1968. The peasant finishes plant-ing potatoes by October or November at the latest. He depends on the rainy season (December through March) to stimulate his crop. The im-pact of rainfall variation on potato-growing, not only from year to year but from month to month, seems apparent, since 260 mm. in April during the harvest (as happened in 1960) does less good than the same figure in January or February. Finally, there is great microclimatical variation among potato-growing regions in Bolivia, which influences Palca's market and income.

The area (generally known as the Tiraque plateau) is one of great ecological similarity: sweeping brown plains with clayey soil suited for potatoes, wheat or barley, and livestock—sheep and cattle. It is also

---

[13] From *Statistical Abstract of Latin America, 1968:49.*
[14] From United States Department of Commerce, *Environmental Data Service,* vols. 1-20. Environmental Science Services Administration, Washington, D.C.

one of cultural similarity: the peasants, by and large, share the same single language—Quechua—and the same material culture, religion, social organization and ceremonies. Spanish is spoken within the town of Tiraque itself, but only a smattering has penetrated the surrounding countryside. The region is of interest for the wide variety of systems of land tenure it presents. Besides the huge ex-latifundio, Palca, there are medium-sized haciendas like Pucara; small haciendas, which were not affected by the reform and are to this day worked by their old patrones or in sharecropper arrangements with the peasants; and small independent farms or *piquerías* worked by peasants who managed to buy plots of land from their patrones before the reform. The area is almost a perfect natural laboratory in which the effects of revolution on different types of land tenure may be studied.

According to Leonard (1952:119-120), the break-up of large Colonial land grants in the Cochabamba Valley proper began in the late eighteenth century and increased rapidly after independence. This process continued up until the reform, so that even in the late 1940s the latifundio was rare in the Upper Cochabamba Valley; instead, there were many minifundios and great pressure on the land (Leonard, 1952:120). It is possible that this process was in progress on the Tiraque plateau also, but at a slower rate. At all events we shall note a tendency in this somewhat marginal area to follow events that happened in the Cochabamba Valley since the reform.

HISTORY

The great hacienda of Palca was a true latifundio—8,800 hectares, according to its old patrón, who claims that it extended in part down to the subtropical valleys *(yungas)* of the Chapáre nearly 40 kilometers distant, and that parts of it were not even measured let alone exploited. It consisted of five sections *(comarcas)* in varied ecological zones ranging from mountain heights above the Tiraque plain to the yungas. My study was confined to nuclear Palca on the upland plain described above, where the hacienda house was located, and which shares ecological similarity with its neighbor, Pucara.

Palca is something of a myth in the area. Its old patrón and local townspeople are fond of reminiscing about how big and beautiful it used to be; how it reached from the mountaintops all the way down to the yungas where even its boundaries were lost in green and mist. The hacienda was famous for its flower gardens and four hundred beehives—the biggest honey producer in the Department of Cochabamba, according to some—and it was also one of Bolivia's largest potato farms. Both peasants and patrón agree on this: a great number of potatoes were produced on the hacienda before the reform, as indeed there are now, and the patrón owned much livestock, principally sheep and fine cattle.

Anyone visiting the hacienda today can see traces of its former beauty: the tall lanes of eucalyptus and evergreen lining the road up to the hacienda house, which is large and imposing though crumbling pathetically in disrepair; the grove of deep pines in front of the house, half turned to jagged stumps now as the peasants chop down more and more trees to make *chicha,* the common maize beer; the house grounds themselves swamped by weeds and the dung of men and animals. In a sense, the house symbolizes the loosening of ties, the breakdown of order and «shapelessness,» which has been one result of the agrarian reform at Palca. The squalor, physical and moral, of the peasant family who have taken over part of the house, reinforces this impression.

Adding to the legendary quality of Palca is the sketchiness of historical information concerning the place. According to the ex-patrón, around 1870 in the time of President Melgarejo, the Indians of Palca acquired legal rights to the hacienda. In 1879, the year of the War of the Pacific, various whites appeared at the farm and induced the Indians to enlist in the army in return for lands farther east in the Chapáre. Several did agree to leave their land, and when they returned from the war, they were told that their lands at Palca had been rented from the government by a family from the city of Cochabamba. Information here is very sketchy—neither the ex-patrón nor anyone else could tell me more than this. By 1889 the farm was in the hands of another family who, so the story goes, lost it in a card game to one Ignacio Hinojosa whose son, Mateo, was the last patrón—a harsh man who bought new land and made Palca the biggest estate in the area.

But if we are in doubt as to the details of Palca's chronicle, we are in little doubt as to the actual daily conditions under which the peons lived in the days before the revolution. If one feels oddly haunted by the past beauty of the hacienda, nostalgia quickly fades when one realizes the brutality and exploitation on which that beauty rested. Without exception the campesinos testify that, under the old order, they had to work from six in the morning to six at night six days a week and sometimes, when there was pressure, even seven—that is, each family had to provide a laborer, father or able-bodied son, to work the patrón's fields. On the seventh day they did not rest but worked their own plots (*chacras* or *pegujales*). The produce of the latter, even, was shared with the patrón according to the system of compañía: the patrón provided the peasant with seed, in return for which the potato crop was shared fifty-fifty with the hacendado at harvest time. In other crops—wheat, beans, barley—the patrón took a smaller percentage. In addition, he took the fruit of one of each ten rows of potatoes which remained to the peasants, a custom known as *prevenencia,* and one of each ten lambs born to the peasant's flock each year (*diezmos*). A small sum of cash had to be paid to the patrón for each burro, foal, or calf, born in the peasant's herd. The peasants claim the hacendado took half their manure. They were unanimous in response to the very simple question: «How did you live?» «Did you have enough to eat?» «We

PALCA

Permanecidos

Echados

Dependents

V. Pozo

D. Guzmán

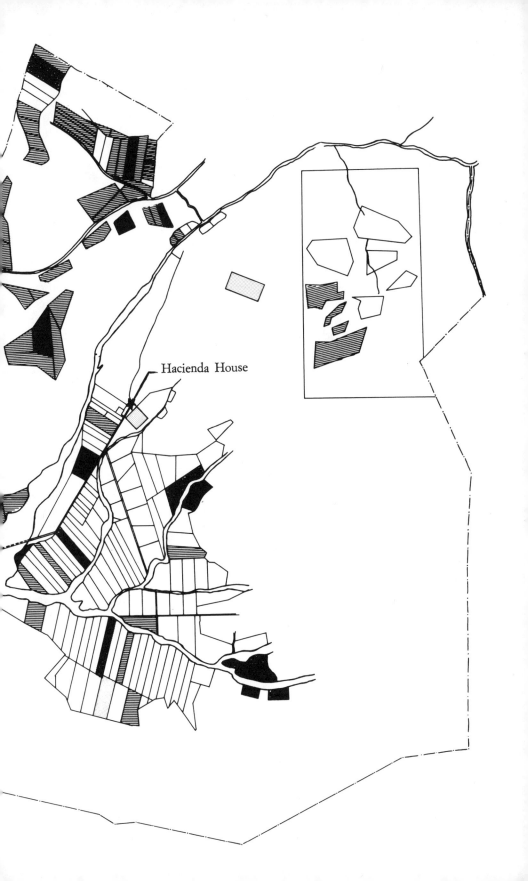

Hacienda House

never had enough,» they in effect replied, «never really enough.» They say that, due to the patrón's work schedule, they lacked time to plow more than a percentage of their fields, sometimes, less than a half. They were willing to work extra for the patrón, at times, for food. Women had to work also, rising very early to prepare meals for men in the fields; they had to carry meals into the fields and were whipped if late. They had to spin thread from lamb's wool and make bags and blankets for the patrón. The women claim they never had time to care for their children properly.

The regime was brutal, enforced with the whip by a mestizo steward *(mayordomo)* from Punata or Cochabamba employed by the patrón and three foremen *(curacas)* chosen from among the peasants themselves. The peasants say if they arrived a little late to work they were beaten with the whip; if they missed a day's work, they received a week's more service in the house of the patrón (pongueaje) or the patrón might take another lamb. The peasants' stories can be vivid—for example, from a talk with Cesario Zapata:

I asked about abuses. He said Vallejos (a mayordomo) was *bad.* Punished his father when the latter got tired harvesting potatoes. Vallejos beat his father in the face with his fists, Cesario said.

Or this from an interview with a peasant who was a child when his father was evicted from the hacienda:

I asked Jacinto why the patrón threw him off the place. He said his father, Pedro Sánchez, missed one day of work when his (Pedro's) brother got married. The mayordomo came to take a burro from Pedro for this, but Jacinto said his father didn't want to give up the animal, and the mayordomo (whose name Jacinto knows only as Ricardo) hit his father in the face with his whip. He hit his father in the eye and put it out. After this, Jacinto said his father pulled the mayordomo from his horse and the horse kicked the mayordomo. After this, the family was kicked out: the mayordomo told the patrón. He said that when his family was evicted, the patrón totally destroyed their house and took all their harvest; he said that Hinojosa (the patrón) chased his father with a revolver and his father had to escape. I asked Jacinto how he felt, seeing all this happen. He said he was only twelve years old then and very small, he knew only fear. «We were all in the hand of the patrón,» he told Eusebio, my field assistant, in Quechua. The patrón kicked them off the hacienda and they went to live in Sakabambilia with friends.

Jorge Icaza, in his novel *Huasipungo,* which treats of Quechua-speaking peons in the highlands of Ecuador, shows there is a point at which the Indians may rebel: when the patrón tries to take away their houseplot *(huasipungo).* Other students (Carter, 1963; Goins, 1954) also stress the strength of the peon's de facto tie to his house-plot, whether or not it is legalized on paper in a court. It is a testimony to the supineness of the Palca peasants, the rigor of the system, that some twenty-eight to thirty families were evicted from the hacienda before the reform, and there was no rebellion. The peasants do not seem to recall even any unwritten rules which, if violated, might have goaded them to revolt.[15] They all felt themselves «in the hands of the patrón.» The women say that they feared, sexually, one of the curacas when they were away pasturing animals in the hills; but there is no evidence here of droit de seigneur, as has been found elsewhere in Bolivia (Patch, 1963:114). The exploitation seems to have been mainly economic. Besides all their other duties, the peons were required to carry the patrón's produce to market in Cochabamba on the backs of their own burros: a long and tortuous process in the days before the construction of the Santa Cruz-Cochabamba highway.[16] They had to care and feed themselves all the while they were away, losing time from their own fields. Each family had to provide a male laborer in turn for a week's household service in the patrón's houses in Punata, Cochabamba, or on the hacienda proper; this man also had to care for the patrón's animals. There was no payment for these services, known as pongueaje, and since there were only about sixty families on the hacienda before the reform, each family got hit with pongueaje about once a month.

In details of everyday interaction, an almost feudal deference was enjoined upon the peasants. They say that, before the reform, they had to take off their hats and kneel before the patrón and call him «Tatay» or «Papasuy» («little father» in Quechua). If they did not do this, although they would not be whipped, the patrón would not like it. «He would not see or hear anything that happened to that campesino,» as one informant put it. In return, the peasant received his plot of land, a few hand tools and perhaps a pair of *abarcas* (sandals made of leather and old rubber tires) at carnival time. The patrón also gave his peons grain for the making of chicha at carnival, at the fiesta of Palca's patrón saint, Santa Rosario, in October, and for the threshing of his own grain.

Everything, in short, even subsistence from their fields came to the peasants largely as a kind of gift from the outside; their services in turn to the hacienda were gratuitous. It is not surprising to find traces of dependency or fatalism, a certain lack of initiative, persisting today after years of living under such a system. The precariousness of their lives—the wide fluctuations of yearly rainfall (only partly eased by irrigation) and the frequent threat of hail and frost—doubtless reinforce such attitudes as well as a reluctance to postpone enjoyment of whatever brief pleasure life may offer.

Houses were tiny—mud huts with *paja brava* (mountain grass) roofs. People slept on the mud floor or on crude beds of clay. Technology was purely of the paleoecotype of Wolf: hand tools of wood and plows drawn by oxen of a type unchanged since the Conquest. Even the most rudimentary elements of sanitation were lacking. The

---

[15] It is possible that they exaggerate now in order to point up how far they have come since the reform. The peasants almost without exception appear grateful to the reform and glorify it.

[16] The highway, for a time the only major paved road in Bolivia, was completed with Point Four aid in 1954. It has reduced, but not solved, the problem of the peasants' isolation.

peasants did not know doctors and would have had no money to pay for modern medicine even if it had been available. Their agriculture was—from the peasants' point of view—almost purely subsistence, they consumed the fruits of their plots. In short, it was a dark, squalid, muddy life, relieved only by sex and occasional binges on chicha. There was no school up until about three years before the reform. The peasants say the patrón installed a school at this time because «he had heard rumors» of the coming reform and wanted to dodge it, just as he bought a tractor, thresher, and two trucks at about the same time in the attempt to have his hacienda pass as a «commercial enterprise.» [17] But the school does not seem to have been worth much: «As soon as a kid learned a little, the patrón threw him out,» one peasant told us. At all events he would not allow a child to stay in the school more than one year.

The whole system worked against the colono, not only on the hacienda proper but in the world outside. Although there was nothing here like the *rurales* of Mexico who could arrest and return a runaway peon to his hacienda,[18] it does appear that in the world outside the dice were heavily loaded against the colonos. Poor and illiterate in their homespun lamb's wool, knowing nothing but traditional farming in that region—where could they go, what other work could they find in a country so heavily agricultural?

---

[17] Though the Bolivian reform aimed to abolish the latifundio, it tried at the same time to preserve large commercial farms which paid cash wages and had received intense capital investment; the aim was to abolish social injustice, but not at the cost of production (Heath, 1959:3). A not infrequent charge heard in Bolivia is that some landowners, through bribery or adroit political rope-skipping (joining the MNR at the right time), managed to have their latifundia declared commercial enterprises, or *empresas*.

It should perhaps be stressed further that the latifundio system bound the landowners also; it was not simply a case of individual malice on the part of owners against their peons. Sr. Mateo Hinojosa, for example, the patrón of Palca, told me in an interview that if he had tried to treat his «Indios» differently his fellow hacendados would have ostracized him. The hacendados seem to have genuinely feared «letting up» on the Indians for fear of loosing a hurricane, a fear not wholly unrealistic in view of excesses committed by peasants in the wake of the reform (Patch, 1963; Heath, 1959).

[18] Town police would, however, return a man who had deserted his family. Palca's peons were apparently always free to leave, yet few did so voluntarily; in effect they *chose* to stay since conditions were even worse for them if they gave up their lands (Lambert, 1967:77). In a sense, we may see Palca as a kind of limiting case of dyadic contract (Foster, 1961, 1965): the peons received little from the patrón in return for what they gave; but they did receive land in usufruct, and sizable and fertile plots relatively in the area, and they had a certain security. Significantly, all but one or two of those evicted chose to return to Palca after the reform, although it cost them a great deal to do this. They suffered much outside the hacienda, as will be shown.

In this region, moreover, the landowners' power seems to have derived more from the social and cultural isolation of the peasants than from population density and labor surplus per se (Burke, 1967:128).

Nor could they count on any kind of decent reception in the halls of town authorities. «All was the patrón,» the peasants are fond of saying. «The townspeople *(vecinos)* had no respect for us.» The patrón had his spies and informers, notably in Tiraque; if the peasants murmured in their cups against the patrón, it could be reported to the latter and severe action taken. It was this mechanism, in part, which led to the eviction of thirty families in the years before the reform, in the mid-1940s during the presidency of Gualberto Villarroel. For example, from an interview with Zenon Rodríguez, an old man whom the patrón evicted:

He said there were discontented people *(descontentos)* in the time of Villarroel ... and Sinforiano Vargas especially talked, was a kind of leader. Sinforiano got drunk in Tiraque and said «¡Viva Villarroel! We're going to throw the patrones out and be patrones.» Hinojosa heard of this through his lawyer, José Montaño of Tiraque, and had Sinforiano arrested with soldiers and thrown in jail in Cochabamba for three months.

From Eugenio Vargas, another of the evicted peasants *(echados)* and only surviving brother of Sinforiano, we received the same story. Also, not only did he have his informers, the patrón had *muñeca* («pull») with the police and military. The severity of the system had an atomizing effect on the peasants which kept them from organizing: this «shapelessness,» apathy, atomization and inability to organize will be a pervasive theme in this work. For example, Irina Ochoa, widow of Cornelio Vargas who became a leader among the evicted peasants, speaks:

I asked the old woman why their family was thrown off the hacienda.... She said when her husband was a bit drunk in Tiraque and knew of Villarroel's reform law that said they weren't going to have to work anymore for the patrón—that her husband shot off his mouth like his brother Sinforiano and that Hinojosa (the patrón) was informed of this. She said that Sinforiano shot off his mouth and was arrested and squealed on Cornelio, said that Cornelio had said the same thing. Hinojosa learned of this and Cornelio was thrown off the place.... She said Cornelio was angry with Sinforiano for this.

Even close kinship did not always stand the pressure. The peasants claim also that they were subjected to cruel treatment while imprisoned in Cochabamba, being taken out often and plunged naked into a cold lake up to their chins from eight in the morning to three in the afternoon, not being allowed to move. Several peasants died from this treatment.

It is significant to note that, while Palca never underwent a genuine jacquerie-type rebellion before the reform, yet in a sense there may be said to have occurred a kind of incipient rebellion in the verbal outbursts of the peons during the time of Villarroel,[19] which led to the

---

[19] Colonel Gualberto Villarroel, the first MNR president of Bolivia from 1943 to 1946. This was a period of marked unrest: strikes in mines and haciendas (Bernard, 1969: 997) precipitated, on one level, by inflation and a massacre of

expulsion of thirty families. None of this was focused or organized; the peasants took no action against the system, nor did outside organizers appear to inform the peasants of their rights under Villarroel's pioneer and very mild agrarian reform law. The peasants, as they themselves put it, simply heard «rumores» and began to «talk,» and the patrón's tough and efficient boom fell on their heads. It must be stressed again that there were no posts of leadership among the peasants at this time except the mayordomos, imposed by the patrón, and the curacas, who were generally the latter's favorites (see Chapter VI). There existed no social groupings above the level of the nuclear or slightly extended family, which might have provided organizational focal points. It seems likely that the implicit and premature rebellion (if we may call it that) during Villarroel's time reduced even further the leadership potential in Palca, since among the evicted peasants were those with at least the initiative and courage to speak against the patrón. Hence the vacuum, the crisis of leadership which resulted when the patrón and his organization were removed. The first secretary-general, or *dirigente,* of their sindicato, for example, Fortunato López, was chosen for no other reason than that he was the only person in the community at that time who could speak some Spanish. The peasants felt that only such a person could help them handle their dealings with the outside world in the absence of the patrón. Today they complain bitterly that López took bribes from the patrón and rode around the hacienda himself on horseback «like a patrón,» and they blame López for the fact that the patrón and his mayordomo were able to persist at Palca over a year after the revolution, until 1954, although with a reduced work schedule.[20] As will be amply documented in Chapter VI, drift, confusion, atomization and problems of leadership continue to plague Palca at the present day.

After their eviction from the hacienda, the echados spent many years wandering from place to place in the general vicinity. Here and there they might be given a piece of land on another hacienda where they lived more or less badly; or they attached themselves to other peasants and scraped along on sharecropping arrangements. With the triumph of the MNR in April 1952 and the election of Paz Estenssoro

---

tin miners at Catavi, on another by a growing crisis of legitimacy stemming from the Chaco War (Patch, 1956). Villarroel was concerned with Indian problems; the MNR during his term organized the First National Indian Congress; and the government legally abolished pongueaje and ordered the establishment of schools (Bernard, 1969:998-999). Villarroel fell and the law was never enforced, but his term may be seen as a harbinger of the 1952 revolution. Cf. Chapter VI, below.

[20] The peasants themselves say «We are very passive» and admit that it was only when campesinos from neighboring haciendas armed themselves and surrounded Palca «on all sides» that they once and for all forced the patrón and his administrator out. During this time, as earlier, the patrón visited Palca only occasionally during the potato harvest, and the administrator lived in the hacienda house.

as president, the peasants claim that they were told by their leaders, notably José Rojas, Salvador Vásquez and Jorge Solíz, that they had an obligation to return to their lands in Palca; in general, this seems to have been their inclination anyway, and after a long hard struggle they succeeded in gaining full title to their lands in 1956. This cost them a great deal of money for lawyers, documents, etc., in many cases they were forced to sell their animals. To this day the echados in Palca are in general poorer than those who stayed. For reasons to be discussed, they did not always receive the same plots they had tilled before, and their plots today are smaller than those who were not evicted.

Further, the latter do not seem to have always welcomed the echados; there was a degree of conflict upon their return which has implications that will be discussed. In general, we may say that the latifundio at Palca is a thing of the past, having been broken up into family farms which, from a structural point of view, resemble the small independent farms of the United States or England. Yet they do not, for various and complex reasons, function as such. While the peons of Palca have gained a great deal from the agrarian reform, it is problematical whether the «profound psychological transformation» cited by Antezana above, has occurred. They are still a long way from becoming a race of modern farmers.

Finally, as has been noted elsewhere (Flores, *in* Parsons, Raup et al., 1951:244), as a frequent result of agrarian reform, population has notably increased at Palca—from roughly sixty families [21] in the time of the patrón to eighty-six at present, representing a total population of 383. One reason for this seems to be that Palca was a kind of «dumping ground» for criminals and their families during and after the revolution, a frontier area with plenty of land where undesirables from other sindicatos could be transported and given plots.

Another factor in the population increase appears to be a general slackening of family discipline since the reform. While before, parents were strict with their children to protect them from the whip, young people today are allowed ample time to go out «walking» in the evening. Teen-agers move about fairly freely in concubinage and small stigma is attached to unwed motherhood. Better diet and improved medical care have probably lowered the death rate. There is a growing number of landless youth living with their fathers. It is ironical that the benefits of the reform present Palca with a problem it never knew traditionally: a growing land shortage which promises to become severe in the years ahead. In this manner the hacienda follows trends in the upper Cochabamba Valley proper and many parts of the nation.

After his eviction as first dirigente, López was badly beaten and driven into Cochabamba where he lived for nine years. He has recently returned to Palca where he has received a small plot and works chiefly as a mason.

[21] This figure includes both those who were evicted by the patrón and those who stayed. After eviction, of course, those actually resident on the hacienda were much less than sixty. Cf. Peinado, 1969:206.

CHAPTER III

TECHNOLOGY AND MATERIAL CULTURE

THE VISITOR to Palca today will see, should he arrive for the first time in winter as I did, the great plain gleaming gold with wheat and barley ready for harvest. Here and there lie fallow fields and the peasants' houses like little loaves, without exception made of mud mixed with straw the color of the plain. The only variation one notices is the sun striking roofs of *calamina* (corrugated iron) or shining red on roofs of tile. In a sense these items are mutations in the midst of the sea, sparks of change in the mud. The peasants assure you they never had such things before the reform.

Moving onto the hacienda and walking around, one finds indeed that there are many such sparks, but always tiny and diminished against the large background of sameness. The peasants' houses are various, for example, but only in detail, within narrow limits. In this they are like the peasants' wealth and their lives, which have become more various since the reform, but always within limits. Some houses are a few square feet larger than others. Some have roofs of tile or sheet metal which serve, the peasants say, better than more primitive types to keep the rain out. Some walls are made of *fachada,* or smooth mud-and-straw, some of bricks of the same material; but the basic pattern is the same: the ex-colono's house is a small, plain, oblong mud building consisting of one room where people sleep, eat, relax and make love, receive guests. Adjacent may be various smaller sheds made of the same material, which serve as storehouses for crops or tools. Outside the house, also, will be a hive-shaped mud oven and a stand made of mud for holding the *perol*, the great iron basin for the making of chicha. A not infrequent pattern makes use of a walled open courtyard or square, as in the house of Don Dionisio Guzmán, secretary-general of the sindicato, and one of the richest men in the community (see fig. 1).

A few of the poorer houses, particularly those belonging to certain aged peasants, are very small indeed and lack windows; informants say these represent the type everyone lived in before the reform. Such houses are little more than huts built low to the ground, with roofs of pure paja brava.[22] They are totally windowless while the others have

---

[22] It must be noted that, in several cases, peasants have built new and more spacious houses to live in since the reform, these lying adjacent to houses of the older type in which their parents lived. The latter are now used as kitchens,

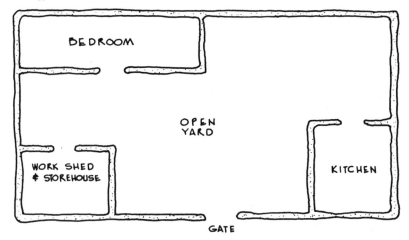

Figure 1

one or two, occasionally up to four gaping black holes in the wall without glass. Between the most traditional houses and the largest houses with tile or metal roofs are many of intermediate type with walls of either *fachada* (smooth dried mud) or mud brick and roofs of dry eucalyptus branches stretched over rafters of the same tree over which the thick mud-traw combination has been spread. In general, these three subtypes of mud house correlate with wealth levels in the community, the poorest people living in the most traditional type and the richest occupying the largest houses. However, it should be stressed that there are cases of peasants who are relatively well-off who have still not improved their houses or adopted modern consumer goods. It is perhaps significant that these people are to be found in more isolated upland regions of nuclear Palca, which are nonetheless productive and where they own sizable plots of land.[23]

Significant, perhaps, also is the fact that there are cases of peasants who according to our figures are neither poor nor isolated, yet they seem to have made almost no effort to modernize. These are among the encogido in the community, and they are also heavy drinkers. Yet such people have usually at least expanded the size of their dwellings and adopted beds or a new tool, such as a wheelbarrow. There are only at most two or three peasant houses which represent the literal image of the past, and as might be expected, their occupants, ragged and

---

storehouses, etc. In short, the tendency Patch (1956: 261) noted for traits not to displace but to complement each other among these people applies to housing as well as to other realms of material culture.

[23] Mariano Alvarez, one peasant I asked about this, replied: «We can't use a bicycle up here.» He claimed to have no interest in buying a radio or phonograph, saying he preferred to put his money into buying good fertilizer, which he needs a lot of, since he has a great deal of land. He, like many other peasants, has a high investment in chicha-making equipment.

grizzled, shy, callado (shut up) bear in every gesture the stamp of the peon.

Palca possesses only one public building, its schoolhouse upon which, significantly, construction has been begun but remains unfinished. A frame has been inserted in one of the windows; part of a roof of corrugated iron and tile has been put on; but the rest remains unfinished, with plants sprouting from an earlier roof of mud, which also was never finished and which has fallen through in places leaving several big black holes. The children attend school in a room in the old hacienda house, which the peasants themselves recognize as being cramped and inadequate. When it is realized that, since the reform, even the most remote and poverty-stricken communities have completed a school; [24] that Palca is not isolated and anything but poor relative to other peasant communities; that, finally, the peasants *want* a school as evidenced by their recognition that one room in the decayed hacienda house is inadequate for their children, the question arises why they have not built one.

Prior to my entrance in the community, as a kind of precondition for my working there, they asked me for $75 to help them buy roofing materials. (They obtained also $75 from my friend Marcelo Peinado of the University of Wisconsin Land Tenure Center and chipped in $75 of their own!) The $225 worth of new roofing materials now lies rusting and bleaching. It appears that the peasants of Palca are able to complete a considerable number of minor individual innovations in their lives; but their sole collective public building stands abandoned to the elements. The fragmented individual innovations stand, perhaps, as a symbol of the atomization of the community; the school is an image of their inability at present to «follow through» a collective project—it too reflects atomization, a theme to be dramatized again and again in this work.

If you enter any house, even on a warm day, it is damp, cold and dirty in the dark room, and you are liable to be eaten by fleas. Across the courtyard may be strung the torn carcass of a sheep drying in the sun for *charki,* flies everywhere, a radio blaring. There is no central heating; floors are of hard-packed mud as they were before the reform. Latrines have never been present. The peasants say their huts were totally without furniture before the reform. Now, without exception in every house I visited, there was a cheap wooden table and chair at least, sometimes three or four tables with several chairs and benches. The peasants without exception have wooden beds now, which they lacked before the reform; then they slept on the floor or on raised cots of clay called *estradas.* But their beds are seldom made and consist of a jumble of ponchos, blankets, rags, anything which lies

---

[24] This is the impression of my travels; also of everyone I talked to in Bolivia, Bolivians and North Americans alike.

to hand on which they throw themselves fully clothed, exhausted after work or drunk after chicha. Lacking is a sense of order, of symmetry; this mirrors, one feels, the lack of organization of their symbolic life, a certain apathy and confusion.

The following from my field notes may give a sense of what it is like; it is the house, again, of Don Dionisio Guzmán:

The bedroom is a shed, oblong, 35 or 40 feet long, with cheap plain wood beds at either end. The roof is of tile, unlike most in this community. Mud floors and walls, damp and cold. On rafters overhead are draped colorful *polleras* belonging to Doña Basilia, wife of Don D., shawls—much colored cloth and clothing of all types which they use in fiestas. Small flags of Bolivia on the wall; all kinds of knick-knacks: old newspapers, pictures of Ovando and Barrientos, a calendar bordered by all of Bolivia's presidents draped in ribbons of yellow, red and green, the flag's colors, like Barrientos himself making you wonder just where the break with the past has been; an educational picture of the Battle of Ingavi showing a general grandiosely waving his sword in the direction of another army across a rolling plain under a rainbow also conveniently colored red, yellow, green; two flags over an old carbine with the motto «¡Viva el 2 de Agosto! ¡Viva la Reforma Agraria!» A sizable table of solid brown wood lies between the beds against the wall; on this a good Crown phonograph and radio.... Guzmán turned this on for us and we got La Paz quite well. I noticed a small shed opposite the open door against which a wheelbarrow was leaning, quite new, and inside the shed were their traditional tools and a brand new American-style pickaxe. At the opposite end of the room, over the bed, a small shrine with babyblue and gold background, cheaplooking, of the Santa de la Cruz.

None of the above, with the exception of the shrine, traditional tools and women's clothing, would have been present before the reform. Of particular interest are the radio, phonograph, and the new pickaxe and wheelbarrow. Many peasants today have radios, often of transistor type ranging in price from 480 to 1,200 pesos ($40 to $100). There is a sprinkling of sewing machines ($30 to $60), a lighter sprinkling of phonographs, and the average young man today has a bicycle which he buys used in Punata for $35 to $50. What is most significant here is that such innovations as the peasants have adopted consist largely of consumer goods and minor improvements on their houses. They have not invested in capital goods which would permit them to alter their ecotype. The peasants of this region lived before the reform and they still live under a system of paleotechnic type (Wolf, 1966: 19-20).

There have been only minor innovations in the realm of capital goods. The new American-style pickaxe and wheelbarrow would not have been in their repertory before the reform (though the patrón might have owned them to use on his own land). The peasants make use of insecticides and chemical fertilizers now, which they say were unknown both to the patrón and to themselves before the reform and which, they claim, keeps their production at present equal to prereform levels even though they work shorter hours now and less arduously. Four peasants possess hand plows of steel, which were unknown before the reform. Tractors are occasionally hired from Punata (at considerable expense) to break up hard ground for planting. But the peasants' basic tool kit remains unchanged since the reform and earlier: wooden plows drawn by oxen; burros for transport within the hacienda; hand tools (sickles, shovels, hoes, etc.) with heads of steel bought in the market fitted to handles made at home. Except for the

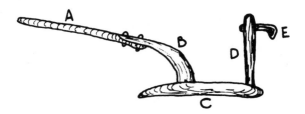

Figure 2. Diagram of a classical Greek plow adapted from Singer et al. (1956, 2:82): A, draught-pole; B, draught-bean; C, stock; D, stilt; E, handle.

steel heads these tools probably date from the Conquest or earlier. Figures 2 through 5 below give a sense of what this equipment is like; as can be seen, it is of the crudest sort imaginable: wood handles made from boles of eucalyptus fitted to heads of steel in the case of hand tools, and stocks of wood (often sheathed with iron) in the case of

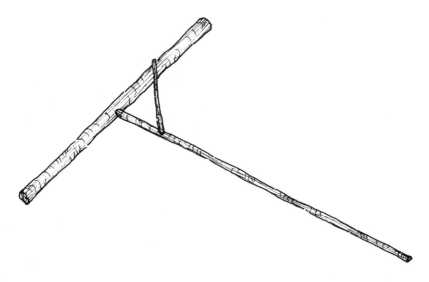

Figure 3

plows. Figure 4 shows a typical axe used by the peasants for chopping timber and in the making of tools and house building. Figure 5 shows other hand tools in common use: on the left is an *azadón,* a pointed hoe used for breaking up the soil along the rows of potatoes during their growth, in weeding and deepening the furrows and piling up earth around the young plants. In the center in the same photo is the *lampa,* or half mattock, used in clearing irrigation ditches, in cooperative labor altering the course of the Palca River during certain times of the year—again for irrigation purposes—and, in digging up potatoes at harvest. On the right is an adze used in stripping and honing eucalyptus branches, for tool handles, roof beams, etc. Other hand tools in use (not shown) are shovels and sickles bought in town, and pitchforks made from nothing more than a fork in a eucalyptus branch, stripped of its bark and honed.

The plow in use at Palca is shown in figure 2 while figure 3 shows the *rodilla,* a T-shaped frame of wood hauled by oxen across the fields to break up lumps of earth in preparation for sowing. The plows do not differ fundamentally from the *arado* dental, the Mediterranean scratch plow found by Foster in most parts of Latin America (Foster,

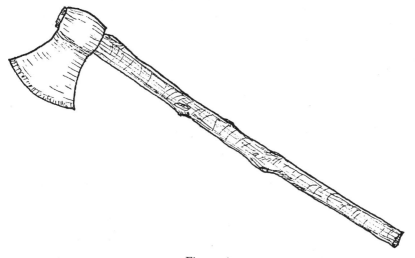

Figure 4

1960:52), or from those described by Singer, et al. (1956, II:82-83) as being in use in the classical world.

In the plows in use at Palca, as in the ancient plows described in Singer, there is a stock, of which the leading point, lying nearly horizontal, did the actual breaking of the ground. «The pull of the draught-team was transmitted to the stock through a beam and pole, and a handle was provided . . . on a separate stilt at the tail . . . . *Such an implement did little more than disturb the surface, pushing the soil and stones to one side*» (Singer, et al., 1956, II:82-83). Italics mine.)

The peasants are aware that tractors, or even steel plows, bite deeper into the soil and are more effective in opening up moist soil from below—important in planting. Tractors are also better for uprooting weeds. The peasants have tried to compensate in many cases by shoeing the wooden stocks of their plows with iron—an innovation since the reform— but they know this device comes nowhere near accomplishing the work which tractors could do. The campesinos since the reform present an interesting blend. They have one foot in the modern age, hiring truck transport from Punata to carry themselves and their produce to market; they ride everywhere within the local

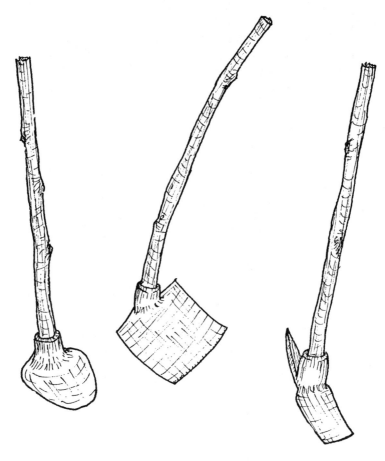

Figure 5

region, to Cochabamba, Tiraque, Punata, in trucks and hire trucks on occasion to haul harvested crops from fields in the hills down to their houses. Yet *within* the hacienda their basic technology of production shows little change from classical times in Europe;[25] they lack even the wheel, with the minor exception of wheelbarrows adopted since the

---

[25] Or even earlier. The lampa, for example, dates from Inca times (Rowe, 1963:211). On the other hand, the plows in present use almost surely derive from classic Mediterranean Europe since the Inca possessed no draft animals and the foot-plow they used was very different from the contemporary type here.

reform. Their technology is still preeminently an adaptation involving human and animal organisms alone in the transfer of energy from the environment to man, i.e., a paleotechnic ecotype.[26]

Most useful for analysis here is the concept of ecotype developed by Erasmus (1967:380), expanding somewhat on Wolf to include variables of productive technology, transport and markets. Tractors and trucks of their own, indeed, are perhaps the peasants' most crucial technological lack. Production is limited by lack of the former, for the reasons above stated. And without trucks the campesinos are dependent on townsmen from Punata with trucks to take them into town for the Tuesday fair. The opening of the Santa Cruz-Cochabamba highway (which runs right by Palca) and the presence of a considerable population of peasants without adequate means of transport has provided the townspeople with the opportunity to set themselves up as middlemen making a profit dealing with the peasants; this has led to economic relations which the peasants themselves view as disadvantageous to them. In short, Palca provides a testing ground for the hypothesis of Erasmus (1967:368, 379) that an agrarian reform that removes the funds of rent which formerly went to the hacienda owner without significantly altering the ecotype will result in no serious change in the lives of the peasants. On the contrary, new forms of exploitation are likely to appear as well as increased chanelling of funds into ceremonial activities. Further, at this point even increased production might not benefit the peasants of this region since crop prices are limited and fall when production rises. It is hard to see how Palcans can significantly alter their lives if they become, as Erasmus puts it, «richer only in foodstuffs» (Erasmus, 1967:362). There is finally the problem of how to dispose of a mass of illiterate monolingual peasants in a nonindustrial country even if capital-intensive agriculture were instituted. At present in Bolivia economic alternatives are rather narrow, and there is small provision, in the Cochabamba area at least, of training facilities for turning peasants into a commercial or industrial work force.

It is worth noting also that these tools of Palca, like so much of the rest of its culture, are stripped, functional, almost brutal. No one thinks of carving or otherwise decorating an ox's yoke or tool handle; the peasants' animals lack even names. There exists nothing like an incipient native sculpture or painting, although the peasants since the reform seem not to lack for leisure. If you ask them why they never whittle or carve, you may have trouble even getting them to understand your question; then they will tell you simply «We never think of it» or «It is not the custom.» They claim the work schedule was so hard before the reform that they lacked time even to teach children stories.

Yet Palca manifests a considerable degree of material culture linked

---

[26] Chiefly a short-term fallowing system (Wolf, 1966:21).

in one way or another to fiestas. Many (though by no means all) peasants own peroles, which range in price from 100 to 700 pesos ($10 to
$60, approximately). *Wirques, p'uñus* and *cántaros,* all various kinds
of baked-clay vessels used to make and transport chicha, are also not
cheap for the peasant but nevertheless are common equipment. When
one adds to this the fiesta dress (bought also in the market in Punata),
which everyone has except certain of the poor and aged, it is easy to
see how a sizable fraction of the peasants' capital investment may lie in
ceremonial objects. Out of a sample of twenty-two families I inves-
tigated on this subject, five had placed at least half their investment in
movable inorganic goods in equipment directly related to ceremonial.
Almost all had at least some investment in such, and as will be seen
later their expenses during the celebrations themselves are considerable.
It is important to stress that the peasants had very little equipment of
this type before the reform because, they say, they lacked money to
buy it. The patrón provided chicha for them at two fiestas, Carnavales
and the fiesta of their patron saint, Santa Rosario, on October 7. At
such times the patrón and his mayordomos provided grain, and the
peasants did the work of making chicha, the patrón's equipment being
used for the *muqueo.* One result of the reform has thus been increased
individual investment in chicha-making equipment and also a good deal
more informal drinking among the ex-colonos. Analysis of the peasants'
technology alone makes us expect that Erasmus' hypothesis cited above
concerning an increase in the ceremonial fund since the reform will be,
at least in part, verified.

The kitchen, usually packed with women and little children, is a
dark, smoky, warm place with a black pot boiling over a fire. The
horno (oven), now as before, is of clay. Wood is still burned in cooking.
Utensils are of the simplest: cheap pots of clay or metal blackened by
use; cheap metal spoons grained and pitted with dirt; a few plain clay
bowls. Water for drinking and cooking is taken, still, straight from the
irrigation ditch which flows by the road or, in some cases, from the
Palca River, when it contains water, or from a spring. Before the reform, the peasants say, pots were of earth solely; now they consist of
both clay and metal. Spoons and forks before were of wood; now, most
peasants use eating utensils made of metal. Dietary staples consist of
boiled potatoes and *chuñu* (potatoes stripped of their skin and dried);
sara mut'i (corn grains ripped from the cob and boiled); a watery soup
made of potatoes and, on occasion, onions and canned pork grease
bought in the market in Punata; noodles; milk, occasionally, and meat
even more occasionally; eggs. *Locotos* (green peppers) are still ground
by the women on a tongue-shaped stone with a round stone muller to
make *llajwa,* a hot sauce the peasants take with their boiled potatoes.
The occasional eating of meat, outside of festive occasions, seems on
impulse. As far as I could tell, a man would simply feel like eating
some *chicharrón*—chopped-up fried pork something like our barbe-

cue—so he would kill a pig and invite relatives and friends to share it. An animal that dies a natural death, even from illness, is also eaten. It is significant that chicharrón is the only dish the peasants know how to make out of pork (besides a crude sausage): another instance of the rudeness, in a sense the poverty, of their culture.

The peasants eat much the same things as before the reform; they have the same staples, but they get much greater quantities now. They have those occasional items like fruit and sugar, which they scarcely knew before the reform.[27] I heard repeatedly on the hacienda that people did not get enough to eat in the old days. At least they manage to do this now.

Clothing shows perhaps more change than other aspects of material culture so far considered; yet here too we witness a blend of the old and new. A peasant's typical workaday outfit consists of abarcas, trousers made of homespun wool, shirt, sweater and hat. Only the homespun pants and abarcas are left from prereform days. Other articles of clothing are made commercially and have been adopted by the peasants since the reform. In the old days they made all their clothing at home on their crude looms, as indeed they do, in part, today. But only a few old men today still wear complete outfits, pants, coats, shirts, hats, of homemade wool.[28]

Further, it is in clothing that the tendency noted by Patch (1956: 161, 261) is very pronounced: a tendency for traits not to displace each other but to act in a complementary fashion depending on context. For example, the men of Palca wear abarcas while working on the farm, but the majority now put on store-bought shoes when they go to town, shoes which are indistinguishable from those of cholo workers of the town. To work they wear pants and jumpers of homespun wool (or store-bought clothes which have run down), but they wear commercially-made suits, hats and shirts to town, and the young men especially are fond of a cheap nylon jacket of a type not unlike that seen on youths in the cities and, indeed, in this country. It seems that changes in clothing symbolize a significant psychological effect of the reform. The peasants without exception say they feel «better,» «more like a man» when they go to town now in their commercial clothes than they did before the reform in their ragged homespun. However, it is doubtful whether the reform's effects in this area are as rosy as Antezana (see p. 6, above) suggests. The little details of everyday life—gestures and movements, a peasant's rough hands—persist; the campesino is still identifiable as such in towns and suffers exploitation and a degree

---

[27] This fact is related to the greater frequency with which they get to market today, with more money to spend.

[28] These are very rough, often with stripes of black wool mixed with brown. The shirt is like a jumper with pockets around the middle not unlike a belt in which coca, still chewed in large amounts, is stored. The coat is narrow, ill-fitting from our point of view, single-breasted.

of subtle exclusion. His assimilation into Bolivian national life may be «inevitable,» as Patch holds, in the long run; [29] but I question whether it is occurring at the rate he sometimes implies (Patch, 1956:183). Evidence from the Tiraque region suggests that this may at times be an extremely slow process.

Women's dress is perhaps more stable: pollera, blouse and *liklla* or *awayo,* a scarf flung around one's chest and shoulders in which a remarkable number of items may be carried on the back. Yet women own these articles made commercially now as well as at home, and what they put on depends on context. On the farm they go barefoot or wear abarcas and their oldest dirtiest clothes. To go to town they may put on their more gaudy store-bought polleras, and they have also adopted, since the reform, a type of cheap webbed plastic shoe made in great quantity by a domestic firm. Most women own hats of the old prereform style, high-domed and round, made of their own lambs' wool. But they have taken up as well store-bought fedoras and, in some cases, the high hard stiff white hat typical of the valley. (In a labor of love Goins [1954:127] has drawn for us the different varieties of this hat.) Again, what is worn depends on context, the newer types being reserved generally for special occasions.

To sum up, in the area of technology and material culture Palca shows a blend of the old and new, sparks of change against a larger general background of persistence. There is a tendency for traits not to displace one another in a neat pattern but to act in a complementary manner depending on context. People are eating better now and enjoying material comforts unknown before. Yet basic tools of production and distribution have not changed. Without a large alteration in these it is hard for the peasants to make a great improvement in their living-standards even though the «funds of rent» formerly paid to the land-owner have been removed. They are still poor, living in dung and mud, with a sizable drainage of resources into subsistence and ceremonial activities. The hypothesis of Erasmus (1967:368, 379) appears tentatively supported.

---

[29] Cf. Patch (1956:144). The blend of cultural traits noted here doubtless represents a continuation of the process of mestoization or «latent acculturation» which Patch noted among the Indians of the Cochabamba Valley long before the agrarian reform (1956:138; also Bernard, 1969:986). One effect of the reform has been to somewhat extend this culture into the highlands. As in other aspects, events in this somewhat marginal area followed those in the valley. Patch's work, incidentally, like that of Goins (1954), shows the limits of a purely cultural approach to phenomena. If you look at culture traits alone in selected villages as Patch does (1956:chs. VII and VIII), arranging them along a continuum from conservative to «emergent-mestizo,» it is possible to convince yourself that considerable change has occurred. But Patch never asks what these traits *mean* in the lives of the peasants. He never fully confronts the problems of standard of living, income and power. As I will show again and again, people may adopt all sorts of new traits, all kinds of minor consumer items, without basically altering their lives (Reina, 1960:101).

FACTORS IN CHANGE

The factors behind the pattern of persistence and change in material culture are subtle and complex. Involved are outside agents and imitation; questions of capital and credit; patterns of leadership, social organization and attitudinal orientations—nearly everything, in fact, with which we will be dealing in this work. It is easier to account for the changes, which are in the last analysis relatively small, than for the basic substrate of persistence. The peasants say, for example, that before the reform they lacked time to make improvements on their houses. Nor would the patrón allow them to cut down trees on the hacienda for the rafters they would have needed to improve their roofs. Besides, they lacked money to buy sheet metal or tile or, for that matter, radios, bicycles, accordions and phonographs. After the reform with the freedom and leisure it provided, they went to work making such improvements as they now have, which they had seen in houses in Punata. They could buy building materials and consumer goods now, because they had money from their produce which they were able to market on their own.

Imitation and more cash would seem to be responsible also for the changes in clothing and food handling and the minor technical innovations which the peasants have made in their farming methods. They learned the use of insecticides and fertilizers (chemical) from the «engineers» of the Alliance for Progress experimental farm above Palca, who visited the hacienda and made speeches and demonstrations. But limitations in resources (conceived very broadly), or perhaps more accurately limitations in their ability to mobilize resources, have kept the peasants of Palca from making a genuine breakthrough in their basic adaptation to the land.

Again, the factors behind this are complex, and only the body of this work itself can hope to render a full analysis of the problem. At this point I will merely state that the peasants seem to know full well the value of mechanized agriculture, but as individuals they cannot hope, as a rule, to amass enough capital to obtain it themselves. More accurately perhaps, they are unwilling to save and risk such capital when weather and disease may destroy their crops and when prices—notably of potatoes, their chief cash crop—vary so widely from year to year. Nor do they appear oriented psychologically to pool their resources in collectives or cooperatives.[30] An atomistic social organization and lack of leadership predispose to a certain apathy. There appear to be no outside agencies, moreover, who can help—in fact this work will show that such agencies, when they exist, tend to be indifferent to

---

[30] Nicanor Sánchez, for example, said the trouble with a cooperative is that «All aren't equal. Some wouldn't pay their quotas, and they would fight among themselves when drunk and it would all be a failure.»

or even exploit the peasants. The people of Palca, like peasants in many parts of the world (see Brewster, 1969: 79), have good reason to distrust outsiders when they arrive on the scene to «help» them.

And there are other blocks to change in the community which I can illustrate in no better way than by describing the fate of two campesinos who made real efforts to break with the past by investing heavily in capital goods not shared by the others. The innovator in Palca, perhaps like pioneers anywhere else, can expect difficulty, a certain amount of criticism from his compeers who are unable or unwilling to take the risks he does. In addition, centuries of ignorance, of total noninvolvement in anything like modern technology, mean that the peasant has no model to follow when at last he tries to avail himself of it. We shall see these factors—ignorance and *envidia* (envy), and perhaps others—abundantly illustrated in the study of the two exceptional men which follows.

TWO INNOVATORS

Don Jacinto Sánchez is a skinny, dark wisp of a man so thin you wonder when he ate last. He is dirt poor, something of a rebel, something of a poet. He told me once (referring to the envy in the community) that he did not «trust his shirt.» He said he did not want his sons to «have to work the land like a burro.» In an effort to avoid this calamity he put all his money one year after a good harvest into a small used truck which cost him 12,000 pesos.[31] But this proved more of a liability than a benefit:

Jacinto said he had a small truck but did not earn much with it because the campesinos of Palca never wanted to pay to ride as passengers, they wanted to ride free and got angry if he tried to charge them passage; and they had plenty of envidia also for him having his truck, and he said he had also to pay a chauffeur 300 pesos a month since he did not know how to drive, and the whole affair was a total failure, he couldn't make a go of it. He said he sold his truck after a year and a half....

It is important to note the persistence of «status» versus «contract» orientations here:

I asked him how it was that they could expect him to give them free rides. Jacinto said that since they were all from Palca, all friends and neighbors, they felt he should not charge them money to ride to town.

---

[31] This is roughly $1,000, a great deal of money indeed for these peasants. I am not sure the sum was as large as this, or that Jacinto's story is true in every detail. But there is reason to believe, from what I observed, that much that I am writing about him is true.

At this moment, driving the peasants to Punata on fair days is largely a monopoly of *cholo* middlemen of Punata, townsmen who have obtained trucks since the reform. As we shall see later, one of these men notably exploits the peasants, and they are aware of this. There is only one peasant of the hacienda who recently bought a truck—Don Víctor García—and the peasants appear also to resent his charging them for services.

This is not to say that they never engage in «contract» relationships. On the contrary, one of the effects of the reform on the hacienda has been a remarkable increase in market activity, as well as *jornal* (paid labor). But the peasants had been acquainted with markets and had engaged in a small amount of jornal for a long time before the reform. They appear unable to shift swiftly to a «contract» orientation within an unconventional context. «Contract» relations within the community are severely limited. It seems that only by not charging money, not using his innovation to rise too noticeably above the level of the other peasants, can the innovator soften the negative sanction of the community.

After selling his truck, Jacinto used the money to buy a mill with which he hoped to make money grinding grain. He bought an old Buick motor to power this mill; I suspect he was overcharged for the motor and incompetent to run it:

> He said the motor cost 5,000 pesos, bought in Punata. It had broken down yesterday and was not working.... He said the mill isn't making money. The motor uses a lot of gasoline, and parts cost a lot. On the subject of his mill he went on at a great rate. To fix the motor costs 4,500 pesos. The pistons are broken—he needs 1,500 pesos to fix these but after this he is convinced that the mill will earn a lot of money. He left me musing on the cost of being an innovator in Palca....

Jacinto was finally unable to mend his old Buick, which ended as a memento in his yard. Still undaunted, he bought another, smaller engine, which led also to consequences he had not foreseen:

> I asked him ... how his motor was running. (It was grinding wheat into flour at the time.) He said that at the moment it was running well, but that he had had trouble with it; said it cost him 690 pesos to pay a mechanic to fix it and for new parts, and practically all he earned with it he has had to pay out for all this. He said that when he bought the motor he never thought he would have to pay this much for repairs, etc. He blames his son Nicanor for having used his machine and having broken the *aguja,* and Nicanor never advised him of this, and for this reason the valves broke down and he has had a lot of trouble. He said he is plenty angry with Nicanor because Nicanor used his motor for two months and never paid his parents a cent. Nicanor «took advantage» of the situation and pocketed all for himself, Jacinto said. He said also that after the fiesta of Santa Rosario, Nicanor was drunk and on one occasion attacked his father, saying (following is my interpreter's translation from Quechua into Spanish): «¿Cuánto vales? ¡Tu Carajo!» And Jacinto said he had to defend himself with a stick, hitting Nicanor hard on both arms, and since that time Nicanor doesn't come to his father's house and, «If he passes me he doesn't notice me.»

The seriousness of this kind of conflict may be seen when it is realized that family authority among these peasants clearly resides with the father, that the father ideally is a figure to whom great respect is owed. In all my time in the field this is the only conflict of this type and magnitude I was privy to. To sum up, Jacinto Sánchez' innovations led to a tragicomic tale of woe, costing him money, the affection—for the time being, at least—of his 23-year-old son, and they brought him the envy and antagonism of neighbors.

Much of his difficulty must be attributed to sheer ignorance in dealing with mechanical problems. I was present in Punata when Jacinto's second motor broke down for the second or third time. A mechanic there told him bluntly that his motor was simply too small to run a grain mill, and promptly offered to sell him a larger one, at a considerable price, which allegedly would serve for this purpose. At last report Jacinto was considering this move, meanwhile continuing to use his small motor to grind grain against the mechanic's advice. Meanwhile, his neighbors were enjoying the spectacle of his troubles:

«All have envy of me because of my motor,» Jacinto said. «When my motor broke down all criticized me and took pleasure.» He said he could not get any credit to fix it, «no one would lend me 5 pesos. There are people richer than me here who could buy a truck or motor better than I, but they would not lend me 5 pesos. When they come to grind their grain at my mill they show plenty of affection *(bastante cariño)* and call me "Don Jacintuy" [32] and try to get a lower price....» The people here are very envious, «so envious,» he said, «that they would not lend him oxen in *ayni* (reciprocal labor) yesterday when he wanted to sow potatoes.... I asked him to tell us in total confidence who exactly envies him, and he said all his neighbors.... He said when they get drunk they say plenty of bad things, gloating that his motor had broken down. «'Your ass has broken, you must be very poor now,'» he said they said. «I don't trust my shirt,» Jacinto wound up.

The case of Don Víctor García is even more dramatic as regards envy in the community. A vigorous and enterprising peasant who came to Palca from Potosí after the reform, Don Víctor runs a *chichería* on the highway in addition to his work on the land. He has accumulated enough money to buy a truck which he uses to carry produce to the local fairs. During my last interview with him, Victor produced a small submachine gun from under his pillow, which he said he had obtained to protect himself from the threats of townspeople in Punata—middlemen with trucks with whom he had entered into competition—and from his jealous neighbors who, he claimed, also had threatened him. Victor and his son ride with their gun constantly in their cab; if they are menaced, «I will spray them a little,» Victor says.

Yet Victor at this point does not appear richer than certain others

---

[32] The diminutive of the Quechua «Don Jacintuy.» The suffix -*y* denotes the diminutive and signifies affection.

in the community, and Jacinto Sánchez is poor now. There are rich men *(ricos)* in the community to whom the invidious sanction does not seem to apply. Why the difference? Perhaps the explanation lies partly in the fact that the ricos in general seem to have arrived at their condition through an intensification of traditional customs rather than innovation. Everyone respects Don Ricardo Rodríguez, for example, by all accounts the wealthiest person in the community, as a «hard worker» and «good farmer» who has managed to send one of his sons to Punata to mechanics' school and even away to Argentina for further study. Ricardo's innovations do not go beyond tile and sheet-metal roofs, a radio, etc.; his dwelling appears like the others, only larger. There is nothing which stands out, nothing which could make others look pale by comparison or threaten them. In short, I am proposing that the «rate-buster» model of Erasmus (1967:378) may go further toward explaining the presence of invidious sanctions among Palca's peasantry than Foster's model of «limited good» (Foster, 1965:293-315), although, finally, it is probable that even Erasmus' concept may not prove wholly adequate to explain the phenomena.

According to Foster, peasants live in a «closed system». All good things, except prestige, are viewed by them as being in limited supply; it follows that a man can improve his condition only at the expense of others. Foster seems to believe that each peasant *knows* this, and that such a cognitive orientation lies behind such leveling mechanims as gossip, envy, evil eye, witchcraft—all kinds of invidious sanctions—as well as complex prestige systems, which allow a man to rise in a socio-religious hierarchy at the cost of his material possessions.

Erasmus, on the other hand, questions the validity of this explanation at least for peasants living at the «upper limits»—i.e., those who, as in Bolivia, have participated in an agrarian reform which has freed them from the «funds of rent» paid to a landowner. Erasmus especially questions the value of the «limited good» hypothesis for peasants whose technical base is changing (Erasmus, 1967:378):

in the kinds of situations described in this paper, where the ecotype is being radically altered by new technological inputs, the expanding world of the peasant is like that of a positive-sum game. He is beginning to see the world as one of unlimited goods in which he is relatively deprived. In my experience, the kinds of rural peoples Foster calls «peasants» do not view the success of other peasants as a source of their relative deprivation. The «rate-buster» model applies to peasantry much better than the model of limited good. The rate-buster incurs enmity by establishing new standards of performance which become an index for measuring the inadequacy of his fellow-workers.... The peasant *entrón* (upstart, upwardly mobile person) is not disliked by his fellows because they believe his relative affluence has deprived them; they dislike him because his success shows that their inability to enjoy a greater share of the goods of the new.... game is a product of their own inadequacy. Eventually, as mobility increases, successful individuals provide a demonstration effect rather than a frustration effect, and invidious emulation replaces invidious sanction. But as long as social discrimination and ethnic identity help maintain barriers in social isolation, the mobility rate may not be fast enough to effect a change in outlook.

Palca is interesting in the above context. Foster's model of «limited good» does not seem to apply here, for one reason because in the case of a most important good—land—the peasants have always had ample.[33] What they lacked before the reform was access to it, ability to work it. The patrón, who siphoned off their labor, to be sure limited their «good» severely; and the peasants clearly saw him (and not each other) as the source of their deprivation.

Further, the hacienda has never had a complex socioreligious prestige hierarchy through which, in the typical Fosterian situation, a man rises in the community at the cost of his worldly goods. The peasants were always so beaten down before the patrón, so overworked and isolated that they never developed this complexity of culture. They were equal in suffering and devoid of the hope of easing their lot by becoming a «boss's man» (e.g., through *compadrazgo*); thus they had small chance of developing the habit of competing with each other, a phenomenon Cotler noted in the haciendas of southern Peru (Cotler, 1970*a*: 417) by which one man's well-being can come to be viewed in terms of the deprivation of others.

This is not to say Palcans do not suffer from envy. They do. But they do not view the success of one man among them as a theft from others. For example, from my interviews with Don Victor García:

> Víctor told a little incident. He said that one day he went into Palca to pick up some wood and stopped by the house of Don Dionisio Guzmán. José Jiménez was there and both Don Dionisio and José began asking him: «Where did you get that truck? With what money did you get it? *Why can't we buy a truck also?*» [Italics mine.] Víctor said he finally told them: «I stole it. Why don't you do the same? Why do you have envy of me? Carajo! » And finally they shut up. I asked Víctor if they were trying to say he stole from *them*. Víctor said no. They just couldn't believe he got the money honestly, that he must have stolen the truck or stolen money from somebody.

Why can't we buy a truck also? There it is, it seems to me: the peasant is simply jealous because his neighbor has suceeded in doing something he might like to have done but has failed to do. He does not regard the truck as a direct theft from himself. Nor does the amassing of wealth alone—cf. the case of Ricardo Rodríguez above—

---

[33] Until recently at Palca, the peasants say there has always been enough land for young people at marriage to move out from their parents' house. I submit that, subjectively, there has always been a certain feeling of space in their lives, though, objectively, good has been limited. How long this situation may last is doubtful. As noted above, population has increased markedly since the reform with no increase of employment alternatives. It will be interesting to return to see whether the land shortage which is developing may not result in a surge of envy, etc., of Fosterian phenomena over time.

invoke invidious sanction, as it should according to Foster's model.[34] The point is: Don Ricardo's (and the other ricos') innovations such as they are, his wealth, have resulted from an intensification of traditionality, not a break with it. He goes with the grain of the culture. Jacinto Sánchez and Victor García, on the other hand, have tried to break radically with the past.[35] They have introduced innovations which the average peasant regards almost magically,[36] with awe, envy, perhaps even a certain fear. What is interesting in connection with Erasmus' idea above is that, at Palca, *the ecotype has not needed to have been altered by «new technological inputs»* in order to bring into effect envy induced according to the «rate-buster» model. It has apparently been sufficient to bring the new technology very strongly into the peasants' consciousness, along with the revolutionary ideology which tells them in effect: You are no longer indios, you are as good as anyone else, why should you not have what they have, etc.? I can testify personally to an attempt by the dirigente of Palca (see Appendix), first to a persistent effort to cajole me into selling my jeep to him for a pittance, then a plot to steal it from me at gunpoint. He appears to have felt that I «owed» it to him for having stayed on the hacienda over a year and for having performed numerous medical and other services for them and for having been accepted with affection into the heart of the community. I fell, in part, into the role of a beneficent patrón and, as such, «fair game» for exploitation (alternately through pleading, cajoling, exploitation through dependency; and then violence) as the patrones had exploited them.

As further evidence for the above, I was told later by townsmen of Tiraque and by others in Cochabamba that the peasants often simply appropriated equipment during the breakdown of local authority after the 1952 revolution, justifying their actions as revenge on the *rosca* (members of the ousted class of landowner). It was at that time positively dangerous for an outsider to drive on certain roads: «the rosca»

---

[34] Another line of speculation is: Palca possesses some of the features of the closed corporate peasant community outlined by Wolf (1955): endogamy, primitive technology, decommoditization of land. It lacks, for the reasons sketched above, the complex leveling mechanisms of the full-blown corporate community. Hence wealth accumulation and innovation within limits are accepted. Radical innovation, however, threatens the peasant's inchoate sense of corporateness. See p. 40, below.

[35] Ricardo has never been *pasante,* has never sponsored a *devoto* to the patrón saint, yet suffers no opprobrium for this. The post of pasante, the one religious post on the hacienda, is not linked to social or economic position.

[36] In the homes of certain peasants at Palca, it is rumored, lie hidden parts of a threshing machine belonging to the patrón, which they seized and dismantled during the revolution. They did not know how to run it, apparently; the secrecy with which they kept it from me, plus the persistency and tone of the rumors made it appear as if they regarded it almost like a relic or prized souvenir. By the same token, the dirigente's attachment to my jeep seems much more than utilitarian.

became a flag which could be waved at anyone as an excuse for appropriating desired equipment.

In short, I am proposing that Erasmus' «rate- buster» model fits the data at Palca. The peasants are very much aware of a world of «unlimited goods,» which they seem to feel they have a right to and will grab if they get the chance. It follows that they will envy anyone in their community who manages to obtain these. But I propose also that Erasmus' model is inadequate to fully explain the Palcan data, since it neglects the role of the community and the psychological heritage of the hacienda. The peasants today are very conscious of the value of the new technology; at the same time, due to ignorance and lack of capital, they regard it as distant from them, alien, identified (I suspect) with the outside, with the patrón or townsman who even today is exploiting them. (After centuries of exploitation the peasants are very sensitive to it!) Hence anyone introducing radical technical innovation becomes a potential stranger or exploiter especially when he tears the web of traditional attitudinal orientations in the community (vital to mechanisms of security and mutual aid; see Chapter VI) by trying to make a profit from his mill or truck, by introducing «contract» orientations where «status» had been traditionally important. Only when levels of capital formation rise to allow a general change of ecotype, only when barriers of language and lack of education are broken allowing greater diversity and richness of life to these people will, perhaps, «invidious emulation replace invidious sanction» (Erasmus, 1967: 378).

A final variable may be the personality of the innovator. Jacinto Sánchez is the son of a poor echado; Victor García, an outsider from Potosí. Ricardo Rodríguez, on the other hand, as well as the other rich men, has held a post of respect in the sindicato, Ricardo having served as dirigente to whom the peasants express gratitude for having helped expedite their land titles during his term in office. He is a respected worker who has many godchildren *(ahijados).* Just before I left Palca, it was rumored that Ricardo was saving money to buy a truck, which he planned to run with the help of his mechanic son. It will be interesting to return to the hacienda to learn whether Ricardo has made this innovation and, if so, how it has been received by the community. At this point I would guess that Ricardo stands a greater chance of inducing a successful emulation effect in the community than Palca's present two innovators, due to his prestige and also to his ability to mobilize greater mechanical knowledge through the aid of his son, thus providing a successful demonstration effect.[37] While the inventor of a new item may well be a marginal man (Barnett, 1953), it seems likely that its advocate, the man who gains its successful acceptance, will stand well in the community.

---

[37] It should be noted that some peasants, at least, are aware of Jacinto's problems and laugh at him. On these he may perhaps be said to exert a negative demonstration effect.

In any case, Palca appears at the moment in a state of flux; it is a kind of laboratory where experiments are occurring. A growing shortage of land (to be discussed later) may indeed finally result in the kind of phenomena Foster has described. Adoption by prestigious individuals of the new technology may, over time, change the ecotype. Whether, in the last analysis, even the introduction of tractors and trucks could help the hacienda in the light of outside factors is problematical. The fate of these peasants may well lie not in their hands but in events largely outside their control in town, city and the nation as a whole. For this reason the community cannot be studied as a closed entity but must be seen as a field of action, interacting with and influenced by events in the larger, national and even international field of action.

CHAPTER IV

MEDICAL TECHNOLOGY AND ATTITUDES

TECHNOLOGY AND attitudes having to do with medical matters show the same blend of old and new features as other areas of culture. Whether the old or new is invoked, whether the peasant avails himself of a doctor or *curandero* or *yatiri* (types of native curer) depends on the context of the situation. However, the factors defining this context are extremely complex, involving economics, values, world-view, kinship. Perhaps because of the uncertainty surrounding the people's health and the mechanisms of its preservation, one finds a large degree of individual variation and apparent contradiction in this area, as well as complexity of motive. I had ample opportunity to make observations, since the peasants are frequently sick, and my jeep saw considerable service as an ambulance (not to mention as makeshift hearse and coffin-carrier). But I could never be certain my understanding of the context of illness, the complex blend of social and psychological factors surrounding it, was correct. But we may be sure of one thing: good health, like a good harvest, is a central preoccupation of the peasant, a frequent source of conversation and a theme constantly invoked as a motive for religious behavior. A peasant cannot work without health, which is precarious enough in the environment of Palca with its crude technology and small cash returns. He prays often for health and harvest because they are so crucial.

Yet there can be no doubt health conditions have improved since the revolution. Before the reform the peons of the Tiraque area lacked modern medical facilities. There were no doctors in the town—the Tiraque clinic was completed only in 1955—and the peons lacked money for medicine even if it had been available. To this day Tiraque does not boast a pharmacy. The patrón never administered medicine to his colonos, nor would he suspend work obligations until a man was virtually on the point of death. The peasants say that if a man were that ill, the patrón or mayordomo might give him two days off to go to Punata, but his family had to provide a substitute to perform his work either in the field or in pongueaje. Medicine consisted of treatment by local curanderos; in particular, children were relegated to these and many died. Infant mortality at Palca ran as high as 50 or 60 percent.

Since the reform the campesinos have come to know modern medicine—the Tiraque clinic mentioned above is now available to them as well as a larger public hospital in Punata completed in 1957. In addition, there is a doctor in private practice now in Tiraque, several private doctors and a private clinic in Punata, numerous pharmacies and practical nurses *(practicantes)* in the latter as well as extensive facilities of all types in Cochabamba 60 kilometers away on the highway by truck. There can be no doubt that the revolution, with its freeing of the peasants from their chain to the hacienda work schedule, has resulted in improved health at Palca. The Cochabamba-Santa Cruz highway has also helped, as has the new public clinic in Tiraque, which provides a doctor, nurse, and modern drugs at relatively low prices. Still, it cannot be said the people of Palca have moved in any consistent fashion into the modern medical world. Nor have representatives of that world always functioned as modernizing intermediaries or «brokers» for the peasants (Wolf, 1965: 97-98). While nominally such, they have often acted in unexpected ways, reinforcing traditional attitudes of suspicion and withdrawal. Moreover, conceptually and intellectually the peasants evidence much continuity with the past; their idea of the *pachamama,* for example, literally means in Quechua «earth mother» and was a female supernatural in Inca times of great importance to highland Indians concerned with agriculture (Rowe, 1963: 295). It has become, as we shall see, deflected into the medical realm.

To sum up, in no other area of life is the blend of old and new more manifest than in the field of medicine. In no other area is the state of flux and apparent confusion of the ex-hacienda peasant so dramatized. Behavior involved in treatment of the sick ramifies beyond the immediate context; health is crucial to the peasant. For these reasons I feel it warrants treatment in a separate chapter.

Diseases of the ex-colonos of Palca are what one might expect among people living in unheated huts at 8,000 feet altitude without sanitation: respiratory ailments—colds, pneumonia, tuberculosis, and a variety of intestinal disorders, which the peasants lump crudely under the term *dolor de estómago* (stomach ache). Particularly deadly among infants are throat and lung infections and diarrhea *(tiricia),* which the peasants believe to be caused by a woman's becoming pregnant while nursing or by jealousy on the part of a nursing baby when he sees another child nursing. Mention might be made also of a variety of diseases of plants and animals which cause the peasant considerable economic loss in certain years and are a factor blocking capital formation. Modern therapeutic methods and the services of veterinarians and plant pathologists are totally lacking in the area.

In the case of human illness, the peasants themselves make the first diagnosis; from a modern point of view they make it negatively, i.e., if they decide that a person is not bewitched *(hechizado),* not invaded by a pachamama and not afflicted by a *karasiri,* they may take him to a doctor. They thus distinguish between natural and supernatural causes of disease. In the case of the former, they do not seem to understand the germ theory of disease; but they know that doctors have effected cures and they have faith in modern medicine in cases which, for one reason ar another, they have decided are not due to occult causes. Finally, a good deal of fatalism is to be seen in connection with the sick, as is perhaps to be expected among people who have lived so long at the mercy of illness and death. If the peasants come to believe that a person's situation is hopeless, they may decide not to waste money trying to cure him. (Such a decision may of course be made for motives outside the medical, like simple greed or selfishness, especially when a person is old, is not a close relative to those who are caring for him, and owns land or animals which could be useful to the latter.) A discussion of disease at Palca might do well to begin with analysis of etiological factors as the peasants themselves see them, and then move to the underlying social and psychological matrices in which they are embedded.

CAUSAL FACTORS

Witchcraft (brujería, hechizado), pachamamas, and karasiris[38]—all supernatural or occult factors—play a large role in illness at Palca.

Illness may also be viewed occasionally in a straightforward Catholic manner as a *castigo de Dios* (punishment from God) as the result of sin.[39] The factor invoked as causal by the peasants depends in part on the type of illness from which a stricken person suffers, in part on the context in which it occurs.[40] For example, psychological disturbance seems to be blamed on witchcraft and, occasionally, *susto* (fright). In one case of serious derangement I was able to observe, the idea of hechizado seemed to be a generalized affair, attributable to no special person or persons within the community, although perhaps caused by persons «outside the community.» Sinforiano Vargas, a man of about fifty with a long history of instability, went suddenly berserk one morning and attacked his wife with a pickaxe. The community, including his son, claimed he was hechizado, but no one was blamed for this, nor was I able to locate any special tensions between his family and others which might have been projected into the belief in witchcraft. In an-

[38] All concepts deeply rooted in the Andean area. See Paredes, 1963; Rowe, 1963.

[39] As Paredes (1963:18) points out, Spanish Catholicism perhaps imported as many «superstitions» into Bolivia as it found among the indigenous populations; at any rate, it opportunistically and syncretistically made use of the latter. This perhaps reflects, on the local level, the peculiarly medieval branch of Western European culture which reached the southern portion of the New World. See Parsons, 1936:ch. X; Foster, 1960.

[40] In general, Malinowski's (1935, I:435-451) theory of magic is supported here: more precise symptoms tend to be subject to more tangible, overt (i.e., modern medical) control; subtle, uncertain and diffuse symptoms, such as those of mental illness, tend to invoke magical techniques.

other case, a peasant from Palca witnessed an accident on the highway where he saw the head of a decapitated man roll some distance on the pavement. He was unable to work for a week after this, he told us, suffering from susto.[41]

Yet witchcraft may be invoked in a context of tension between individuals and an individual may be accused of being a *brujo* (witch) or a devil; however, I witnessed no action, communal or individual, taken against such a person, although he may lose respect and become an object of gossip. For example, Francisca Claros, a big childless woman with a strident voice, who was often drunk, was commonly believed to have administered a potion to her husband Ignacio to make him impotent, while she betrayed him flagrantly in intercourse with Casimiro García. The community felt Francisca had emasculated Ignacio, for he did nothing about it; the three lived in a drunken *ménage à trois* on the top floor of our hacienda house, and some peasants believed Francisca had cast a spell over both men. The plight of Don Casimiro García was believed especially sad; he had «lost control,» as the peasants put it, having given himself over to sex and chicha. His daughter Hilde believed that Francisca had a «bundle» wrapped in cloth on her stomach under her pollera, which she used to bewitch her father. Hilde thought that if she herself could get hold of that bundle and serve her father Francisca's feces «dried, ground and toasted,» she could break the woman's hold on him. Implicitly, she thought of her father as a man under a spell, a sick man who could be cured only by such methods. For her part, Francisca hated both of García's daughters, especially the youngest, Delma, a pretty girl who was attending the government training school for teachers near Punata and who often rode in our jeep. The peasants describe a scene with Francisca on her knees in her muddy yard, muttering prayers to all directions that Delma might «die in one of the cars she's always riding around in.» I shall return to this family who embody to an extreme degree the kind of uprootedness and anomie which has been, for some peasants at least, one result of the reform.

At the other end of the continuum, physical illness with familiar and precise symptoms (injury, cough, fever, etc.) is often considered outside the realm of the occult. But even here much depends on the context in which the sickness occurs. One peasant told us that, although there are no professional witches in Palca, witchcraft is always suspected when a person who has always been healthy suddenly falls ill. Illness involving swelling or «when the face turns black» are often attributed to brujos. Witchcraft also tends to be invoked when illness occurs in a context of tensión, even if symptoms are precise. For example Julián Ramallo married a girl who had lived months in concubi-

---

[41] This did not seem to involve «soul loss» as noted elsewhere in Latin America (Steward and Faron, 1959: 131), or any special techniques of curing. The man appeared simply upset after seeing the accident and took some time to recover.

nato with his neighbor, Evaristo Marín. The latter broke with the girl, who married Julián later in civil marriage and became ill. While pregnant, she began suffering from a bad cough and vomiting, and Julián decided she was hechizado. However, it took him some time to decide this; my notes on this case are worth quoting, for they bring out clearly the drift in the peasants' lives, the doubt and uncertainty (one is tempted to say) which they evince, caught in limbo between traditional and modern. They show the opportunistic blend of ancient and modern techniques, which the peasant makes use of in his quest for all-important health:

Julián said his first wife, Abiana Rojas of Waca Wasi, died of witchcraft. At first he said he didn't realize this and took her to a local curandero thinking it was due to a pachamama. The curandero couldn't cure her.... (he) tried to cure her by burning *c'oa* (see Glossary) in a room to fill it with smoke to invite the pachamama, and he killed a wild rabbit by cutting it open alive and placing its open guts on the chest of the sick woman. The idea of this, Julián said, is that it will draw the pachamama out and let the sick person get well; it is supposed to take the sickness out of the body. But this treatment didn't work with Abiana; she didn't get well, and Julián took her to a small clinic in Punata—he doesn't recall the name of the doctor there. The doctor couldn't cure her, so Julián took her to a yatiri from Charcas near Sucre, whom he met casually in Punata. The yatiri said the woman was hechizado (bewitched by Edwarda Marin, mother of Evaristo, with whom she had lived earlier, who had done this for reasons of envidia...).

Julián spent 2,000 pesos all told—nearly $200—and still failed to save his wife. This money was divided between the Punata doctor and the yatiri from Sucre; the curandero, Sinforiano Vargas, a local man who is also a *partero* (midwife) charged nothing for his services.[42] The price of folk medicine, in short, is not low, even if measured only in money. But yatiris and curanderos sometimes knowingly cheat the peasants, and in any case they absorb time and capital which, from a modern health standpoint, could be more profitably spent on doctors. The prevailing belief in supernatural factors of disease causation means the peasants often go first to curanderos; only later, after hardship and expenditure of money, do they finally arrive at the doctor's. This gives the disease a tremendous head start, in the worst cases, and in others— because of depleted capital—it keeps the peasant from being able or willing to follow through on treatments. Other factors blocking «follow through» (I witnessed *no* case of any seriousness where a doctor's prescribed course of treatment was carried out in full and to the letter) are ignorance of the germ theory of disease [43] and a certain lack of

---

[42] To charge money from one's neighbors, to introduce considerations of contract where status had previously been important, was a factor in the resentment stirred up against the innovators discussed in Chapter III.

[43] In no way is this meant to deny Simmons' cogent point that it is not enough *only* to educate people, to inform them of modern concepts in order to diffuse modern health practices. On the contrary, the Palcan data support his

trust in the representatives of modern medicine, in some cases well deserved. When the peasant no longer feels sick, he no longer sees himself as sick; he has no money for what he regards as extravagance, and the doctor who tries to tell him about the menace of hidden infection or rabies cropping up later after a dog bite is talking about phenomena outside his world view. The tendency to delay treatment until too late and to drop it as soon as some improvement is manifest was cited to me by medical people as one of the most important obstacles to improved health among the peasants.

Treatment of mental disorder, moreover, may also involve a vacillatory eclectic approach. Sinforiano Vargas, mentioned above, ran the gamut of local medical beliefs as to disease causation. The community in general considered him hechizado because of his long history of instability—wandering out of his house from time to time and going anywhere, without money; once he was even picked up in the streets of Santa Cruz. But when he was first brought to my attention he was suffering from the specific physical problem of chest pains at night, as if something were «sitting on him,» and his family took him into Tiraque for treatment of this. The doctor there told me it was a psychiatric problem; ultimately, after his assault on his wife, we captured him in the hills and drove him to the psychiatric ward in the city hospital in Cochabamba but meanwhile he had been treated also by a curandero because his son Casilio began to wonder whether the illness might not be caused by a pachamama, and, «If it's a pachamama the doctor cannot cure him.»

Significantly, Casilio had his father treated by the doctor and the curandero simultaneously until his final breakdown.

Pachamamas, to be sure, are viewed as causal factors in a wide range of illnesses, most often physical, where symptoms exist which are more complex than, say, a cough, and where no specific tensions appear which can be projected into witchcraft. It is not easy to learn from a Palca peasant exactly what a pachamama is. Some of the literal meaning of «earth mother» survives when the peasants burn c'oa to the pachamama before planting potatoes (but not other crops) in the hope that she will grant them a good harvest.[44]

---

contention that popular beliefs constitute more or less complete explanations of illness and its cure, deeply rooted in the culture, and anyone seeking to effect change must come to terms with the «most receptive and resistant points with regard to modern medicine» (Simmons, 1965:1A).

[44] Yet crop failure or sickness among plants is never attributed to the pachamama but to *los tiempos* (the weather) which the peasants think may be due to a *castigo de Dios* (see Chapter VII). The pachamama was also invoked as the reason why Palcans had not exploited a spring on their lands near the border of a neighboring hacienda, Cañada. They feared that if they opened this spring for irrigation purposes, the pachamama would get angry and «men would die». Further study disclosed that the peasants feared it would lead to conflict with Cañada which is much drier than Palca and needs the water more (all their fields are

But with the passage of time, with, perhaps, replacement of the indigenous gods by the Catholic, the word pachamama was deflected into
other regions and has taken on other meanings. Mariano Alvarez, for
example, told us that a pachamama «sleeps in a silent place. When we
open up springs, pachamamas may be there.» He believed they come
out and get into a person and make him sick. Mariano said also that,
when there are storms, lightning rays can fall from the sky and land in
«corners» in the hills, trees and broken rocks where they also «sleep»
and come out later and make people sick:

«Curanderos cure these with c'oa,» he said, «just as they do illness caused by
pachamamas.» I asked him again what a pachamama is. He said he really doesn't
know what it is—only that curers cure ills caused by pachamamas.

José Vargas and Raymundo Sánchez also admitted they do not
know what a pachamama is, but were positive in asserting that it causes
human illness, but not illness of plants. Macedonio Najera believes
pachamamas can be found in «far places» like the wild rock bed of the
Palca River on the road to Pucara, and if you pass there sometimes
they enter you and make you ill. But he no more than the others could
form for us a clear idea exactly what pachamama is, although he was
positive in telling us that it is the «custom» there to believe in them as
causes of illness. A new house or oven may be blessed by the priest
«to keep a pachamama from living there.»

In particular, pain and swelling appear likely to be attributed to
a pachamama, and pervasive is the idea that it is due to a type of
foreign entity or small god which has entered the body and must be
drawn out. The peasants believe illness caused by a pachamama may
be cured by local curanderos, while witchcraft can be dealt with only
by yatiris from the altiplano or from Las Charcas near Sucre. In general, affliction with a pachamama is regarded as less serious than that
with hechizado.

Treatment of illness caused by a pachamama shows the same eclec-
ticism, the same tendency to switch pragmatically back and forth between old and new methods, as that involved in witchcraft. In one
case which came to my attention, Guillermo Flores had his young wife
treated by a local curandero for swelling in her arms and dizziness.
This had no effect; the swelling spread through her body and she began
to urinate blood, whereupon Guillermo had her treated briefly by a
druggist in Punata, and when this had no effect, returned to the curandero. Toward the end he lapsed into fatalism, convinced that the
girl was going to die, got drunk and beat ther when she was ill, and
told her: «Die. I want to marry another woman.» In another case, a

---

temporales, i.e., without irrigation). It is tempting to suspect that the conflict
with their neighbors was what the Palcans feared, and fear of the pachamama
was their way of articulating this. The pachamama thus appears as an articulation or objectification of the peasants' general anxiety.

man—apparently in despair because he had been told by a curandero that his wife would not recover from her illness—nonetheless refused our offer to drive the sick woman into Tiraque to the doctor because it would «cost too much.» He evinced, in fine, no striking faith in pacha-mamas but clung to the curandero because it was cheaper. Fortunately, the woman survived.

Karasiris constitute the final factor in disease causation in Palca. This idea is also ancient in the Andes, deriving, according to Paredes (1963:30-31), from precolonial belief in invisible beings who entered people's dreams to suck out their fat. The Indians later projected this belief onto the Spanish, notably executioners and then priests, believing (with poetic justice) that the latter sucked fat out of the people. Specifically, the Indians came to believe that priests «walked» at night to extract fat out of the bodies of men like vampires, causing them to fall ill and die. This belief persists at Palca in modified form. There, karasiris are said to «walk» at night between Easter in March or April and the months of June or July. But the peasants do not believe any longer that priests themselves engage in this activity, only that they have taught other men the black art of extracting fat from a man's belly with a needle, leaving a tiny mark, after which he suffers abdominal pain and dies. The karasiri, meanwhile, is thought to sell the fat to convents which pay well for the «oil».

The following is an example. Around the beginning of June, Luciano Rojas fell ill with stomach pains after drinking, and the community believed it was the work of a karasiri:

They (various informants in the community) said that Luciano had been sick since Sunday night with *dolor de estómago* (stomach ache) and they all believed it was due to a karasiri who is from Waca Wasi (literally «Cow House,» a neighboring small hacienda), or at any rate a man who came from afar and did his dirty work here. Luciano was drinking chicha in Waca Wasi Sunday. After leaving the chichería during the afternoon, he fell asleep in a field. When he awoke he noted that his pants were untied and his shirt was out, at the same time that—isolated and alone as he was—he saw a man walking in the distance. His sister arrived about this time, Luciano said, and saw the man also. Shortly after this he became ill, and for this reason all believe he has been afflicted by a karasiri. The peasants asked us if we would go to Boqueron Khasa (a neighboring community high in the mountains, formerly part of the outlying reaches of Palca under the patrón) in order to bring a yatiri here who is a specialist in treating afflictions brought on by karasiris, and we consented....

The work of karasiris, in short, is regarded as serious illness by the peasants, requiring the attention of specialized curers. In the above case, the work of the folk curer not only failed to help Luciano but did him positive harm, which only medical treatment in Tiraque later was able to rectify. The peasants in this case manifested the same drifting exploitation of both modern and ancient methods of curing as in other cases.

It is important to note, further, that the karasiri who was purported to have done the evil to Luciano was thought to have come from «afar.» Similarly, crop failure due to disease or the weather is thought sometimes to be the result of a castigo de Dios; but always this castigo is conceived as the result of sin committed outside the community, «perhaps in the *pueblos*» (towns), and I never heard an individual singled out as responsible. It is almost as if there were fear in the community concerning such an accusation. There is little evidence in Palca of illness invoked as a mechanism of social control which Simmons (1965:3A-4A) notes as having wide occurence among Latin American peoples.[45]

Yet Palca does possess a karasiri of its own who suffers a modicum of opprobrium—one Agabito Linares, ragged, filthy, in a conical old-fashioned hat, one blind eye weeping yellow. This man, drunk and often sleeping in the road, is widely believed to sleep with his mother-in-law, and I have seen him cruelly beaten for this at a drunken party. *But it was as a sexual delinquent he was beaten, not as a karasiri.* A drunken quarrel between the wife and mother-in-law suddenly erupted, involving the women who turned on him and beat him bloody (see Chapter VI). The peasants believe Agabito sleeps with his *suegra* and that he is a karasiri, but only one informant stated that the latter is a direct result of the former. I never saw illness blamed directly on Agabito. It appears the karasiri here is a marginal man upon whom communal anxiety about illness can conveniently, in a generalized way, be projected.

TECHNIQUES OF CURING

We have already touched, in passing, on methods of curing. They are rudimentary in the extreme compared to those found among cognate or neighboring peoples—for example, the contemporary Quechua of Peru (Mishkin, 1963:469) or the Aymara of the Bolivian altiplano (Tschopik, 1963:568-569.) Invasion by a pachamama requires that the foreign entity be extracted by various means: burning of c'oa in a closed room; killing a rabbit and applying the hot guts to the affected area as a poultice. In the case of the wife of Guillermo Flores, the curandero bathed the woman's swollen arm in hot water in which c'oa had been boiled, like tea. Then, with c'oa, he tied up the arm as in a poultice, and this was kept on till the next day. Sometimes both c'oa and the animal are used in the poultice: c'oa is applied first and the hot split rabbit on top of it. The curandero customarily works only at

---

[45] One woman in the community told us that when the mother-in-law of Agapito Linares (mentioned below) became ill in the hospital, it was due to a castigo de Dios as a result of her sin. But I heard no general gossip in the community to this effect, nor did the woman appear to suffer any general community sanction, ostracism, etc., for her «sin».

night and only on certain days of the week. The inadequacy of such treatment in the case of Doña Agustina Flores is obvious. According to a doctor with whom I discussed the case in Cochabamba, she probably died from a form of septicemia.

Treatment for the effects of witchcraft is more complex and expensive and the opportunity for calculated cheating on the part of the curer appears greater. For example, the following was used in the treatment of Julián Ramallo's wife mentioned above:

Julián said they took the yatiri to their house in Palca and at midnight the yatiri had all the candles put out and he spoke with a spirit. Before doing this, he put a handkerchief on the floor with money on it —not much money— and he let fall coca from his hand onto this. From the way the coca fell, he decided it was brujería.
At midnight, then, in total darkness, the yatiri spoke with a spirit; he asked the spirit the name of the witch who had bewitched the woman and was making her ill. The spirit replied that Edwarda Marín, mother of Evaristo, had bewitched Abiana for reasons of envidia, because she had left Evaristo's house and married Julián. The yatiri told Julián that Edwarda had buried clothing belonging to Abiana along with a doll in a grave in the cemetery in Tiraque, and it was necessary to get these out of there. The yatiri promised to go alone to the cemetery and take out the doll, and when he did this, he told Julián, his wife would get well. Before leaving, he wanted to be paid, and Julián gave him 600 pesos ($50), and the yatiri left and never returned. Juliá's wife died shortly after, two months after giving birth to her boy who still lives.

The belief that a person is bewitched by means of a doll or miniature of the sick person, who has been dressed in the latter's clothes and buried by the witch, appears common in the region. Sometimes the peasants believe the witch has stuck needles into the doll, and that it is necessary to find the doll and remove the needles for the sick to recover. Also common is the belief that the bewitched individual is afflicted with a toad implanted by the witch, which the yatiri extracts by rolling an egg over the afflicted part. Coca and money are common in diagnosis, and sometimes the curer expects to be served wine and pisco, as well as chicha. Pachamamas may be called on to aid in the cure. In short, treatment for witchcraft can involve the same assumption as that used for pachamamas: a foreign body has entered the sick person which must be taken out. Finally, contagious as well as sympathetic magic may be invoked in brujería, as in the case of Hilde García who believed she could cure her father of the spell cast over him by his mistress by serving him the latter's feces «dried, ground and toasted.» Therapy for witchcraft, like other aspects of Palcan life, consists of a mixture of many things.

As for karasiris, I was able to view only one instance of a yatiri at work curing illness caused by this; it was the case of Luciano Rojas, and here the chief idea seems to be the reverse of the principle of treatment involved in other cases, i.e., to restore to the sick man material which the karasiri allegedly extracted from him. Treatment consisted of feeding the sick man copious quantities of raw blood from a

freshly killed sheep mixed with fat from the belly of the animal and
wine. Later, milk and wine were prescribed (it all had to come from a
black sheep and a black cow) for a period of two weeks. After five
days of this treatment, Luciano's wife appeared at our door in tears
saying that Luciano was feeling worse than ever, had not been able to
defecate and was suffering pain. We drove him to Tiraque where the
doctor told us that the blood prescribed by the yatiri had dried the
man's intestines, in effect had paralyzed them, and it was necessary to
treat him with enemas. My assistant had difficulty explaining to Luciano's wife what an enema was and the complexities of its administration; in the end he had to help her. In this case the yatiri's treatment, in addition to costing over $20, worked positive harm to the
patient. Yet it is important to stress that neither Luciano nor his
family expressed anger at the yatiri for this. At Palca, the peasants say,
nobody apparently gets angry with the curer when he loses a case, nor
are curers viewed as witches.

It remains for us to mention finally a category of part-time specialist
who perhaps may be placed most conveniently under a medical heading: the *parteras,* or midwives. Although some women are aided in
childbirth only by their husbands, most peasants are attended by parteras who, at Palca, are five in number, four men and one woman. Sinforiano Vargas, until his recent mental illness, appears to have been
most in demand; he charged nothing for his services and, the peasants
say, «He has a good hand.» Modern medicine seems to have made little
progress in this specialty: I was able to locate only one man on the
hacienda who took his wife to a hospital to have her child. Palca's
obstetrical techniques are as rudimentary as the rest of its culture. No
special food or care is given a pregnant woman. She works up until
the moment when labor pains begin; the partera is usually summoned
at this point, who gives the woman *matés* (teas) made from coca leaves
and from *flor de ramo,* an herb found locally in the bed of the Palca
River.

While labor is in progress, the partera massages the mother's body
to «help get the baby out,» and when birth is completed, the partera
cuts the unbilical cord and throws the placenta out. The peasants say
parteras always wash their hands before working; but soap is unknown
at Palca, and the flies, mud and dung everywhere hardly make the place
(from a modern point of view) an ideal spot to be born. I witnessed at
least one mother's death from septicemia; the high infant mortality has
already been noted.

After birth, also, maté is again given to the mother, and the partera
bathes the baby in lukewarm water and swaddles him in tight cloth.
The mother's waist is also swadddled tightly in a similar cloth band to
help her «stomach ache»; the teas are also supposed to be good for this.
If the pain does not diminish, there are other techniques. For instance,
Gregoria Najera, a pretty, husky, and very slovenly young girl had four
babies, all but one of whom died:

She said the first three times she was all right, the mate and cloth sent the pain away. But last time the pain didn't go away and Pedro Saavedra (a partero) had to suck the soles of her feet to suck out the pain, and finally he succeeded and the pain went away.

We note again here, as in the case of pachamamas and certain cases of witchcraft, the belief that pain or illness is caused by the entrance into the body of a foreign entity which must be extracted. This belief appears common throughout Latin America, among peoples as diverse as the ancient Inca, Tupí forest tribes and the nomadic tribes of the Chaco (Steward and Faron, 1959:131; 307-308; 390; 419). However, these peoples made use of shamans to extract the intrusive object; curing was involved with religion and therapeutic techniques were rich compared to those I found in the Palca area. The curanderos of the latter can hardly be considered shamans since they lack the vision of a spirit-helper, imbibe no drugs, and make no effort to divine the cause of past events or predict the future (Steward and Faron, 1959:308). Their techniques tend toward the magical more than the religious (Goode, 1951:53-54) and are, again, rudimentary.

The pervasive concept of illness here, finally, involving penetration of the body by foreign material or extraction of vital material from it, implies that the people experience their bodies (or, as Fisher and Cleveland [1958:x] would put it, have a «body image») as something permeable, helpless to a degree, with weak and fluid boundaries. As Foster has shown, in the absence of scientific knowledge, the symptoms of folk illness are broad and vague and «lend themselves to almost any kind of interpretation» (Foster, 1952:9); the parallels to projective areas of culture are obvious. And Fisher and Cleveland (1958), building on Schilder (1935), G. H. Mead (1934), Freud (1949) and Parsons and Bales (1955), have adduced a considerable amount of evidence to suggest that how an individual subjectively experiences his body, how he «meaningfully organizes the sensations from his body» (Fisher and Cleveland, 1958:x), discloses a good deal concerning his «ego» or «self-concept»; specifically, they hypothesize that one's body image is a sensitive indicator of an individual's social relations, especially those early «significant others» internalized in his socialization; that the body image is a replica of and container for the central systems of the personality.

Fisher and Cleveland show that, in our culture at least, body images of people with interior symptoms of disease tend to have body images which «are characterized by boundaries which are pictured as *easily penetrated ... fluid and vague* rather than definite and explicit. It is as if the individuals feel *stripped* of their body exterior and experience the body interior as *directly exposed* to whatever impinges upon them. They experience their bodies as being *open* rather than closed» (Fisher and Cleveland, 1958:83). (Italics mine.) «Stripped,» «directly exposed,» «open»—I suggest that these words come close to the peasant's feeling when he says «We were all in the hand of the patrón,» and when he talks today of his helplessness before the power of frost and hail, i.e., «los tiempos» on which he blames crop failure and which may or may not be due to a castigo de Dios.

Fisher and Cleveland show also that weak body boundaries correlate negatively with what they term «self-steering behavior» (1958: 117-118), i.e., the ability to be «an independent person who has definite standards, definite goals» and can steer his own special course forcefully through the many alternatives life can offer. Vague and fluid body boundaries could, however, fit the diffuse, encogido, alternately passive and explosively violent behavior which will be outlined for many peasants in these pages. Only future research can determine the degree to which Palca's medical beliefs, the chief realm of its «folklore,» reflect the peasants' general life situation.

An important aspect of medicine at Palca is the considerable variation in quality of treatment which the individual peasant receives. Before the reform, all suffered equally from the lack of modern facilities; they were equal in this as in their other lacks. But since 1952, a degree of variation has sprung up. At Palca, as among ourselves, some people receive better treatment than others, although (with them) always within rather narrow limits.

Treatment depends, as we have seen, on type of symptom and on the context in which illness occurs. Whether a person receives modern or «folk» treatment depends on such variables as suddenness of onset, previous conflict or tension, the physical environment of onset, etc. But above and beyond these factors, the quality, the degree and intensity of treatment which a man received depends on the resources (broadly conceived) which he is able to muster. At Palca, as elsewhere, the man with wealth in money, land, animals and kin stands a better chance of obtaining thorough treatment than a man who is poor in these things. Particularly important are *human* resources—resources in friendship and in kinship. It is hard, for example, to imagine that Doña Agustina Flores would have suffered so at the hands of her husband Guillermo if she had had a strong father or brother to speak for her. Guillermo is said to have beaten her and made her go to work almost immediately after her confinement, after which she fell ill, and I myself found her sick and abandoned in the road one night while Guillermo had hurried on to his house to care for his oxen.

Similarly, I have seen Miguel Lizzaraga, a vigorous peasant of about thirty, race to Tiraque on his bicycle to see his father Victor at the office of the private doctor where we had taken him in my jeep; the old man was suffering the effects of violent alcoholism after the Fiesta of Santa Rosario. Miguel paid in full for his father's treatment; surrounded by friends and relatives—the old man is liked and respected in the community—he returned home and soon recovered from what was probably little more than a great hangover. But Miguel's distant uncle Andrés, an aged widower who had come from outside the community, who had no close relatives in Palca and had been given land there since the reform by the dirigente—Andrés died alone [46] in Miguel's dark hut, untended and, toward the end, unfed. «What am I going to bury you with?» Miguel told the old man, when the latter asked him to kill one of his own sheep to feed him. Miguel told us that Andrés was going to die anyway, there was no use taking him to a doctor. The fact that Miguel inherited Andrés, bit of choice land after the old man's death may have contributed to his fatalism.

Negative sanctions on the part of the community (neighbors' gossip,, etc.) do not appear to have sufficient force to alter this kind of situation. Nor does the revolutionary sindicato (peasant league formed, since the revolution, of all adults on the hacienda) in spite of its avowed aim of effecting change, of «making a better life» for the peasants, take action; if anything, its stance reinforces the status quo. The sindicato assumes responsibility for a sick member of the community only if he is wholly without kin at any degree of removal: I never witnessed such a case. It exerts negative sanction on a man only if he refuses to bury his distant kin but says nothing about an obligation to care for him. The customary law is: he who buries a dead man inherits his land. The dirigente (head of the sindicato) can transfer the right of burial to another if his relative refuses to bury the dead; few do this since the value of the land to be inherited usually far exceeds the cost of burial. But, as is evidenced above, burial expenses can be sufficient to be used as a weapon to silence a dying man's appeal for better care.

Resources may be manipulated to lighten the medical burden of the influential and deprive the poor. Felisa Ochoa, twelve-year-old daughter of Manuel, a poor man, was bitten in the leg by Ricardo Rodríguez dog. Don Ricardo (cf. above) is the richest man in Palca, a respected ex-dirigente with many godchildren, including the present dirigente, Don Dionisio Guzmán. At first Manuel, believing the wound minor and not wanting to «bother» Don Ricardo, treated the child at home by rubbing burnt hair from the same dog into the wound. (Contagious magic can apparently be invoked in such cases.) When the child's leg was badly swollen and she was in great pain from infection, Manuel went to Don Dionisio who declared that Ricardo was responsible and should pay all the medical expenses involved. Result: Ricardo paid for a few injections of antibiotics and then stopped, although the doctor in Tiraque wanted to continue for two more weeks to avoid risk of infection of the bone. But as soon as the child showed some improvement, Ricardo balked at paying more, and Don Dionisio did not insist on his completing the treatment. He laughed when we told him the doctor wanted the dog's head for examination for rabies; «All dogs are *bravo* here,» he said. By chance, the child survived with no bad effects.[47] Throughout the

---

[46] Of tuberculosis probably.

[47] This case strained my «scientific» detachment. In the end I secretly paid for oral antibiotics to be given to the girl for a period of fourteen days; we slipped the pills to the girl's mother. When the girl recovered and was back running with her skinny little legs behind the sheep, the dirigente's attitude was: «See,

case the girl's father, Manuel Ochoa, showed himself apparently humble and self-effacing, willing to go along with whatever the dirigente and his padrino, Don Ricardo, desired. The case shows how differentials in wealth and influence interact with details of everyday social behavior to work against the poor. Manuel himself said he could not afford to continue treatment simply because he did not have money; and the dirigente drifted away from his original idea.

To sum up, I have shown something of the complexity of behavior at Palca in connection with treatment of the sick and have analyzed some of the variables influencing that behavior. In general it can be said that culture connected with curing shows the same rudimentariness, the same drift, contradiction and lack of organization and leadership as other aspects of the peasants' lives. More, however, needs to be considered. So far I have presented mainly the internal factors, the internal dynamics of the situation. But as has been stressed earlier, the hacienda, especially since the reform, cannot be studied as a closed system but must be seen in all its complex relations with the outside world. Various kinds of cultural «brokers» have sprung up since the reform who impinge on the hacienda and influence its life. Representatives of modern medicine, doctors, nurses, practicantes, and others stand among these; I turn to them now to complete my picture of the medical situation at Palca.

MODERN MEDICINE AS A CULTURAL «BROKER»

It is safe to say, I think, that representatives of modern medicine have had an impact on Palca above and beyond the purely medical. In most cases the doctor or nurse simply «does his job»; the peasant, seeing the effect of this, has been, on the whole, not unfavorably impressed, and modern medicine has made notable progress considering the base line from which it started.

The peasants furthermore trust the doctor, in most cases, at least within limits. But modern medicine costs, and the peasant is tempted to cut corners, not only by frequenting curanderos (who are not above quite calculatingly cheating them), but by seeking out personnel with dubious qualifications who administer modern medicines.[48] Such per-

---

I told you so. She was getting better. You worry too much.» It occurred to me that I may have encouraged the peasants' tendency to drop treatment on the assumption that «They'll get better anyway.» I did not desire, however, to sacrifice the girl for the education of the community. As it was, she still risked death by rabies.

[48] In Bolivia at present it seems that nearly anyone who wants to may set himself up in business as a druggist or practicante and sell medicines and write prescriptions. Medicines, many of which are restricted in use in the United States by law, can be bought over the counter in Bolivia. Drugs tend to be sold under their technical, rather than brand, names.

sons, druggists and *practicantes* are sought out because the peasant wants to cut corners, because he is out for a «bargain»; ironically, he often pays as much if not more for such treatment than if he had gone to a doctor in the first place. For example, old Fortunato Ramallo, father of Julian, was a great *tomador* (drunkard). One time he fell in a street in Tiraque and needed eight stitches in his head. Victor Rojas, a *practicante* of that town, treated him and charged him 120 pesos. The government-sponsored clinic would have cost perhaps one-third that amount.

Similarly, when Alejandro Muriel began suffering from paralysis of his legs, he went to Rojas who charged him 60 pesos for an injection and a prescription. According to a highly respected physician of Cochabamba, Dr. Julio Rodríguez, the prescription was for a Vitamin B_1 preparation and was totally worthless for anything Alejandro could have been suffering from. We drove the peasant into Punata later to the hospital where he saw a qualified doctor for 5 pesos and picked up a prescription for 100 pesos. The latter finally cured him.

The *practicante* Rojas indeed deserves further comment. A big florid man with a red moustache, in Western clothes, no stranger to chicha, he was always talking about how much experience he had working as a nurse for the Shell Oil Company in the Oriente, for the «Dutch engineers» («ingenieros holandeses»). Meanwhile his wife bullied the patients. For example, while Alejandro Muriel was being treated, she interjected at one point to say that if Muriel didn't follow instructions of the *practicante* he would lose his legs. Mrs. Muriel burst into tears at this, staring straight ahead of her in what seemed to me naked dread. I saw that it would be very tough on the family of this young couple if Alejandro could not work. Rojas told his wife to stay out of it and she left. Rojas' wife looked as poor as any peasant, his kids also, two and three years of age. Their house is small, one-story, mud floor, thatched roof, little better than a peasant's. I saw that Rojas was probably in a bind too.

Significantly, when, as a kind of experiment, we informed the dirigente of Palca, Don Dionisio Guzmán, of the kind of treatment Alejandro received and suggested the peasants would probably do better at the clinic, Don Dionisio said that Victor Rojas was his compadre; he did nothing we could see to try to dissuade his people from visiting Rojas, and they continued, for a time at least, to go to the *practicante*. However, after a period of some months, Rojas and his family left, bag and baggage, for Puerto Todos Santos in the Chapáre. Our presence in the area, our constant recommendation of qualified medical personnel in Tiraque and Punata plus our willingness to transport sick peasants in my jeep, had caused a decline in his business.

Rojas stands as a kind of symbol. Where there is such unemployment as in Bolivia at present, such stagnation and at the same time geographical fragmentation and transitional values between ancient and modern, such men are common. Economic necessity presses them into such work, at the same time the confused values of the peasants in medical matters provide them with opportunities for exploitation. As the country moves toward greater homogeneity through expanded communications networks and education, as qualified medical personnel increase in number and spread through the campo, the practicantes will decline in number.

But at the moment this is a slow and tortuous process. The situation is complicated by the fact that *even government qualified and attested individuals and groups engage in activities of dubious moral merit from the peasant's point of view.* These people could be, from their credentials and formal structural position in society, modernizing cultural «brokers» for the peasants; they do not always, in actual practice, perform that function. In plain English, individuals and groups who purport to help the peasants are cheating them; the peasants are not blind to this, and attitudes of suspicion and withdrawal are reinforced. This is highly evident in the field of health. For example, while I was at Palca, an organization operating out of Cochabamba sent representatives to the hacienda with the aim of setting up a dispensary there. The organization had an official-sounding title, SEPSA *(Servicio Popular de Salud)*; [49] leaflets were handed out among the peasants; and I was able to verify that, although it was a private and allegedly nonprofit organization it did have the approval of the Ministry of Health with which it was working in «cooperation.» [50] As can be imagined, the need for local dispensaries staffed by competent nurses is great in the Bolivian countryside, where lack of roads and impassable terrain make it hard for medical personnel even to reach certain localities, especially during the rainy season. Such a dispensary is needed even at Palca because doctors in the area lack jeeps or cars and will not in any case leave the towns to make calls in the campo: many children still die during the night of respiratory ailments because there are no means of getting them to town.

The peasants, in short, were initially receptive to the idea, promoted by the organization's field agent, of contributing a small sum on a cooperative basis to buy medicines and equipment and pay the salary of a permanent nurse at Palca. Low-cost drugs, a visiting doctor, and free transportation to hospital were also promised, at first. But when, during successive visits, the agent changed his offer, telling the peasants finally they would have to pay for transportation (which they do at present anyway), and the doctor's fee would be much higher than first

---

[49] Dr. Julia Elena Fortún, in a recent paper, mentions this organization among many others who are contributing to Bolivia's development. I am concerned to show, however, that structural change, multiplication of bureaucracy, may not, on the level of everyday life, lead to behavioral change.

[50] A word used by my friend, Miss Cora Goodson, a North American public health nurse in Cochabamba acting as advisor to the Bolivian government's Ministry of Health. «Of course,» she added jokingly «there are many thieves in the Ministry of Health.»

mentioned, and the nurse's also, the peasants began to regard the scheme as a cheat, a «thing of business,» and rejected it.

Similarly, the doctor at the Tiraque clinic did little to help the cause of modern medicine at Palca when he tried to charge 600 pesos for an autopsy to the family of a man who had hung himself, and then quickly dropped this allegedly legal «requirement» when the peasants vigorously protested. The leader of the Palca community, the secretary-general of its revolutionary sindicato, Don Dionisio Guzmán, told me privately after this incident that all the town authorities were *suwas* (Quechua: thieves). Yet it is significant that he adopted a purely defensive attitude toward, for example, the Cochabamba organization mentioned above. When I suggested that he might help stop such abuses by going to the city and reporting them to the campesino Federation, he said: «Why do so much? We're dropping it and that's enough.» The peasants here do not conceive, and do not as yet importantly utilize, political structures created by them during the revolution as channels for upward articulation of their interests.

From the point of view of the larger society, looking downward, so to speak, there is little institutional control of what actually happens on the local level. Much depends on individuals e.g., the first doctor at the Tiraque clinic, who left in the early part of our stay, seemed to be a man very different from his successor who demanded the autopsy. But the peasant nevers knows how an individual in this role—or other brokerage roles, for that matter—will behave. A certain illegality is always possible. It is not a situation to breed trust.

There are, finally, more subtle problems involved in the inculcation of modern health attitudes at Palca—factors whose impact is hard to assess. The peasant, who dreads spending time in the hospital anyway, away from his kin and familiar surroundings, is not reassured by the *gente decente* (aloof, aristocratic) attitudes of doctors, many of whom are only spending their «year in the provinces» after medical school,[51] and can't wait to get back to set up a lucrative practice in the city. Doctors will not leave the towns to make country calls; they will not go to the scene of an accident, but one must extricate victims as best one can and bring them to the doctor. There is finally the question of the technical quality of Bolivian medicine itself, the modern sector of which has, to a North American, like so much in Bolivia, the façade of modernity rather than the thing itself. There is, for instance, a single mental hospital in all Bolivia, in Sucre, but according to a former dean of the medical school of the Universidad Mayor de San Simón in Cochabamba, Bolivia lacks a single true psychiatrist, a man who would be accredited in Europe or the United States. My own observations on numerous visits to hospitals in the countryside and in Cochabamba; conversations with doctors, nurses, medical students and members of

---

[51] Bolivian law requires that graduates of medical school practice for at least one year in certain designated regions of the country.

the United States consulate in Cochabamba who have lived some time in Bolivia; my service as a volunteer ambulance driver during the disastrous rainy season floods in Cochabamba in February 1968—all combine to indicate that Bolivian hospitals lack up-to-date sanitation and equipment; [52] that rote-memory learning in the schools blocks the study of medicine, so that to become accredited students must «get out of Bolivia» to study in Colombia, Argentina, the United States or Europe; that archaic attitudes and practices survive even in the modern sector. The condition of health practice among the peasants must be seen in the context of a situation where even the «modern» practices being promoted among them are hardly fully so in a scientific sense.

---

[52] The lack of even basic equipment such as sterilizers and X-ray machines is great, particularly in public hospitals set up for the poor. Miss Goodson informs me that there are perhaps four fully qualified registered nurses in Cochabamba. No food is served patients in public hospitals; a man without family or friends simply dies if he has no money.

CHAPTER V

ECONOMIC ORGANIZATION

ANNUAL WORK CYCLE, DIVISION OF LABOR

LIKE MATERIAL culture, and all other aspects of life, economics manifests a blend of stability and change, old and new; yet it is in the economic area that the most striking change has occurred, the change which may be called truly revolutionary: the removal of all rents and services paid to the patrón and the division of the latter's land among his ex-peons. The main thrust of the agrarian reform, its tremendous mobilizing force, was directed to this end, and there can be no doubt that it succeeded.

Yet the frame of economic life, the loom (so to speak) on which the peasants weave, has not altered with the reform. Crops have not changed, nor has the yearly cycle of work, which is remarkably consistent throughout the entire region of the Tiraque plateau.

January-February — Rainy season. Hoeing and then harvest of new potatoes. Cooperative labor on the Palca River moving stones to build dams to divert water to the fields for irrigation. Occasional emergency work on the river to avert floods.

March-May — Harvest of some new potatoes and regular potatoes; harvest of the main part of the potato crop in May.

June-July — Wheat, barley, corn and lima bean harvest and threshing. Also small amounts of oats (for fodder only) and *ocas* (subsistence only). Irrigation and preparation of land for sowing of all crops.

August-September — Sowing of beans, wheat, barley, new potatoes; also minor quantities of ocas and maize mainly for home consumption.

September-October — Sowing of potatoes; also minor amounts of *papalisa* (see Glossary) for subsistence and oats for fodder only.

November-December — Hoeing and weeding of all crops.

Labor is arduous, as may be imagined from the large stretches of land which must be worked with crude tools. Men walk considerable distances to reach many of their fields, and then plow for hours behind their oxen during the cold months of June and July, breaking up soil for plowing; at this time Palca resembles some Oriental print, some timeless vista—lonely specks in the brown immensity moving in silence behind toy oxen. Sowing of potatoes, the main crop, is accomplished with two teams of oxen hauling plows. One plow opens a furrow; a man follows, spreading chemical fertilizer; another follows him sowing seed; another with dried manure; then the second yoke of oxen plows a furrow right alongside, covering everything. It is a long task, but one

considerably easier than the harvest of potatoes, which requires that a
man work many hours bent over, tearing the tubers from the ground
with his pointed azadón. Threshing, on the other hand, is a festive occasion, especially when there is a large amount of grain available *(gran
trilla)*. The wheat or barley is piled high in a flat place. Four or five
horses are bridled together and driven into the pile, and then whipped
around and around within a circle formed by the peasants holding a
continuous line of rope and leather thong *(waska)* to keep the animals
from escaping. It is great fun, under the pure sky, in the keen wind;
everybody gets drunk. The host always provides plenty of food and
chicha, and thirty or more peasants show up just for the fun of it. It
was not very different in the old days, when the patrón also gave out
chicha to the peons threshing his grain.

The basic division of labor also has not changed. Men still perform
not only the main work of the fields—they sow, harvest, hoe, thresh.
They work on the roads when they are washed out after the rains and
on dam building in the Palca River to divert its current for irrigation
purposes. (These are, in fact, the only tasks for which the community
as a whole cooperates; it is significant that they are traditional, having
been accomplished in this manner before the reform as far back as
anyone I talked to can remember.) Men chop timber and do the work
of house building—any job which requires male strength. Women's
work may be summarized in the peasants' own words translated from
Quechua: «la cocina y el pastoreo» («the kitchen and the pasture»).
The woman's main task is to cook for her men before they go to work,
serving breakfast about nine or ten A.M., after which she takes the
animals (mostly sheep, with a few cows and, when they are not in use,
oxen) to the hills to pasture. She returns with her beasts from the hills
«with the sun.» While sitting watching the animals, occasionally throwing stones or clods of mud at them to keep them from straying, she
nurses her baby and works incessantly spinning thread from lamb's
wool with her *pushka,* or wooden hand spindle.

Cena, or dinner, is prepared by the woman upon her return home or,
if an older female relative is living with the family, she may do this.

Little girls of six or seven [53] begin to help in the house, cooking and
carrying babies around, slung on their backs as their mothers do, in
their small *awayos.* (Quechua: *lliklla,* a shawl slung on the back and
tied in front of the neck in which sundry things are carried). At about
eight or nine years they begin to pasture sheep near the house when
the animals are not taken to the hills—that is, just after the harvest of

---

[53] Legally, young children are supposed to attend school. However, the
school at Palca is so irregular and so inefficient by any standard or dimension
(see Chapter VII) and the peasants' orientation toward traditional tasks so
strong, that a large percentage of families simply do not send their children to
school. School attendance is especially low in the case of girls.

grain crops when they are left to graze on the cut stalks. As early as ten years of age, girls may be entrusted with the care of babies for a week when parents are away in the hills harvesting. At twelve or so they start going with their mothers to help shepherd flocks in the hills, and a teen-aged girl may be sent out alone with the animals, freeing her mother for housework—washing, cooking, caring for small children, making chuñu, etc.

Nursing babies accompany the mother, slung on the back or under the teat in an awayo. Small children of six or under may also go with the mother. Or if, as is often the case, there is an older relative at home, a grandmother or grandmother-in-law, they may stay there. Boys of eight begin going to the fields with their fathers and «putting their hand on the plow.» Men and boys may return to their homes for lunch or they may dine in the field on chuñu wrapped in cloth which they carry with them.

I noted no variation from the above pattern. No allowance is made for crippled children, retarded or disturbed children simply because there are none. With the exception of one young woman with a with-ered leg (which hinders her not at all in her normal tasks) and one man who lost a hand meddling with fireworks at a fiesta, Palca is com-pletely able-bodied. Data which might explain this phenomenon are hard to come by. One suspects, however, that the high infant mortality rate reflects a Spartan attitude toward the handicapped.

The basic division of labor according to sex alters only gradually with age. Men continue working in the fields until quite remarkable ages—their sixties and seventies in many cases—until quite literally they sicken and die. The same is true of women, although older women tend to stay in the house cooking and caring for children; they go less into the hills with the animals.

The division of labor is not rigid in the sense that women may help in the fields, notably during the sowing of potatoes when they join the line of mutually aiding men, dropping the seed in its place in the fur-row. I have seen lazy sunny days in June after the grain harvest when the pressure of work is off and whole families down to tiny tots will be seated in a cornfield shucking the corn. Not uncommonly, women carry lunch to men in the field and eat with them and, during the potato harvest, women go to fields in the hills with their husbands to cook for them and for their helpers. They remain there until the work is finished, living with their men in improvised canvas tents.

Similarly, a man seems not to mind doing the cooking if his wife is ill or carrying a small child on his back in an awayo. The making of chuñu and marketing may be managed by either women or men: the former go to the fairs with greater frequency when it is a question of selling a small amount of produce or a small animal up to the size of a sheep or pig; men handle transactions involving larger quantities of produce and the sale of cattle. Still, women often go to the fair with surprising loads, such as a heavy bag of potatoes; this presents them with marketing problems, as we shall see. Quite often, man and wife go to the Punata fair together, sell their produce and get drunk together.

Still, though the division of labor has not changed essentially in structure since the reform, it is safe to say that it has changed in emphasis, in intensity and its day-to-day existential meaning for the peasant. The arduous prereform work regime for men has already been discussed; the men do the same work now but under less grueling conditions. The same applies to women. Older women state that, before the revolution, they had to rise much earlier than now, as early as four in the morning, to prepare food for the men going to work about six A.M. for the patrón. They pastured sheep at an earlier hour, and the patrón, through his mayordomo, gave them lamb's wool out of which to spin thread, and they also had to make blankets and potato sacks for the hacienda, one sack for a *tupu* (about 100 pounds) of potatoes per year. The women complain with some bitterness that they lacked time to care for their children properly.

Prereform marketing, interestingly, to the degree that it involved the peasants in the outside economy, was performed mainly by women. It was the women who managed to obtain the time off necessary to go occasionally to Punata to barter small quantities of goods or to make the tiny purchases in cash the peasants made then: matches, kerosene for a *mechero* lamp, a can of lard, etc. The men carried the patrón's products to Cochabamba on the backs of their burros, but this in no way involved them in the city market.

Palca has always had a degree of part-time specialization beyond its basic division of labor. Medical specialists—curanderos, yatiris and parteras—have already been discussed. Suffice it to say that the local curers, with the exception of certain itinerant types who spend most of their time on the road, are peasant-farmers like everyone else; curing is a part-time occupation with them. Except for Sinforiano Vargas, Palca does not possess a bona fide curandero. The peasants, while I was present, visited curers in nearby Sak'abambilia and Boqueron Khasa.

Weaving is another specialty which shows stability since the reform. A few women still weave clothing of lamb's wool; yet due to the influx of store-bought clothing and potato bags made commercially, they weave much less than formerly. Most of the weaving which is done locally at present is accomplished by two men who charge a small amount of money for specific orders, e.g., a pollera or a pair of pants, woven on crude wood looms which have not changed since the reform. There appears to be no resentment on the part of the community of this type of contract arrangement within its borders, perhaps because the charge is so low—much lower than the price of commercial clothes—and because the work and its machinery are traditional.

Other part-time specialties on the hacienda do represent minor innovations since the reform. They include the making and selling of chicha for cash;[54] a mason who learned his trade during a nine-year stay in the city of Cochabamba and now works as a *jornalero* (hired day-laborer) building houses;[55] and two men who play *zampoñas* and *qenas* (types of reed flute) and earn an occasional pittance playings at parties. Youths occasionally earn $10 or so as devil *(diablado)* dancers at fiestas in the region (see Chapter VII), which are considerably larger and more drunken than before because of the larger amounts of cash the peasants have at their disposal. Yet specialization remains minor. Abolition of feudalistic services to the patrón and subsequent relative freedom to dispose of their time has not led the peasants of Palca to seek employment on a large scale (mainly on commercial farms in the yungas of La Paz) as Burke found on the altiplano (1967:105, 110). With the development of commercial agriculture in the government-sponsored pioneering projects in the Chapáre, if they succeed, Palca's people may find themselves confronted with similar sources of outside income. At the moment they lack these. Yet even if such outlets become available, one cannot assume they can be permanently filled without affecting the hacienda's production. While there are seasons when men could be spared, there are others (sowing, harvest, threshing) when any large exodus of manpower from the farm would (granting the labor-intensive methods of production in use) cause a drop in production. The marginal product of labor, as yet at any rate, is not zero (Lewis, 1955:327; Schultz, 1964:ch. 4).

To sum up, division of labor on the hacienda shows the same basic pattern as technology: agrarian reform has not led to massive and fundamental change but only to sparks, isolate details. Men still make their living raising potatoes and grain crops, and for women it is «la cocina y el pastoreo».

TYPES OF LABOR

Organization of labor also shows considerable continuity with the past. Change in this area represents shifts and intensification of tendencies already present under the patrón. Although particular types of

---

[54] Santo Gonzáles and Angel Rojas, who sell chicha in this manner, earning up to $300 a year each, seem to evoke no resentment in the community for the charging of money for chicha; neither did the schoolteacher (see Chapter VIII). The role of chicha-seller is one the peasants have grown used to; it does not represent an innovation which stands out, hence is not subject to individuous sanction according to the «rate-buster» model. These sellers are also liberal in extending credit to their neighbors.

[55] F. López (see p. 20). After eviction from the hacienda, he learned his trade in the city of Cochabamba and eventually returned to Palca where he inherited a small amount of land and the sindicato allowed him to stay. His income (not large) comes chiefly from his jornal labor.

work tend to be organized in a certain manner—potato sowing, for example, is usually done by means of reciprocal labor *(ayni)*—still it is true that the nuclear family works together on this occasion, and jornaleros may be hired, all working together in a single field. In labor matters, as in so much of the rest of their lives, the peasants hold to no rigid pattern but do what appears convenient at any point to accomplish their work.

At present, eight types of labor may be distinguished at Palca: (1) festive labor; (2) reciprocal labor; (3) cooperation among kin; (4) communal labor; (5) jornal, for a wage paid in cash or in kind; (6) dependents' labor; (7) labor contributed by townsmen in the sharecropping or compañía system; (8) voluntary labor. Of these, the first five types are most common; by far the main part of the work of the hacienda is accomplished through these. Voluntary labor, where a man with nothing much to do on a particular day lends a hand to a friend out of apparent sheer goodwill and friendship, is rare indeed but does occur. At least, in these cases, labor was extended with no tangible reciprocity in sight, and the peasants, when interviewed, said none was expected.

Festive and reciprocal labor fit the patterns outlined by Erasmus (1955:8-12; 1965:174). In the former, peasant A helps peasant B at some task and is in effect «paid» on the spot in festive coin. At Palca this consists of food—soup and plenty of boiled potatoes with ground peppers—coca, cigarettes, and chicha above above all, so that everyone gets drunk. There is no obligation to return the labor. At Palca purely festive labor occurs only when there are great piles of grain to be threshed, and the peasants go from house to house threshing and drinking in turn. «When you give chicha, there's no lack of volunteers,» they say; people willingly contribute not only their labor but their horses to the task.[56] It is logically usually only the wealthier peasants who need to make such a gran trilla. They have more to give and receive more aid than the average.

Food and chicha, again, may be seen as the rough equivalent of wages (Chayanov, 1966:22) paid to friends and neighbors on a farm Chayanov designated as a «half-labor type.» [57] The expense is not trifling—ten or more *puñus* (medium-sized clay jug) of chicha at 20 pesos (a little less than $2) per puñu—plus the potatoes, cigarettes, etc.; but

---

[56] Festive labor here corresponds to the *minka* form found in highland Peru and Ecuador (Erasmus, 1955:6). It is perhaps further evidence of their general poverty of symbolic culture that the Palcans have no name for it.

[57] Chayanov (1966:22, 274) designates as «half-labor» or «farmer unit» farm an organization which «uses paid labor in addition to family labor power, but not to such an extent as to give the farm a capitalist character.» For Chayanov, such a farm would be expected to show some modification in a commercial, profit-oriented direction of the consumer-labor balance he saw as typical of the family peasant farm, but not enough to give it a capitalist character. This is indeed what we find at Palca.

the work gets done rapidly and feelings of friendship are reinforced. People go around for days afterward talking about the gran trilla at Don Dionisio's.

The donor's prestige is maximized and he is more or less assured of future help when he needs it. Resources are thus built in people, and when the dirigente, especially, gives such a «bust,» he helps reinforce and validate his position.

In reciprocal labor, A helps B, and there is obligation to return the labor. The peasants state, however, that they are not rigid about the exact date of repayment, and a man who desires may send a replacement, for example, a grown son. Food and chicha are also provided to ayni helpers, though in smaller quantities than on purely festive occasions. Reciprocity extends to the mutual borrowing and lending of tools and animals, notably oxen teams and burros, and seems to function smoothly: I never witnessed or heard of conflict pertaining to this. Ayni comes into play chiefly among social equals during the sowing and harvest of potatoes and for house building—situations calling for extra manpower which everyone in the community knows about. As one peasant expressed it to me, a man will not fail in his obligation here: if he did, he would soon want helpers when he needed them. The fact that most ayni helpers are friends and live close to one another on the large hacienda and are, sometimes, kin, also works for the smooth functioning of the system. In addition, Palca's relative wealth in foodstuffs reinforces the system, removing complaints heard against ayni elsewhere in Bolivia: that hosts «fail to serve adequate meals, enough chicha, etc.» (Leonard, 1966: 49).

Festive and exchange labor have genuine adaptive significance for the peasants. It is vital to get the grain crops threshed and stored safely away before the wind and hail of the winter month of June can damage them. Large numbers of men are needed for this, as well as for the potato harvest from the extensive fields which, if the nuclear family alone had to work them, would run well into the sowing time for grain crops and new potatoes. On the other hand, for purely cultural reasons, the peasants like to have most of their potato sowing finished by the great fiesta of their patron saint, Santa Rosario, on October 7. They work hard in ayni for this, and there seems to be a festive aspect to all cooperative labor; as more than one peasant said to me drunkenly, lurching and pounding my back: «This is our life, our life, you see?» Palcans engage in festive and exchange labor for reasons of both adaptive necessity and «social entertainment,» which indeed fit the evidence Erasmus has drawn together pertaining to similar customs from widespread parts of the world (Erasmus, 1955: 131, 133; 1965: 179).

Festive and exchange labor, like the other kinds, have their roots in prereform days. At that time, of course, most of the work of the hacienda was done by means of massive forced labor—forced cooperation, if you will—by the dependent peons of the patrón. Still, threshing of the patrón's wheat and barley was a festive occasion much like that which occurs at the house of a wealthier peasant now; the patrón through his mayordomos handed out grain from which the peasants made chicha; they brought their horses and worked and ate and got drunk much as they do now. They also engaged in voluntary exchange labor among themselves, although to a much lesser extent than at present. Exchange labor was confined to house building and to the mutual borrowing and lending of burros used to carry the patrón's products to market in Cochabamba. The peasants say they engaged in a small amount of ayni in sowing and harvesting in the fields, but since they were usually able to sow only a fraction of what they sow now, ayni was rare. The nuclear or slightly extended family was the most frequent work group on the peasants' subsistence plots.

Palcans do not complain—as Andean peoples studied by Erasmus appear to have (Erasmus, 1955: 184)—about the poor quality of festive work or the difficulty of controlling worker-guests. For peasants such as these, who are so unspecialized technologically and are «rich only in foodstuffs,» exchange and festive labor appear a convenient solution to the problem of completing tasks «which must be done faster than one man can do them and those which exceed the strength of a single man» (Erasmus, 1965: 181). Until such time as capital-intensive agriculture is introduced on the hacienda, along with increased use of cash and contract in economic relations, we may expect these types of labor to persist. Growing pressure on the land, however, may in time increase the number of laborers willing to work outside their minimal plots for a cash wage (Pierson, 1948: 70).

For there can be no doubt that such wage labor has increased markedly since the agrarian reform. As is the case with festive and ayni labor, jornaleros are hired for tasks requiring sizable groups: sowing and harvesting (more often the latter, when day laborers are paid either in cash or in kind); house building; hauling of grain or potato crops from distant fields to a peasant's house when a townsman's truck may be hired on a day-to-day cash basis. Before the reform, an industrious peon such as Ricardo Rodríguez might, by «working until the night» every day, produce a trifle more than the others, which he could sell in the markets of Tiraque and Punata. With this he might pay a youth from «outside the hacienda,» from Waca Wasi or Chaqo, a «bit of silver» for a day's work. But that was all. Today, jornal labor is common. As in the case of festive labor, jornal tends to be asymmetrical: wealthier peasants hire poorer ones or youths without families or land. The main reason for this seems to be a desire on the part of the community to preserve a certain consonance between a man's labor activities and his socio-economic position. Thus, the most frequent employer of day laborers (for 10 pesos, a little less than a dollar a day, or 2 to 4 arrobas of potatoes) is Don Dionisio Guzmán, dirigente of the sindicato. The peasants say that his position does not fit with working in reciprocal labor with all but a very few members of the community. The growing number of landless youth, again, implies that jornal labor is likely to increase. Specialization—for example, the case of Fortunato López mentioned above—may also increase the amount of wage labor eventually.

Much work on the hacienda requires no extra help at all but is handled by the nuclear or slightly extended family or a man and his son working alone. This includes *barbecho* (breaking up fallow land with the plow for sowing) and the sowing and harvest of minor crops such as lima beans or maize. Poorer families with less land indeed do not hire jornaleros; they themselves serve as such, and their grain crops are not large enough to require a festive threshing. The only occasions when they might need the help of a large work force—the sowing and harvest of potatoes—can be handled within the context of reciprocal labor.

There are several points which must be stressed about the economic role of kinship at Palca. The first is that, often, it is impossible to separate it out rigidly from reciprocal labor. Since brothers have mutual obligations to help one another during the potato harvest, for example, it is hard to see it as anything but a special form of ayni. Further, work obligations within the framework of kinship which, at first glance, appear asymmetrical, may in the long run prove reciprocal. For example, Moisés Lizzaraga, a youth of eighteen, could always be seen out helping his grandfather, Melchor Andia. Melchor, however, was never seen helping Calixto Lizzaraga, Moisés' father, with whom the unmarried youth lived. The latter said simply that he had a duty to help his grandfather. It appeared a case of pure one-sided kinship obligation until we realized that Moisés was the only male heir to Melchor's lands, and the old man and his wife were close to eighty.

Still, labor within the context of kinship may have an asymmetrical aspect. Though fathers help sons and vice-versa, the latter's obligations are stronger, as are those of married men who are *ahijados* (god-children) to the compadres who have sponsored their marriage *(padrinos)*. As can be imagined, a rich man who can afford to sponsor many weddings has at his disposal a larger labor force when he needs it than a poor man; at Palca, as elsewhere, possession of resources in one area makes for access to resources in another. A positive feedback mechanism makes for mutual convertibility up to a point between resources in money and kind and resources in people.

Finally, kinship obligations transcend the boundaries of the hacienda. The husband of a girl from Pucara, a good friend of ours, goes frequently to Pucara to help his father-in-law. Similarly, the father of a widowed woman who married into Palca from Waca Wasi visits her often to help her out. There are other cases. Such aid does not appear infallible but flexible according to need and the quality of interpersonal relations within individual families; still, one is struck again and again by the ease and apparent generosity with which the peasants lend each other a hand *as long as it follows traditional paths*. For the fact is that new forms of cooperation seem very difficult for them to adopt. The case of the school, cited in Chapter II, is an example. Soon after I began work at Palca, the community turned out en masse under the direction of their dirigente, Don Dionisio Guzmán, and rapidly put up such equipment as they, along with Marcelo Peinado of the Land Tenure Center of the University of Wisconsin, and myself had contributed. But there it stood, half-finished still one year later when I left the hacienda. Don Dionisio, whenever I broached the subject, stated that although he «had no sons himself» (and by implication had no stake in the school), he would speak to the peasants. He did so only once at a meeting of the sindicato, without much force. Other men said the teacher was no good; still others, that their child was attending school in Tiraque, why should they spend money and labor on the school here?

As a community, in short, Palca turns out effectively for only two tasks: for repairing the roads after the rains and for work on the Palca River changing its course for irrigation purposes. Both projects are deeply traditional, having been accomplished before the revolution under the direction of the mayordomos. Both are crucial to life on the hacienda—for the entrance of trucks involved in marketing and for production, respectively. Today the peasants work under the supervision of their dirigente, Don Dionisio, whose skill and firmness in these traditional tasks contrast sharply with his ineffectuality elsewhere. The Palca sindicato turns out en masse, as does the sindicato of neighboring Waca Wasi, which also uses the river for irrigation; each family head is responsible for providing at least one able-bodied male. There are few slackers. When there are, the peasants say they just «leave a bit of work behind» for them to do.

The final type of labor at Palca—which I have called for lack of a better term «dependents» labor—consists partly of aid which orphaned youths perform for families which have taken them in. I observed only one case of this at Palca; the young man was treated essentially like one of the family, like one of the growing number of landless sons who work and live with their fathers expecting to be granted land from them when they marry or, at least, when the father dies.

But most «dependents» labor is performed by those evicted from other haciendas (four families in all) who were granted land at Palca after the reform by the dirigente (see p. 21). This phenomenon may perhaps be viewed as a direct outgrowth of the fact that the hacienda traditionally has always had plenty of land relative to the Cochabamba Valley proper; it has always been something of a marginal or frontier area. The patrón, for prestige purposes, had much land in pasture for his fine cattle, which the peasants have since put into crops. The outsiders say they are «grateful» to Don Dionisio for giving them their plots and, accordingly, they work for him. From our observations, this work is not infrequent, nor does it seem wholly voluntary since I have heard the dirigente, in a fit of rage at a meeting, threaten one of the outsiders with eviction, and the status of the peasants' land tenure at present is such that, probably legally he could evict. The parallel with the past is obvious. Erasmus (1967:366-367) and Ferragut (1963:139) have shown how, in some cases, the ignorance and confusion of the peasants, certain long standing habits of interaction, have allowed the dirigentes of haciendas to step into the patrón's role and behave like new patrones. To only a limited degree can this be said to be true of the dirigente of Palca.[58] However, increase in the number of landless youths in the community (with no external migration so far), plus proposed changes in the agrarian reform law (which at present exempts the ex-colonos from taxes at the same time it forbids their selling or mortgaging their land) might alter this situation. If the dirigente of Palca or other rich men can buy up land and work it with the labor of a glut of landless youth, they might, in part, recapitulate the past. Population increase in the entire area would favor this trend, as would the purchase of the cooperation of leaders in the Federation of sindicatos— peasant leaders higher in the national political structure. Still, the fact that land and power are shared among many rich peasants, who lack the separate income sources in the cities which were available to the patrón, means that no one man or group is likely to attain power equal to the latter. Gratuitous service on a total basis is not likely to be reintroduced, nor will wealthy peasants become as free of vagaries of the market, of price fluctuations, as the patrón. In the last analysis, mounting pressure on the land will probably lead to hardship and a degree of fragmentation of wealth and perhaps—in the long run (see Conclusions)—temporary or permanent migration to the tropic areas, which are at present undergoing settlement for agricultural purposes in the northeastern part of the Department, the region known as the Chapáre.

LEVELS OF WEALTH, ECONOMIC MOBILITY

Still, the fact that we feel it necessary to even discuss the above possibilities shows that one of the effects on the reform at the hacienda has been to create not inconsiderable differences of wealth; more precisely, it has cleared the way for these. In the old days, the patrón's vigorous work schedule with its liens and taxes had a strong leveling effect on the peasants. Now, the freedom of people to work as they choose, to exploit to whatever degree possible their varying amounts of strength, energy, intelligence and luck, has led to differences. This trend is expectable from what we know of the polymorphism of human groups and fits with evidence from widespread parts of the world (Wolf,

---

[58] However, as will become abundantly clear later, the reform seems to have provided him with opportunity to aggrandize himself in other ways at the expense of the community.

1966: 16). Economic variation among peasants often increases following removal of their funds of rent paid to a landlord, i.e., an agrarian reform.

Sheerly quantitatively, income levels have risen, whether measured in cash or in subsistence crops which the peasant no longer needs to share with a landlord. There is no one in the community, not even the most grizzled old man living alone with his wife, who complains now of going hungry. There is no one who never goes to the fair. Economic alternatives have widened a little with the increase of specialization: jornal labor, diablado dancing, selling of chicha on the hacienda, etc. With the removal of the patrón's diezmos levy [59] on livestock and with freedom to go to the fairs, peasants are selling more animals. Barter has increased, with more and more women from Punata coming out, trading small quantities of valley products—onions and green peppers— for potatoes and grain. Palca's peasants are not poor compared with the average per capita income of Bolivia in 1967 of $165.[60] A few poor peasants may earn a little less than that; the majority earn, even in a bad year, considerably more.

Yet the source of income on the hacienda remains chiefly what it was before 1953: the sale of potatoes and grain. Only distribution has changed. Wealth differences always existed in a small way among the peasants before the reform: Ricardo Rodríguez, for example, was somewhat better off than the others and hired a small amount of jornal labor in his fields under the patrón. There were always minor differences in wealth caused by such variables as individual industry and talent, variation in family size (which in turn affected its work force) and distribution of land in inheritance. Some people received more productive plots than others. In short, the emergence of «rich» and «poor» (in the peasants' own words) represents no genuine nova at Palca but an intensification of earlier tendencies. Also, it must be stressed that wealth differences at present form part of a «ranking» or prestige hierarchy, using Fried's (1967: 191) terminology; they are hardly sufficient to qualify as «stratification.» Wealth differences among the peasants are not insignificant, involving as they do differences in quantity and quality of land held and yearly income,[61] yet

---

[59] See p. 13.

[60] From United Nations Statistical Yearbook, 1968: 587.

[61] In 1966, Ricardo Rodríguez and Francisco Cossío had cash incomes of about $2,000 and $2,500 respectively. (This does not include barter income or crops consumed for subsistence.) Sinforiano Váldez, one of the poorest peasants, with a large family and working in *compañía* arrangements, earned a little over $100. Middle-income families in a sample of twenty-two families stratified according to income by Sr. Marcelo Peinado of the Land Tenure Center of the University of Wisconsin and kindly lent to me by him, had cash incomes which clustered about a mode of a little more than $500 to a little ever $600 per year. There are a few peasants earning up to $1,000 per year and more than a few earning less than $300. Amounts of land held also vary widely; in general, those evicted by the patrón hold considerably less than those peasants who stayed on the hacienda.

they are not inconsistent with the scale of limitations symbolized by the material culture discussed in Chapter III. No one has gathered together enough capital as yet for a tractor, or for a house made out of anything but mud, or for a breakthrough into a neotechnic level of cultivation or notably different life style. The negative sanctions involved in this have been discussed earlier, as well as the natural hazards in the area and price fluctuations, which act both as leveling mechanisms on income over time and, psychologically, to discourage risk-taking. The price of a bag of potatoes ranged from 120 pesos to 50 pesos while I was at Palca—$10 to $4 per bag—and while this did not, due to their good harvests, radically affect the peasants' income during that time, it is easy to see how it might have. The market price of potatoes is based on supply and demand in the markets of the provincial towns and in Cochabamba to which all potato and grain-producing areas contribute within a range of at least 100 miles. The microclimatical variation of Bolivia is such that some regions suffer plant disease or hail and frost in one year while others nearby do not. Those whose production remains unimpaired profit from the relative scarcity and higher prices in that year; next year, the situation may be reversed. The market, further, is at present limited by lack of roads and the vast unpopulated areas of Bolivia.

The peasants claim further they cannot escape the market by «waiting it out.» With the storage facilities now available to them (simply a bare shed with mud walls and floor), they say potatoes lose weight when kept too long; they cannot escape the conditions of supply and demand by holding their crops off the market until prices rise. The peasant is thus bound by forces he cannot control, and among the outlays he must make each year for ceremonial, illness in the family, replacement of gear and, above all, for chemical fertilizer, he treads a narrow path. He is free of the patrón but not from circumstance, and the situation promises to grow more acute as potato farming begins on a large scale at Pocona and Comarapa farther on up the highway toward Santa Cruz and in the south around Tarija—areas free from frost where commercial agriculture is being introduced.[62] Potatoes from Pocona and Comarapa were, before I left, already affecting prices in the Cochabamba market. Even as it is, the richest peasants at Palca have bad years which keep them from rising too far above their fellows.

No one has brought up the idea of saving money at interest in

---

[62] I owe this information to my field assistant, Eusebio Soliz, who spent much time in the Cochabamba market, and to Ing. Teddy Monasterios, for a time head agronomist at the Alliance for Progress Experimental Farm above Palca, who is widely recognized as one of Bolivia's best experts on the potato. He feels the Palcans would be well advised to drop potatoes as a cash crop and go intensively into sheep.

banks,[63] though a Cochabamba bank recently opened a branch in Punata. Certainly there is no one who has been able, in Wolf's words, to «shoulder aside less fortunate fellows and move into the power vacuum left by the retreating superior holders of power» (Wolf, 1966: 16). The dirigente has been able to aggrandize himself to a degree, and the not inconsiderable differences of income among the peasants have been noted. Still, there is no one on or off the hacienda who has been able to take over a position of dominance equal to the patrón. Further, such trend toward differentiation as does exist involve somewhat different mechanisms than those cited by Wolf (1966: 16). According to Wolf, dominant new groups like the Kulaks of Russia or the rich peasants of China arise through a simultaneous dissolution of traditional ties to a landlord and ceremonial bonds within the community which had been having a leveling effect. The upward-mobile peasant rises through violation of «traditional expectations of how social relations are to be conducted and symbolized,» through turning Protestant in a Catholic community or abandoning ceremonial expenditure.

At present, this model needs modification in order to explain the Palcan data. While ceremonial expenditure can be considerable on occasion and may be said to be obligatory insofar as it involves payment for deaths and weddings, Palca has never had a complex socioreligious hierarchy such as has been found elsewhere in Latin America. There is but one ceremonial post on the hacienda—that of pasante, a man who makes an act of individual devotion to the patron saint, Santa Rosario, during her fiesta on October 7. A man may also serve as pasante for fiestas on neighboring haciendas; the post is obligatory only insofar as, once having made a pledge to the Virgin or saints, a man must fulfill it for fear of supernatural punishment. It is a dyadic contract between the man and the saint; as far as the community is concerned the matter is wholly voluntary and unconnected with the holding of political office in the sindicato or even prestige. (This attitude held also under the patrón.) The leveling force of this ceremonial post, further, is muted, since the pasante pays only the cost of his individual devoto and does not bear the burden of the whole fiesta like the *alférez* or *el obligado* of southern Bolivia (Erasmus, 1967: 362). Thus the wealthy peasant at Palca can hardly be said to have violated «traditional expectations» since these were relatively few to begin with. If anything—as shown in Chapter III—intensification of certain conventional values: hard work, care for the land, intelligence in crop planning and marketing and manipulation of fictive kin ties, have paid off for men like Ricardo Rodríguez. By investing in his son's education as a mechanic he has made a move at once progressive and traditional—progressive, in that it may be viewed as a form of reinvestment toward the neotechnic;

---

[63] There is some indication, however, that hoarding occurs among these peasants, which would indeed fit their general security orientation and coincides with evidence noted elsewhere in the Bolivian countryside (Leonard, 1966: 94-95).

traditional, since the community respects a man who works hard and provides for his son. The fact that Ricardo has never been pasante bothers no one.

The other means of economic advance has been the sindicato, particularly through access to the office of secretary-general, or dirigente. As mentioned above, Erasmus (1967: 366-367) has cited evidence from southern Bolivia showing how, in many cases, leaders took advantage of their sindicato positions to advance their interests at the expense of the community and «preserve the vertical patrón-peón coalitions they were supposed to eliminate» (Erasmus, 1967: 366). Don Dionisio Guzmán as dirigente of Palca, has to some extent done the same thing. Making use of longstanding orientations of the peasants, their «gratefulness» for his giving them land, he has turned some of them into parttime peons working his fields. There is evidence also that he has ordered trees cut for timber and pocketed proceeds from the sale; engaged in favoritism in land distribution and pocketed monies entrusted to his care for the communal fiesta of Santa Rosario. While the very creation of the sindicato with its various new statuses and roles was an innovation of the reform, economic mobility since the reform has proved to be in part the result of individuals acting according to traditional patterns within those roles. In short, Eric Wolf's model of postreform mobility may need modification in still another direction for Bolivia. Wolf writes as if such mobility were a matter of individuals breaking with the past and becoming, in effect, entrepreneurs concerned with saving capital and increasing production. The Palca data suggest that such differentiation may be the result as much of structural opportunity as of individual psychological decisión; that individuals do not act in a vacuum but within a framework provided by structure; and that the political-structural changes occasioned by the agrarian reform —the sindicato and its posts— have granted space within which much that is traditional could continue under new names. New roles have been created, but new behavior is not guaranteed in them. Such considerations assume importance when one realizes how extensively agrarian reform movements in Latin America have been involved with the formation of such rural leagues. The Palca data suggest that, unless the menu of economic alternatives for peasants can be widened at the same time, such leagues will add to the already overburdened market of political, rather than economic, entrepreneurs.

PRODUCTION, MARKETING

Production and marketing have also undergone marked structural change in Bolivia since the reform; these subjects have been scrutinized by a number of students, notably anthropologists and agricultural economists (Burke, 1967; Clark, 1968; Erasmus, 1967; Heath, 1959).

Peinado's dissertation (1969) contains particularly useful economic and historical information concerning the hacienda of Palca [64] where he studied briefly.

Yet in this area, as elsewhere, structural change does not guarantee behavioral; the need for intense, qualitative, behavioral analysis remains as strong as ever and nowhere more striking than in the field of economics. Because a peasant becomes a family agriculturalist involved in markets does not mean he acts according to attitudes and motivations analogous to Europe or the United States.

In terms of simple gross output, then, disregarding for the moment considerations of efficiency such as output per man-year and output per unit area (Burke, 1967: 85-87; 90-91), Palca has always been one of the most productive farms in the region. Yet production fell sharply immediately after the departure of the patrón and remained low for several years, returning only slowly to prereform levels, which the peasants now claim to have attained. In this the hacienda followed a trend general in the nation (Clark, 1968: 166; Heath 1959: 7-9), but not for the reasons Heath and others have noted: breaking-up of infrastructure, reversion to subsistence farming, exodus to the city, and lack of leadership.[65] While it is true that the prereform leadership structure —the patrón and his surrogates— was more efficient in some ways, in that it forced each peasant to work longer and more arduously than at present, there is no evidence that eviction of the patrón has led to decreased cooperation among the peasants as Heath claims.[66] Rather, cooperation (of a voluntary sort, at any rate) has increased. Nor can it be said that the peasants of Palca have reverted to subsistence farming. The factors involved in decreased production here are similar to those Clark (1968: 164, 166) has cited for regions of the altiplano: climatical factors and politicization of the sindicatos.

A series of dry years in the 1950s grew so severe that on two occasions peasants took the statue of Santa Rosario from her perch in the Palca chapel and walked to Tiraque in a long procession behind her, praying for rain. They say that aridity accounted also for a decline in forage and, hence, manure; the fact that the patrón managed to make off with a portion of his animals intensified this. Even now the peasants cite a shortage of manure relative to their extensive fields as one of the reasons for entering into sharecropping (compañía) relationships.

But by far the most important factor mentioned by the peasants in

---

[64] Cited in his dissertation as hacienda T.

[65] Palca *has*, I hope to show, severe problems of leadership. I do not believe, however, that they constitute quite what Heath claims: a direct cause of production decline.

[66] It should be stressed that Heath (1959: 8-9) deals mainly with proliferating minifundio areas where, doubtless, cooperation has broken down. Palca's large peasant plots work against this, requiring cooperation. Bolivia is so geographically various, it should be obvious by now that generalization even within local regions can be difficult.

the decline of production after the reform was the heavy politicization of the sindicatos in the days of the MNR (Movimiento Nacionalista Revolucionario) presidents Paz Estenssoro and Hernando Siles. Then (1953-1964), as now, the sindicatos were linked to organizations *(centrales)* in the towns of Tiraque and Arani and thence in a pyramid of command to a Federation of campesino sindicatos in Cochabamba. In addition, the peasants were organized into a militia and called on for frequent guard duty at the centrales and also for quotas of food and cash to defray the cost of political meetings, travel expenses for political leaders, etc. With the advent to power of the tutelary military junta in 1964,[67] much of this has been streamlined. The centrales have been reduced to single men in the provincial towns, whose duty it is to act as intermediaries between the syndicates based in the campo and the Federation office in the city of Cochabamba, which in turn links up to the government's Ministry of Peasant Affairs in La Paz. In 1968 during my last months in the field, the government was again trying to beef up peasant organization in the provincial towns as a power base for the shaky regime of General Barrientos (see Chapter VI); but it is doubtful whether the centrales will ever be reconstituted as they were during the early days of the reform. Guard duty and heavy quotas of food and money have been abolished and the peasants have been «allowed,» as they phrase it, to go back to work; they are grateful to the present government for this and state that since they have been permitted to work full time on their plots, production on the hacienda has returned to prereform levels even though they work shorter hours than under the patrón and less arduously. Also involved in this recovery of production are the use of insecticides and chemical fertilizers (unknown before the reform) and the fact that, with increased population, approximately one-fifth more land is under cultivation now which the patrón kept in pasture for his showy flocks. The peasants have learned from the agronomists at the Alliance for Progress Experimental Farm *(granja)* above Palca how to use a blend of manure and chemical fertilizer, which allows the maximum rate of production consistent with preservation of fertility of the soil.

Yet despite all this it is hard to determine to what degree present production has surpassed prereform levels. We were unable to obtain prereform business records from Palca's ex-patrón or his son, who alternately boast in interviews that the hacienda before the reform was *bastante mecanizado* (pretty well mechanized) with two tractors and four trucks, sowing 2,000 bags of potatoes a year and reaping 20,000 which is, they say, much more than the *flojo* (lazy) peasants produce now; and in the next breath they admit that a greater population using chemical fertilizer is producing more «in the last few years» than they did as patrones. The peasants for their part state that, after the eviction of

---

[67] Ending in the untimely death of General Barrientos in an air accident in April 1969.

the thirty families mentioned earlier, the patrón bought two trucks (one of which was soon wrecked in an accident), a tractor and a thresher in a belated attempt to have his farm classified as a commercial enterprise.[68] These machines doubtless made up partially for the loss of labor of the thirty evicted families; whether production equaled present-day levels is, however, doubtful when it is realized that a considerably increased population in nuclear Palca using chemical fertilizer is cultivating approximately one-fifth more land. Posited against this is the uneven quality of that land—former pasture in the hills—and the peasants' labor. We conclude production has probably increased on this portion of the hacienda, although it has not doubled as Peinado (1969: 203) thought.[69]

Output per man-year has probably decreased and output per unit area increased (Burke, 1967: 85-87; 90-91). A smaller percentage of the gross hacienda product is going to market since an increased peasant population is consuming a higher proportion of it, and the patrón owned more livestock than the peasants now own put together, although most peasant families have more animals individually than they did in the old days.

In short, one must conclude that so far the agrarian reform has not revolutionized production on the hacienda, though it has improved it and led to a much more equitable distribution as far as the peasants are concerned. Labor appears as the most immediate short-run factor limiting production at the moment; the greater incentive and «pride of achievement» stressed by certain writers in connection with family farming (Smith, 1965: 16-17; Powelson, 1964: 52-53) are not so far glaringly apparent at Palca, though it must be stressed that, according to figures on production contained in the University of Wisconsin Land Tenure Center's sample of twenty-two families stratified according to income, a rich peasant may produce as much as three to five times the amount of the main cash crops as a poor man. Achievement incentive (conceived perhaps ethnocentrically in terms of eagerness to work toward the amassing of cash and machinery) doubtless exists in a man like Ricardo Rodríguez; but for most peasants their limited technology, hazards of nature and the price structure probably make it not worth their while to work harder than they do. The sacrifice they would have to make in order to mechanize, in the realm of leisure and security-reinforcing ceremonial and informal drinking patterns, is too much to ask in the face of such risk and in the name of items so costly

---

[68] The thresher was, according to rumor, broken up into relics (see p. 36). The patrón and mayordomo made off with the tractor and truck.

[69] This statement must remain speculative, based on interviews with peasants. Most peasants talk about recovery of production, not a great expansion of it. My differences with Dr. Peinado derive from conflicting views on prereform production based on separate interviews with the old patrón. I also had much more personal contact with the peasants than he did.

and alien.[70] Despite the changes brought by the reform, therefore, it is possible to see Palca at this moment as caught in a kind of circle. No serious change, as Erasmus (1967) pointed out, is likely to occur without a breakthrough into the neotechnic. But without changes elsewhere, in employment opportunities, leadership, and the price and credit structure, it seems unlikely that there can be a change in values on a scale sufficient to lead to such a breakthrough.[71] Further, even if such a breakthrough were made, it is a moot point whether Palca in the long run could compete commercially with other areas in Bolivia less hazardous for potato farming (see p. 73). At the moment we might say that Palca is engaged in a kind of culture of security, which stresses material production to the extent that people have food to eat and enough cash left over to buy minor consumer items and maximize other values such as informal chicha-drinking and fiestas. Up to a certain threshold, prosperity (and entrepreneurial ability in certain contexts; see Nash, 1966:41, 71, 76-80) may even intensify traditional patterns such as drinking and reciprocal labor. Palcans are not, and within the near future do not promise to become, farmers in Wolf's (1966:2) sense of agriculturalists aiming at expansion of a business enterprise.

Neither have they reverted to subsistence agriculture. On the contrary, although consuming more at home, they have also become more involved in the fairs and markets of the provincial towns and even, on occasion, Cochabamba. With removal of the patrón's heavy tax on their labor and time, most peasants are working a larger percentage of their fields; they are producing more as individuals and buying and selling more. Marcelo Peinado's (1969:162) figures covering all crops at Palca show that the peasants in the year 1966-1967 sold or bartered roughly 75 percent of all their crops. Of these, potatoes were by far the most important, constituting 9/13 of the hacienda's production; it is also the chief cash crop since roughly 82 percent is sold in markets.

---

[70] This is the consumer-labor balance long ago pointed out by Chayanov (1966); as Chayanov showed, it varies subjectively from family to family. Often during my walks on the hacienda I saw fields badly in need of weeding. Such fields belonged not only to poorer members of the community, to men stigmatized as flojos or tomadores, but to men with varied income. Other peasants told me the patrón never permitted such neglect. Significantly, also, the fields of the richest peasants: R. Rodríguez, F. Cossío, Don Dionisio Guzmán, appeared generally well kept.

[71] Innovation on the part of prestigious individuals may, however, lead to an emulation effect (see p. 40). If, over time, such innovative emulation should occur, it would cast doubt on the hypothesis of Schultz (1964:37) that no significant change can occur through reallocation of factors in traditional agriculture. This idea seems to me nothing but a projection onto the objective level of Chayanov's essentially psychological and subjective consumer-labor balance. As such, it is questionable, as peasants like R. Rodríguez demonstrate. One wonders how much the hacienda could produce, using the factors now available: increased land under cultivation, increased population, chemical fertilizer, if the patrón were still forcing the work.

My calculation of individual peasants' marketing within the University of Wisconsin Land Tenure Center's stratified sample of twenty-two families kindly lent me by Sr. Peinado showed that—as might be expected—percentage of crops marketed by a family varied directly with its production and level of income. Rich peasants producing three to five times the amount of poor peasants might market 80 to 90 percent of their production, notably of potatoes; poor peasants, 60 to 70 percent. The greatest contrast lay between Ricardo Rodríguez and Francisco Cossío, prosperous men selling 89 and 91 percent of their potato crop respectively,[72] and Sinforiano Váldez selling 25 percent. The latter, significantly, is not only a poor man stigmatized as lazy and a drunkard by the community; he also has a large family. Certain poor old peasants living alone market a surprisingly large percentage of their production which, however, is very low; they live much as before the reform in cramped ancient houses and constitute an exception to the general correlation cited above between income level and involvement in marketing.

The structure of marketing, moreover, has changed since 1953. Whereas before the reform most of the hacienda's produce went straight to the Cochabamba market on the backs of burros, excepting only that portion necessary to keep the peons alive at a minimal level of subsistence or involve them minimally in barter and cash transactions at the Punata fair, distribution today is fragmented. Much produce is bartered or sold throughout the year in small quantities at the Punata fair or to *truequeras* (women who engage in barter) who come to Palca from widely scattered regions and trade locotos, onions, tomatoes and, sometimes, chicha for potatoes or grain. The peasants cite the presence of the Santa Cruz-Cochabamba highway as the main factor in this increase in local barter. Produce is sold also at the Tiraque fair on Sunday and at the (new since the reform) Monday fair at the Kaña Kota bridge above Palca, thought these fairs are very small compared to Punata. This increased participation of the peasantry in local fairs and markets has been noted elsewhere in Bolivia (Clark, 1968: 166-167) and appears to be a widespread result of the reform. As is the case elsewhere (Clark, 1968: 167), a large part—probably the largest portion of the chief cash crops of grain and potatoes is sold to town middlemen with trucks who visit Palca after the harvest and buy directly from the peasants. A considerable portion is siphoned off by townsmen with trucks who work with the campesinos in compañía (sharecropping arrangements). In general, my interviews with women vendors in the markets of Tiraque, Punata and Cochabamba indicate the Cochabamba market receives less and the provincial markets considerably more, than they received before the reform, though some produce originally trans-

---

[72] Percentage of crops marketed by these rich peasants approach the percentage of his total crop which the patrón marketed before the reform, at least for the year 1966-1967 (see Peinado, 1969: 204).

ported to the provincial towns eventually finds its way to the Cochabamba city market after passing through the hands of middlemen.[73]

Yet despite this not inconsiderable involvement in markets and a cash economy, culturally and psychologically Palcans remain peasants running family economies oriented toward home satisfactions (Wolf, 1966:14-15). Land for them is preeminently a «source of security rather than opportunity» (Erasmus, 1967:373). They do not plan their activities primarily in accord with the market—allocate seed for planting each year in accord with what they estimate prices to be. There are no business reports or crop bulletins, nor could the people read them even if there were. There are no government subsidies or price supports[74] to cushion market risk, and the climate is never reliable. In view of this it is not surprising that Palca (and the whole region, for that matter) plants all it can every year in order to be sure of food; that security is of first importance and the market second. The latter receives attention from the peasant only after he has extracted from each year's crop the amount he thinks he will need that year for his family's subsistence and for seed. This lack of planning and concern for security paradoxically leaves the market less secure than it might be.

Other structural and psychological factors interact to inhibit cash-capital formation among the peasants. The lack of trucks has already been mentioned: a number of town middlemen are making a fair living buying from the peasants of the Tiraque area and selling in Cochabamba; prices are invariably higher in the city than they are in the provincial towns and the standard unit of sale—the tupu— smaller, so that the peasant's bag constitutes 9/8 of the size of the bag in use in the city. It is safe to say that the peasants could raise their yearly income by one-fourth to one-third if they could take the bulk of their cash crop directly to the city and sell it.

Lack of transport affects the peasants in other ways. For fourteen years, until 1968 when Don Victor García obtained his truck and one other townsman from Punata began coming to Palca, the people of the hacienda depended largely on one man, Don Venustiano Villarroel, to take them to the Tuesday fair in his truck.

This man, strong as a fist, thick, in a rakish fedora rolling along

---

[73] Influx of commercially raised products, e.g., tomatoes and other vegetables from Vallegrande, have made up partially for any decline in the Cochabamba market; this trend may be expected to increase (see p. 73). Cochabamba is indeed «rich in foodstuffs,» cheap and of good quality.

[74] Miss Katherine Barnes of the University of Wisconsin Land Tenure Center team told me in personal conversation in April 1970 that peasants have begun to make organized demands for price supports in potatoes and tomatoes in the Cochabamba market. Over time this will doubtless affect the provincial markets.

There is also a weather report broadcast each day at 6 A.M. over Radio San Rafael from Cochabamba; but as far as I could ascertain, few Palcans listened to it.

on stumpy legs, is perhaps typical of certain town middlemen who have risen to a degree of wealth through the reform. A poor man before, he scraped together funds to buy a truck after the revolution and began using it in transactions with the peasants. The range of his operations is remarkable. As he phrases it, he wanted to «help» the peasants of Palca when he saw they had no way of getting their goods to the fair; he began coming to the hacienda and taking them to Punata «for nothing,» as the peasants say: he does not charge for transporting produce, as other truckmen do, only persons, and that cheaply—2 pesos (about (24 cents) per person one-way.

However, once in Punata he drives straight to his house where his helpers—sons, sons-in-law and neighbors— unload the produce under the eye of his mountainous wife whose tongue and fist the peasants fear even more than Don Venustiano himself. The peasants say Don Venustiano «forces» them to do business with him; that once «you are there it is not possible to escape»; that he treats them «like a new patrón»; yet, significantly, they continue riding his truck. I know definitely of one youth beaten in the face by Don Venustiano when he tried to take his produce elsewhere. The peasant women especially fear Don Venustiano's wife, Doña Basilia, who is close to six feet tall and must weigh two hundred pounds, who clubs them with her fists when provoked and screeches «India» («Indian») [75] at them. The prices Venustiano pays in his house are considerably lower than the Punata market; the peasants claim his scale is dishonest, and I was able to compare his *chimpu* (mark on a potato bag) with that of the market. There is no doubt that it took many more of the peasants' potatoes to fill Venustiano's unit of measure than the market measure would have required.

Significantly, also, Venustiano would never permit us to view market interaction with the peasants inside his house. While always bluff and cheery on the surface, he was really angry, I discovered later, when we first tried to interview him and he tried to persuade his compadre, Don Dionisio Guzmán, dirigente of Palca, to evict us from the hacienda on the ground we were «Communists.» He never allowed us beyond the sitting room near the vestibule of his house, where we were politely served a glass of chicha and ushered out. Some peasants told us definitely that he feared we would «orient» them. The data presented in the above paragraphs is derived largely from extensive consistent testimony of the peasants.

Don Venustiano works in compañía with the peasants of Palca and other haciendas. (The campesinos say he does not cheat in this.) He visits the hacienda after the potato harvest and buys directly from the

---

[75] Term of contempt or dislike applied to the peasants before the reform. Supposedly it has been done away with, to be replaced by «campesino.» The townspeople nonetheless continue to use it frequently, especially when aroused against the peasants.

peasants—again, apparently, in this context not attempting to bilk the peasants but offering prices competitive with those of other *comerciantes*. He has done favors for Palca with his truck, notably transporting sand and rocks free of charge from Punata to the hacienda for the peasants' school. He has built up compadre relations with influential peasants such as the dirigente of Palca [76] and he is padrino to Palca's *capilla* (chapel or little church). He will not infrequently treat a peasant to chicha during the course of business in his house, especially since the beating of the youth mentioned above angered the Palcans to such a degree that Don Dionisio invited another Punata truckman to come to Palca. With this man, Don Miguel, coming to the hacienda every Tuesday; with the purchase by Don Victor García of his truck; and with the increase in trucking in recent years all along the Santa Cruz-Cochabamba highway (a peasant can always hitch a ride if he is willing to pay for his passage *and* that of his produce), Don Venustiano is suffering from competition and admitted as much to us before we left. But he is still a force to be reckoned with. Through the sheer «muscle» of his family (his sons and sons-in-law), which is regarded in the town of Punata as a rough and dangerous group, and (I have been told), money to bribe the right people, he has been able until recently to preserve a virtual monopoly on the Palca Tuesday trade through his influence in the Sindicato de Transportistas in Punata. This group, formed since the revolution and roughly analogous to a truckers' union in the United States, supported Don Venustiano in his efforts to keep all other truckmen out of Palca on fair days, and our interviews with Don Miguel of Punata and Don Victor García disclose both were threatened by Don Venustiano and others with fines or violence if they persisted in operating in the hacienda at that time. Neither Victor nor Miguel acceded to intimidation. Both continue to operate between Palca and Punata, and both have carried loaded submachine guns in their cabs.[77]

---

[76] The dynamics of power in this situation are interesting and show how anyone impressed with the structural changes in the campo, formation of the sindicatos, «politicization,» etc., must take traditional factors into account. After the beating of the young man by Don Venustiano, I said jokingly to another young peasant of the hacienda, Nicanor Sánchez, «What's happened to the Reforma if you allow this? Don Venustiano isn't even as big as Eusebio,» (my field assistant who is five feet tall). I asked if the sindicato or Don Dionisio couldn't straighten out someone like Venustiano. Nicanor said, «Sure, the sindicato could control Venustiano, but Venustiano is compadre of Don Dionisio.» It is interesting that Don Dionisio finally was angry enough to invite another trucker to the hacienda. He never banished Venustiano from Palca, though he threatened it; at last report Venustiano was still visiting the hacienda.

[77] Lest anyone be surprised at this, Bolivia's violent history must be remembered: it is preeminently an «area of weakened action» (Lambert, 1967:116, 132). The Cochabamba Valley has been a particularly violent region where, between 1957 and 1961, two caciques battled it out in a virtual civil war (Malloy, 1968:

Don Venustiano Villarroel, then, looms important in the marketing system of Palca. Through friendship, compadrazgo, chicha and the performance of favors; through opportunistic shrewdness, force and bribery he has built up a complex web of relations oriented, on one hand, to the city of Cochabamba where he trades, on the other to the hacienda. Preeminently, he stands in the structural position of middleman or broker between the peasants and the city, and insofar as he is involved in the sheer transport of produce, he actively mediates between them. But it is hard to conceive of him as in any sense a modernizing broker. His interest lies in the status quo—in a peasantry as isolated and ignorant as possible and thus not subject to influences which might compete with him. In interaction with my field assistant and myself, Venustiano has expressed the conventional view of the townspeople that the campesinos are all great drinkers, and he shows himself not illiberal in helping them toward this end. He participates minimally in their fiestas and drinking bouts and is—like nearly everyone in the region—fluent in Quechua.

The question at once arises: Why do the peasants, who (verbally at least) dislike this man, who complain that he bullies and cheats them and treats them like a «new patrón»—why do they put up with it?

The answer to this question involves both structural and psychocultural considerations and illustrates again the validity of Erasmus' (1967: 366-368) hypothesis that an agrarian reform which removes the funds of rent paid to a landlord without substantially altering the ecotype will lead only to new, albeit relative, forms of exploitation. Erasmus was concerned mainly to demonstrate this within the political structure of the sindicato; our data indicate that it exists within the market system as well. Erasmus, moreover, stressed the importance of isolation, geographical or sociocultural, or both, in preserving traditional features among a peasantry (1967: 373-374). He showed that geographic isolation (as in southeastern Bolivia) or cultural distinctness (as in the case of the Mayo Indians of Northwest Mexico) can lead to persistence. Our data indicate that *both* kinds of isolation can exist in area of Bolivia commonly thought of as commercial and active (Erasmus, 1967: 364; Patch, 1960), right alongside the Santa Cruz-Cochabamba highway—the principal and (at the time I was there) the only paved transportation route in the country.

The peasants lack trucks. For a long time this made them dependent on one man, Don Venustiano, to take them the 18 kilometers or so to Punata. This amounts to de facto geographic isolation, which damp-

---

318). Anarchic conditions prevailed in the entire country between 1960 and 1963 (Malloy, 1968: 457-461). As I write, I read in the Cochabamba newspaper *Los Tiempos* dated November 27, 1969, that Jorge Soliz, a prominent peasant leader from the upper valley and former Minister of Peasant Affairs, has been machinegunned four kilometers outside the city on the highway to Santa Cruz.

ens the peasants' potential for innovation by helping to perpetuate economic relations which hinder the amassing of cash capital.

Yet even in this relatively simple situation cultural and psychological factors are involved. The peasants own burros. They were accustomed, in prereform days, to haul produce for the patrón on the backs of their own burros to the city of Cochabamba by a much more tortuous route than that in use at present, i.e., through the valley of Sacaba. Why would they not use burros now to go to nearby Punata? The quantity of produce a peasant takes to the fair every other Tuesday or so is not beyond the capacity of his few animals, nor is Punata considered distant: a young man thinks nothing of spinning off to town on his bicycle for a day of recreation any time he chooses.

The answer seems to lie in the fact that, often, the quantities which are taken to the fair are very small—a few eggs or potatoes wrapped in a woman's *lliklla*; or animals—sheep, pigs, chickens—are taken, none of which fit easily on a burro. Also, it is true that very soon after the reform, with the completion of the paved highway in 1954, the trucks of middlemen began arriving in the Tiraque region. Once having ridden in a truck the peasants began to see it as necessary. (It would take «too long» to go to town on burros, they say now. They would «waste too much time».) Factors of prestige probably enter here, since Palcans are envied by neighboring peasants for their generally richer soil and larger plots.[78] They are considered well-off. It seems likely they might feel shamed seeing their neighbors ride by in trucks while they are loping along slowly on their burros. The latter are used to go to the fairs in Punata and Tiraque only by peasants living very close to the towns, and by poor, ragged, extremely traditionally dressed people living on remote heights above Tiraque and in certain deep valleys difficult of access north of Punata[79]—people whom Palcans regard as definitely having a lower standard of living than themselves.

The peasants dress up on Tuesday; going to the fair is something of a festive occasion for them and they prefer no delay. Moreover, Venustiano takes them straight to his house where their bundles are unloaded; this is convenient for Palca's women who, often, are the ones who go to the fair while the men stay behind to work the hacienda's large fields. The women say that, once there, it is too far to the

---

[78] Girls marry *in* to Palca from neighboring farms on the Tiraque plateau, seldom out. Significantly, Palcans do not intermarry with people from the remote heights or even from parts of their own hacienda higher up, from Palca Alto. They say the «way of life is different there,» that women from that area «don't know how to cook the food we like,» etc. (see Chapter VI). Differences here probably amount to class differences. I know of no Palca male who married off the hacienda since the reform.

[79] Bolivia's geographic fragmentation is so extreme that, in general, level of altitude (affecting quality of land) and accessibility to roads are more determinative of level of income and certain details of traditionality than nearness to town per se.

market for them to carry their bundles, especially if they be sacks of potatoes or grain, while all the time Venustiano and his wife are among them and around them, talking to them, «forcing» them inside. Many women see this as an advantage since, even if they were deposited in the marketplace, they would have to carry their produce around to the scales, etc.

Venustiano's cheap truck fare has already been mentioned. Some peasants cite this as an advantage and are apparently impressed by it, not realizing or ignoring the fact that Venustiano more than makes up for this kindness later on. Most important, perhaps, is the fact that Venustiano gives the peasants cash for their produce without delay; they do not need to wait sitting in the sun of the marketplace for hours selling their goods. They do not need to higgle-haggle. This is important in view of the campesinos' diffuse orientations to the fair. The peasants attend the fair for many reasons besides the specific cash purpose of selling their produce. They freely tell you they go to visit friends and compadres (compadrazgo relations with townspeople have increased remarkably since the reform); sometimes they go just to «take a walk» *(dar un paseo)*. Above all they go to drink chicha, and on any fair day the murky chicherías of the town are packed with men and women drinking and talking and, sometimes, getting into fights. Peasants interviewed admit to spending 20 or 30 pesos on chicha (approximately $2 to $3) on the average each time they go to the fair. When it is realized that a glass of chicha costs half a peso, and that many peasants—occasionally whole couples—attend the fair at Punata every two weeks or so, one can see they spend not inconsiderable sums relative to their yearly income in informal drinking. Not infrequently, peasants do not return to the hacienda until Wednesday night or Thursday, drunk, bleary, having spent most or all of the money they received for their produce. The quality of drift and confusion, noted so often in these pages is distinctly evident in the peasants' behavior in town. Fair days are also, as mentioned above, occasions when relations of friendship and compadrazgo may be renewed, and compañía plans entered into for sowing and harvest of the year's crops: sometimes compañía relations coincide with ties of friendship and fictive kinship, often not. The bare mud room of the chichería is the peasant's bar, his club, and the place where some of his business plans are laid.

There are indications also that it serves as a shelter, a womblike refuge from the strain of life. Erasmus (1967: 377-378) has developed a concept he calls the «*encogido* syndrome» to refer to shy, withdrawn rural people who «had been under the patrón-peón system for so long that they were still patrón-ized (subjugated in spirit or low on the pecking-order).» «Somos muy patronizados» («We are under the yoke of the patrón»), certain Venezuelans told Erasmus. Palcans say «We are very passive» and «We are accustomed» to Don Venustiano who treats them «like a new patrón». It is hard not to see a purely psychological element in the peasants' continued dealings with this man, «The lack of confidence and feelings of powerlessness endemic among low-status groups» (Erasmus, 1967: 377).

These peasants, further, like others of the region, are still cultur-ally distinct from the town and identifiable as «Indian» despite the revolution which aimed at incorporating them into national life (Eras-mus, 1967: 373-374). They are identifiable in town by walk, gesture, and (not seldom) clothes; by coca-chewing, and the wearing of abarcas, and their thick rough hands. My notes are filled with incidents of town-speople who, in moments of irritation, have referred to peasants as «Indios» or «coqueros» (coca-chewers),[80] sometimes to their face and sometimes—as in the case of joking between young people of different sexes—in contexts of considerable cruelty. For example, Ciriaco Guz-mán became friendly with a pretty young *truequera* from Punata named Doña Marina. My field assistant, Eusebio Soliz, accompanied him and another youth from Palca, Julio Vargas, one market afternoon when they visited the girl:

They all went to the cattle market where they met Doña Marina selling chicha from a large p'uñu. Doña Marina appeared very happy and smiling and offered them big glasses of free chicha, after which they all took turns buying and getting mildly drunk and Ciriaco kept joking saying he was going to marry Marina, that she was the only girl his mother and father liked; and Julio and Eusebio kept joking saying it would be a good match, etc. Doña Marina was drinking with them laughing and smiling a lot and selling a fair amount of chicha and going along with the goodnatured youthful banter, and Eusebio says the chicha was good; but very suddenly Doña Marina got angry and said savagely to Ciriaco: «I have other men whom I know better than you. I will never get married to this «Indio». Eusebio says Ciriaco said absolutely nothing to this; that he seemed to be tremb-ling and soon wanted to leave, which they did, Ciriaco walking quite fast.

Marriage does not occur between the peasants of Palca and environs and the townspeople of either Punata or Tiraque. Punata police do not stand on ceremony with the peasants. One hears not infrequently in the towns that the campesinos have been «corrupted» since the reform; that they have «turned lazy,» have «no respect anymore for people of the town and want to make themselves equal to us» *(igualarse)*; that they are badly raised *(malcriados)*. This point of view is not unlike that held by many ex-patrones and sounds familiar to any North Amer-ican who listens in his country to stories of how Negroes no longer «know their place.»

In our presence town shopkeepers showed courtesy in dealings with peasants, often indicating to us by side glances, smirks and sighs their impatience with a man's clumsiness in calculation or naive greed. Peasants' dialectical differences (almost all people of the Cochabamba region speak Quechua) frequently amuse townsmen. In short, though the peasants claim they feel much better *as men* in town than before

---

[80] Other choice epithets, notably of Doña Basilia, mountainous wife of Don Venustiano, include «mulas» (mules) and «caras de chuñu» (faces of chuñu).

the reform, it is hard to imagine that they do not still suffer there or
that they are fully incorporated into the town scene on an equal basis.
The long hours so many spend, sitting in cramped dark chicherías,
gorging themselves noisily on potatoes and drinking themselves into
oblivion only to rise and drink again—it is hard to imagine this behavior as not involving a certain retreatism or escape from life's bruises.
One peasant told my field assistant frankly: «If you had our life, you'd
drink too.» Behavior when drunk often includes maudlin weeping and
recalling of lost loved ones and children, «remembering the past,» as
they say. The pain derives from real reasons and apparently hurts so
much that the peasant is willing to surrender some of his cash to
purchase an anodyne. Drunken behavior can include also moments of
the wildest inflation, when the shyest, most shut-up peasant, one on
whom the stamp of the past is most apparent, becomes suddenly bois-
terous and bold, sometimes even megalomaniac as in the case of the
dirigente of Palca, surely one of the most encogido men on the hacienda
as far as the outside world is concerned who, when told I was leaving
with my jeep, went wild at a meeting and shouted drunkenly: «I'll
get him! I'll get him! Even on the highway. I'll get him! » Many encogido people perhaps drink precisely to enjoy such elevation. The important point is that beneath their structural participation in marketing
these peasants are less incorporated into regional life than is apparent.
Much traditionality persists. Illiterate as he is, the campesino is cut
off from such variety as the town offers, such as magazines and newspapers. He probably suffers from anxiety. His relations with the town
are truly rudimentary, stripped. Despite relations of business and
friendship with many townspeople, the peasant appears, to a degree,
still encapsulated.

There are, in addition, definite structural factors impinging on the
peasants which impel them into market relations they themselves view
as unfavorable. Although the open market offers a man 10 to 20 pesos
more for a bag of potatoes, say, than does Don Venustiano, the town
of Punata exacts a 5-peso tax on each bag sold in the market; when
this is added to the fare the peasants have to pay to transport their
goods in trucks other than Venustiano's (5 pesos per bundle), one can
see how—especially in view of the peasants' diffuse orientations to the
fair—the scales are tipped in Venustiano's favor. The little more they
might make haggling in the market is not worth the extra effort or the
sacrifice of their valued leisure time. Don Venustiano, further, to whom
they are «accustomed,» in a way protects them from the hurly-burly.
Only recently, before I left, the peasants of Palca were beginning to
trade with Punata middlemen who give them better prices than Venustiano.

A good deal of barter takes place on fair days alongside market
cash transactions; the peasants barter with townspeople and among
each other, trading products from the Tiraque region for valley products: maize and onions, chiefly. Truequeras come frequently to the

hacienda and trade chicha for goods; it can easily be shown the peasant loses financially on this deal. For example, during an all-night drinking party held upstairs in the old hacienda house involving five peasants (Casimiro García, Ignacio and Francisca Claros, Justino and Gregoria Najera) and two truequeras from Punata, a small p'uñu of chicha was exchanged for half a tupu of potatoes. Another half bag was exchanged for another jar as everyone got more drunk; in effect, Justino and Casimiro García between them traded a bag of potatoes worth at least 80 pesos (about $7) for two jars of chicha worth half that much on the market. Justino said that in the time of harvest truequeras bring a lot of chicha to Palca; he said he realized he was giving his potatoes away cheaply, but they wanted to keep drinking.

The same thing happens when chicha-sellers visit the hacienda: the peasant drinks and, when he runs out of money, is often willing to dispense quantities of potatoes or grain for quantities of chicha far below the value of what his produce would obtain in the market.[81]

Again, we are faced with the prominent role chicha plays in the peasants' economic operations, from production (reciprocal and festive labor) to the market where goods are often weighed and sold to the accompaniment of a glass. Chicha is the grease, so to speak, on the wheels of commerce; it is cheap to make and to buy and only the large quantities the peasants consume in contingent, informal drinking relations make it a significant expenditure. The peasants themselves know this: one man told me definitely that the people of Palca would live better if they did not drink so much. Another, Jacinto Sánchez, said (significantly) they would need a «revolution» before they would give up chicha, because it was the costumbre. Angel Rojas told me he would gladly take his potato crop to Cochabamba and sell it there for higher prices; he knew, however, that, strange as he always felt in the city, and running perhaps into delay in getting a ride back to Palca, he would probably go to a chichería and drink up all his money.

In summary, analysis of market participation on the part of Palca's peasants shows they indeed partake much more in local commerce since the reform both in barter and cash transactions. Local fairs are larger and more active than before and new ones have sprung up; the general trend cited by Clark (1968) applies to this region as elsewhere in Bolivia. Also, as Clark has shown, this involves a reciprocal process: with the increased amounts of cash available to them, the campesinos of this region are buying more commercially made goods: tools, items

---

[81] This, as might be imagined, a complex matter. For example, Doña Rosa, a vendor from Punata, told us she «preferred not to sell chicha here to these coqueros.» Why? «Because when they go broke drinking they want credit; if you don't give them credit they get angry and make a lot of trouble. And if you do give them credit, they forget it and never pay. They forget that we come here to do business; it isn't the same thing as when they make chicha themselves and invite their friends.»

of clothing, bicycles, radios, etc., all the consumer items mentioned in Chapter III.[82]

This process has also helped many middlemen to enter and swell the market. Yet as I have shown in Chapter III, and as Reina (1960: 101) has demonstrated in Guatemala, a people may incorporate any number of such minor consumer items into their lives without bringing about any fundamental alteration in the latter. And detailed behavioral analysis of what actually occurs during marketing operations shows much that is traditional continuing beneath the surface of new structural forms. The peasants, saying «We are very passive» and «We are accustomed to him,» continue doing business with a local middleman who cheats and treats them, in their own words, «like a new patrón»; they do this for a combination of historical, psychocultural and structural reasons. He arrived first at Palca right after the reform and made close ties with the headman there; he offers the peasants immediate satisfactions in a context where their orientation to the market is diffuse rather than specific and where the open market offers net prices, which are hardly sufficiently higher to make it worth the peasants' while to trade there. It is probable that the peasants' psychological orientations, the behavioral details they show in everyday interaction, have their roots in prereform conditions and tend to perpetuate themselves by perpetuating a certain isolation from the townspeople Erasmus, 1967: 373-376).

The role of tradition in the peasants' market orientation is complex. There are sound economic reasons for their diffuse orientation. If one thinks solely in terms of cash, and of the short run, leisure and contingent informal chicha-drinking work against capital formation on the part of the peasants (though not on the part of the town sellers and politicians). On the other hand, chicha might be said to help build capital in the broader sense that it helps strengthen ties of friendship and compadrazgo and facilitates working of the compañía system and reciprocal labor—all means by which a man builds resources in people and obtains a form of insurance in a context where cash credit is lacking and weather and prices are precarious. We have already seen how resources in people may be advantageous in medical and labor matters.[83]

---

[82] It must be noted that most of the consumer items which cost the most are imported: Japanese transistor radios, English bicycles, Italian accordions used at fiestas, etc. Development of native manufacture in this area could doubtless spur employment and save valuable foreign exchange; how strong a push toward the modern such small-scale industry can provide is a matter of debate among students (Heilbroner, 1963: 120; McCord, 1965: ch. VI). In the Bolivian context, in view of the *empleocracia* mentality, the deep, comfort-loving, middle-class orientation of the «revolutionary» elite (Malloy, 1968: ch. XVI), one wonders how willing those bureaucrats at present profiting from the licensing of imports will be to surrender their privileges.

[83] See pp. 55-56; 70. It should be stressed that the peasants do not necessarily intend or see the effects of their behavior; I am speaking here of latent functions

And cash spent buying drinks or sponsoring weddings helps build resources in people; the two are convertible and complementary and, at present important to the peasant. In the end, we are faced with the feedback mechanism or «circle» mentioned on p. 79. As long as the peasants remain on their present paleotechnic level, psychological satisfactions and many structural and cultural features *which are adaptive at that level* work to keep them there. Leisure, so often seen by students as the peasant's aim in life, counterposed to work and productivity (Erasmus, 1961:262; Nash, 1965), needs to be viewed here, in part at least, as having economic value. Traditionality even in technology [84] may serve better for the peasants than innovation as long as they lack the capacity (involving changes in *quantity* of money and *quality* of people) for breaking into the neotechnic. It is hard not to view the peasants of Palca at the moment as other than resting on a plateau from which it will be difficult to rise.

The same issue must be faced in connection with the region as a whole. While there can be no doubt that a significant commercial lift has been given to the Upper Cochabamba Valley and the Tiraque region in terms of a widened market and increased flow of capital, and while there can be no doubt either that a number of townspeople and peasants are enjoying an active prosperity relative to the stagnation of pre-reform days, it is, I believe, a moot point whether commercial development of the area has not also reached a plateau from which it will be hard to rise. Despite the considerable structural involvement of these peasants in markets, as long as the market for agricultural goods remains as limited as it seems to be and as long as the campesinos spend so much money on chicha, chicha-making equipment, fiesta expenses, etc.[85]—in short, on traditional items—when will they experience the «significant impetus to economic development over the coming years» which Clark envisions for the altiplano? (Clark, 1968:172). How can such a «significant impulse» derive from the market in consumer goods which the peasants have constituted since the reform?

(Merton, 1957). The peasants are, however, articulate about the benefits of compañía as insurance. At the moment the situation at Palca works against both the cash-oriented innovator like Don Victor García, and the drinker maximizing mainly psychological satisfactions, the tomador.

[84] Just as Ricardo Rodríguez has prospered relatively by intensifying traditional farming methods, modernizing only to the extent of using insecticides and chemical fertilizers (and of course investing in the education of his son), so the Palcans would probably be better off using their burros to go to the fair. In Chapter III I showed the cost of large innovation to these peasants.

[85] Even Palca's religion, I hope to show, is heavily involved with its security orientation. Relative to Erasmus' work mentioned above, and the theories of Steward, White and others regarding technological determinism, the data here show that, though you cannot have important change in other areas of culture without technological change, neither can you have the latter without the former. It is an empirical problem in each case where it might be easiest to break the «circle.»

Where, among these basically home-oriented, security-oriented peasants are the «new incentives, attitudes and motivations ... which derive primarily from the development and use of managerial talents?» (Clark, 1968:171). Cash-oriented entrepreneurship is undoubtedly *there* in some peasants, but in too diffuse a mix for such «modernization» as yet. Nor do middlemen [86] like Don Venustiano (who may over time get rich) appear motivated to help serious change in the agricultural base from which they are profiting. There is finally the problem of integrating economic activity in this area with others in a nation badly fragmented geographically. (Development of commercial agriculture in other areas may do more than merely bypass these peasants. It may destroy their market, forcing them to migrate or sink into subsistence agriculture; traditional peasants, like the miners before them, may be asked to pay the cost of development. See Malloy, 1968:ch. XIV.) At this point one can only put forth the hypothesis that, without outside infusions of capital, credit and educational facilities, without proliferation of at least small-scale industry, any strong impulse toward further change in this region will be slow.

CREDIT AND EXTENSION SERVICES:
THE COMPAÑIA SYSTEM

Yet an extensive structure does exist which aims at dealing with the peasants' credit problems: this is the federal government's agricultural bank, the Banco Agrícola de Bolivia which maintains an office in the town of Tiraque. This organization, whose representative states as his purpose the facilitation of purchase by the peasants of the region of seed, tools and equipment, ultimately «to advance,» accomplishes little in this direction for either the ex-colonos of the haciendas or the piqueros (small independent farmers) of the area. The main factor seems to be lack of funds: the bank simply does not have enough money to make loans to all who seek or need them. The situation is complicated for the ex-colono by the fact that, according to the agrarian reform law, the condition of his tenure is different from that of the piquero, who may be either a former peon who succeeded in buying a plot from his patrón before the reform or an ex-hacendado who was left with a portion of his estate, his «small property» (*pequeña propiedad)* after the reform. The piquero may sell, mortgage or more or less do what he chooses with his land; the ex-colono may not. According to the present Bolivian law, the ex-peon who received his land during the reform in «dotation» (*dotación)* may pass it on to his heirs, but he may not sell,

---

[86] Thus, «new» brokers, as opposed to the traditional cultural brokers of the prereform system, the patrón and his employees and allies, need not work for change. See Wagley, 1964:45; Dandler-Hanhart, 1967:9.

divide or mortgage it, or even, strictly legally, work it in compañía or sharecropping arrangements, though in the Cochabamba area this latter provision is ignored.[87] The aim of this entailment (Nelson, 1964:75-76) was to protect the ex-colono from manipulators presumably more skilled in business than he who might buy up land cheaply and reconstitute the latifundio. History, notably events during the last century during the time of Melgarejo, shows Bolivian Indians vulnerable to this kind of usurpation. The law aimed also at avoiding fragmentation of the land through inheritance.

But the result for the peasant is that in effect he is denied credit facilities which were set up to aid him, since he cannot legally offer up his land as collateral for a loan. The situation in the Tiraque area is confused by the fact that certain peasants have apparently received loans in the absence of security—one afternoon the bank's representatice showed us a file containing numerous «bad debts» on which he claimed he was having difficulty in obtaining payment; he said the bank lacks the money or inclination to continue this policy.[88] He said that if the peasants legally form production cooperatives, inviting government representatives out, electing officers and so on, they may obtain credit from the bank; but the ex-colonos of Palca as yet show no inclination in this direction apparently out of fear that, in a cooperative, there is a leveling effect and hard workers end up doing the work of the inefficient and the lazy.

It is interesting also to study at Palca who the campesinos are who have obtained loans from the bank. If the bank is conceptualized, structurally, as part of the total cultural brokerage system which articulates with the hacienda, and if cultural brokerage is, further, a matter of two-way interaction involving persons both on and off the farm, then who those individuals happen to be is important. Just as Don Venus-

---

[87] The ex-colonos at present do not pay taxes on their land; piqueros do. For a time there was a law before Congress to change this and to tax the ex-peons' land. I am told by my friend, Katherine Barnes, just returned from Bolivia, that this law has been permanently shelved, although the peasants (of the Tiraque area at any rate) expressed eagerness to pay taxes since it would increase security of their land titles. According to Dr. Fausto Merida, attorney for the campesino Federation in Cochabamba, payment of taxes would reinforce presumption of ownership on the part of the ex-peons and they would then probably be entitled to sell, mortgage, etc. It is perhaps a moot point whether the Federation leadership wants the tax law, since insecurity of title has been a means whereby, so far, it has been able to mobilize the peasants, raising the bogeyman of the return of the «rosca,» etc. See Chapter VI.

[88] García (1964:434-437) has criticized the Banco Agrícola for holding what he calls «free-trade superstitions,» for judging the needs of revolutionary peasants according to criteria of a «good business deal» under the old regime. But these peasants are less revolutionary than the rhetoric of their leaders. Whether scarce resources shold be spent trying to reinforce a system of agriculture here which appears limited and which, in the last analysis, may have to be transformed, is problematical. See my Conclusions.

tiano Villarroel was able to reinforce his near monopoly of the Tuesdav
Punata fair trade at Palca through his «in» with, not just any man, but
with the dirigente, so it is significant that the only peasant on the
hacienda who has managed to obtain (and default on) a bank loan is
one who, in the minds of outsiders, might seem to be among the most
«awake» *(despiertos)* or «civilized.» He is also a man who has moved
around more than most outside the hacienda and is more aware of facilities available. He is Saturnino Achá a grizzled warped-looking man
with a bad eye, who came from Oruro before the reform and served as
a curaca (foreman) for the patrón. He speaks a little Spanish and is
somewhat literate and more active in town than the other peasants;
before I left in the fall of 1968, when the campesino Federation was
trying to beef up political organization in the region, Achá was elected
to head the central in Tiraque, where he at once concentrated on obtaining bribes (cf. Chapter VI). He was spending most of his time drinking
in chicherías and talking of fines, while his fourteen-year-old son
worked his fields and his wife sat in jail for his debts.

Demetrio Cisneros of Kaña Kota, one of the most Hispanicized
peasants in the region and a revolutionary leader (see p. 133) similarly
defaulted on a debt to the bank and shortly before I left was being
threatened with jail for this. The bank agent in Tiraque told us that
it was indeed often (though not always) the most «advanced» or educ-
ated peasants who come to the bank for loans.

In short, I am suggesting that, in places like Palca and in certain
contexts, these may be the kind of people who move into incipient
brokerage roles: marginal men who have lost their roots in farming
and no longer seem to respect it; who, in trying to relate to the outside
world, fall into a kind of limbo. The smattering of learning they have
received provides them with a certain sense of superiority to their fellows, as well as awareness of the outside world—where they go nowhere. Such cases must be taken into account by writers who lay
stress on literacy leading to «empathy» in «modernization» (Lerner,
1958; Rogers, 1969: 45-46). The Palca data suggest that, in a region
offering essentially only traditional agricultural employment, other
things may be more important than literacy in the attempt to raise
living standards. If one is to invest in literacy, it must be of a sufficient degree of intensity to help people to truly «move out,» truly to
move to the city and find roots there in new occupations, or it must be
involved in a program of genuine life significance to the peasants, i.e.,
agricultural education. Otherwise it may lead only to status incon-
gruence.

In addition, the fact that such men as Achá (and Casimiro García
also) have obtained credit and defaulted on it works to block the hacienda's articulation with the state's credit structure, since the bank is
less willing than ever now to lend money to the peasants even if it
were available. At present, the bank lends to certain piqueros in the
region; I was told this is not always beneficial to the farmer since the

bank charges 12 percent interest and pursues repayment of the loan as soon as the harvest is in. It does not give the farmer time to «wait out» the market. Since the piquero is subject to the same weather and disease problems as the ex-colono and, indeed, often has less land, when he has a poor year he may have very little to show for his work after he has paid off the bank. «It's hardly worthwhile to plant potatoes when you have so little capital,» one piquero, a former hacienda owner who had been left with only a minor plot, said to me.

Another source of credit, small and in kind, is the Alliance for Progess Experimental Farm above Palca, which recently has begun to dispense good quality seed to the peasants. The granja has also done extension work at Palca, teaching the campesinos the use of insecticides and fertilizers, what mix and types to use and so forth; it employs an extension agent with a jeep who has worked mainly by means of demonstration. His efforts certainly constitute a factor in the recovery of production mentioned earlier; yet the amount of change the experimental farm can effect directly in the peasants' lives is very limited. The granja has only relatively small quantities of seed available; it is high priced from the peasants' point of view, and those campesinos who need credit—the poorer, unlucky or inefficient ones—are afraid of getting deeply in debt. They prefer to split the risk in sharecropping arrangements with other peasants or with townspeople. So far, only two men on the hacienda have received credit in seed from the Experimental Farm.[89]

And, once again, it is worthwhile inquiring into who these men are. One, Angel Rojas, is a vigorous and hard-working young peasant who paid back his loan in full and had, just before my departure, received credit for plowing the following year. The other man who received seed from the granja is Casimiro García, cousin of Don Victor who, like Achá, is a marginal man produced by the revolution (see Appendix). Like Achá also, he defaulted on his debt of close to $100. We will have occasion to refer to Don Casimiro García later in this work; suffice it to say at this point that he came to Palca from Potosí in 1960 after divorcing his wife and engaging in political activity which endangered his life. He has more schooling than anyone on the hacienda (through the sixth grade) and reads and speaks a fair amount of Spanish; he is a kind of decayed minor chieftain who has turned to drink and lives in an open *ménage à trois* with the wife of another peasant in the ruined hacienda house. He never goes to Tiraque anymore because, the townsmen say, he has built up so many unpaid debts there. He has enemies also because, during the postrevolutionary viol-

---

[89] It is perhaps indicative of a certain atomism in the community that, of three men who, on one occasion, attended a demonstration of seed and fertilizer use at the granja, no one told anyone outside his immediate family what he had learned. «If they had wanted to know, they could have gone also,» one man said to me. See Chapter VI.

ence in the region, when the centrales were strong and García held the post of «Secretary of Justice» in Tiraque, he abused women there.

Other, more explicitly formal extension services are available; but the situation from the peasant's point of view is similar to that of the agricultural bank: a mechanism has been set up, but functions only minimally. The bones exist, so to speak, but they are broken. The federal government's Ministry of Agriculture maintains an office in Punata with a jeep, veterinarian, extension agent and female secretary; while this group seems mildly active in the upper Cochabamba Valley proper it has made almost no penetration of the Tiraque area only 18 kilometers away. The reasons for this lie in attitudes held by both groups: distrust and ignorance on the part of the peasants; distrust and disdain on the part of the urban middle-class technicians who evince attitudes largely unchanged since the Conquest and who, further, are not always above corruption. For example, from an interview with Don Manuel, the veterinarian:

He said he had visited Pista Pampa twice and Huaca Huasi once (small haciendas in the Tiraque region). Neither Palca nor Pucara had ever invited him. He went on to say that often it isn't worth it for him to visit the peasants because he goes and uses up gas and maybe one or two are there to have their animals vaccinated. «Nunca tienen confianza», he said. «Siempre desconfían y yo sé cómo son». («They never trust you. They are always distrustful and I know what they're like.») I told him what had nearly happened to us in Palca, about the planned robbery of my jeep, and this seemed to touch a spring in him. He said he did not know that particular place, but he knows the campesinos in general. «No tengo confianza en ellos, indios, bárbaros, salvajes.... Están acostumbrados a hacer cualquier cosa.» («I don't trust them, indios, barbarians, savages.... They're used to doing anything.»)

Such attitudes are not very different from those evinced in the sixteenth century when, shortly after the discovery of the New World, a massive theological controversy arose among the learned of the Church as to exactly where the natives should be put in the *scala naturae*; and Fray Tomás Ortíz, citing Aristotle, expressed the opinion that the Indians belonged in the same category with animals, logs and stones and hence «could be forced to obey the most prudent» (Reyeros, 1949:34). Who the «most prudent» are can, of course, be decided by the most powerful. With values like these persisting,[90] it is not surprising to find that structures rationalistic or «modern» in form hardly function in accord with their avowed aims. If modernization can be conceived in a sense as a process of communication (Rogers, 1969:48), and extension work is a grass-roots instance of this, one wonders how

---

[90] See Gibson, 1963:382: «Social and cultural themes appear not as institutions but as attitudes that are expressed in institutions. They appear more viable, less changeable than the institutions that express them.» See also Potash, 1963: 393: «It is not institutions in the usual sense of the word that have slowed and complicated the transformation of Latin America *but the survival of a system of values.*» (Italics mine).

much communication can occur in a context where people continue to be experienced as objects, almost as things (González Casanova, 1965:32). Further, my hypothesis set forth on page 7 needs modification and expansion. If haciendas like Palca may be viewed as «internal colonies» (González Casanova, 1965:27), and agrarian reform an attempt at «decolonization» (Chevalier, 1969-974), the attitudes of *both* colonialists and colonized must be understood to make sense of the system. The evidence suggests that these continue to reinforce each other and complement each other in a rough system of pretentious «estate-like» orientations (Pearse, 1970:27) long after the estate or hacienda has been officially abolished.

Don Hugo Rojas, the extension agent, said of the campesinos they can «forget in a minute anything you have done for them and simply try to take advantage of a situation».[91] He said he visited Palca three times to make demonstrations of different types of fertilizer, but it came to nothing because of the apathy and lack of interest on the part of the peasants and because they *desconfían* (distrust) so much. Don Hugo recognizes this distrust as the result in part of the ignorance in which the peasants were kept so long under the patrones and also, now, by their own leaders who want to keep them manipulable. Don Hugo also recognizes that the peasants' distrust is often justified when outside agencies claiming to help them and formally created for that purpose turn out in practice to cheat them. (see chapter IV on the health organization which visited Palca). Once again one can see, coming, to focus on the local level,[92] the failure of bureaucracy, of «brokers» in a structural position to aid the peasants and committed ideally to that end, to perform their avowed function. Corruption is the means by which officials piece out the gulf between the prerogatives of their role as they see them, and the resources legally available (Moore, 1966: 57-58).

---

[91] There is doubtless truth to this charge, which fits with conclusions made by many students of peasant life (Brewster, 1967:66-96; Katz, 1967:99). Peasants doubtless lack empathy (Rogers, 1969:38, 45; Lerner, 1958). Granted the narrowness and harshness of their lives, and their victimization (colonization) by superior power-holders themselves lacking empathy, it follows logically. It offers an example of the complementary and mutually reinforcing attitudes in the internal colonial situation cited in the above paragraph.

[92] The following is an example of this, which occurred not at Palca but at its neighboring hacienda, Pucara. (All the peasants of the region know of it.) Representatives of a respected nationwide agency run by Franciscan priests arrived at the hacienda and persuaded many peasants to pool their potatoes after the harvest, promising them free transport to Cochabamba where they would obtain higher prices. In the end, peasants who subscribed to this idea received a *lower* price than that offered by private middlemen in the area, and the transportation in trucks turned out to be expensive. The agents also sold chemical fertilizer to the peasants which the latter found to cost nearly $2 more per bag than the price charged in Punata. It must be stressed the priests themselves did not perpetrate this, but employees they trusted, their field agents. The peasant again appears at the mercy of individuals free of institutional control.

The agents' attitudes of disdain and detachment from the peasants, moreover, have other behavioral correlates. According to a Peace Corps volunteer stationed in Punata, who has worked in close cooperation with the Ministry of Agriculture there and has had ample opportunity to observe its personnel in action, Don Hugo himself has set up appointments to talk with peasants and then simply did not show up. Don Manuel, on the other hand, acts condescendingly toward them, calling them «*hijo*» (son), etc. The peasants have expressed objection to this; said one to my friend: «Does he think I'm his *pongo*?» (house servant under the old regime of pongueaje). In fact, we might explain the greater (though still minor) success of the agronomists of the experimental farm over the government's official agents in «selling» new methods to peasants of the Tiraque region by the fact of the proximity of the farm (whose blooming fields are themselves a manifestation of the effectiveness of those methods, properly employed), and by the fact the agronomists themselves are, as the peasants call them, «*ingenieros*» (engineers), a «new breed of cat»: young technicians, earthy, not afraid to pick up a tool or mount a tractor. Indistinguishable racially from the peasants, products of agricultural training in Cochabamba and in Colombia, they seem to have bypassed the formalistic learning of the gente decente and many of the latter's values. As such, they show more tolerance and are freer to act as agents of change.

Yet in the last analysis neither formal nor informal extension and credit mechanisms set up to aid these peasants play, at the moment, an active role in their lives.[93] For those short of seed or fertilizer in any given year, the campesinos depend mainly on their own ancient system, the system of sharecropping, or compañía.

This system existed before the reform at Palca and, indeed, all through the Cochabamba region (Leonard, 1948:22). Palcans deeply resented having to share their crops in compañía and their animals in diezmos and even half their manure with the patrón; but they were used to it, they knew no other system, and when, early in the postreform years, townspeople from Punata and Tiraque began arriving at the hacienda to make barter, and at the same time offering potato seed and chemical and natural fertilizer to the peasants in exchange for half their harvest, many accepted. The reasons for this are complex. Primarily, it represented continuity, a seamless link with the past. After

---

[93] This is doubtless, in part at least, the result of conscious policy on the part of the Bolivian government and certain international aid organizations who have given priority in the allocation of resources to the promotion of colonization and commercial agriculture in the lowlands to the east. Since the latter have really just begun to get underway (and it is a crucial matter for research as to how successful they turn out to be), they scarcely as yet offer employment alternatives for people from places like Palca who would be uprooted by any radical shift in their traditional agricultural system. It may be that Bolivia can do no better at the moment than simply leave places like Palca more or less alone until other kinds of work have been developed in the nation.

division of the patrón's lands, and with the free time available to them, many peasants had greater access to land than they had ever known, certainly more than they had seed available for. In addition, the peasants say they suffered from a lack of manure during the first years following the reform due to the aridity of that time which diminished their animals' forage; the fact that the patrón through his mayordomo was able to make off with many of his animals added to the scarcity of manure on the hacienda. When townspeople came bringing seed and fertilizer, they were in a position to help many campesinos; indeed it is probable that, without sharecropping, many would not have been able to stay on the hacienda, especially the thirty or so families which the patrón had evicted and who spent their resources on lawyers fighting to return to their lands, traveling here and there with legal papers, etc. (see p. 21). Many of these people spent all their money and sold their animals in this struggle; even today they are generally poorer than the other peasants, have less land and work more in compañía. Yet it is safe to say that most, even the very richest peasants, have at some time or other worked at least a portion of their lands in sharecropping arrangements. Crops may be poor in any given year, or ceremonial expenses—death, weddings, the cost of being pasante at a fiesta—may use up money normally spent on seed and fertilizer. As might be expected, the poorest, unlucky or least efficient peasants work most in compañía, as do the growing number of youths with little land. If they can avoid it, the campesinos will not work their best lands under this arrangement.

The peasants occasionally farm in compañía with each other as well as with townspeople. Under the most frequent arrangement the sharecropper brings seed and chemical fertilizer, the peasant invests his land, labor, tools, manure and animals, and the harvest is split fifty-fifty. Sometimes the townsman brings manure also (in this case the amount of chemical fertilizer he brings is less), and the harvest is again split in half. Sometimes the townsman contributes only seed; in this case he takes only one-third of the harvest. The townsman, it should be stressed, extracts the seed he invested from the harvest before it is divided; in the sample I studied, this ranged from one to thirteen tupus of potatoes, with four or five most common. The townsman provides chicha and, sometimes, coca and cigarettes at both sowing and harvest, and sometimes brings workers with him to help with the harvest; he pays these in kind from his share of the latter.

Compañía relations sometimes coincide with ties of friendship or compadrazgo, more often not. Sometimes the vecinos visit the hacienda to barter with the peasants; and this relation, nourished by drink, ripens into compañía. There are abuses in the system from the peasants' point of view. The townsmen sometimes bully the peasant, trying to get their investment back if the crop fails, unwilling, so to speak, to split the loss. Sometimes the townsman tries to get the campesino to sell all his harvest to him on the spot, threatening that if he does not, he (the townsman) will withdraw his friendship, will not work anymore in compañía with him and so on; and the peasant sometimes gives in. It is hard to account for this behavior by any other mechanism than that these peasants are still at some level humble and used to being bullied; as they put in the context of the Punata market, «We are very passive.» The «vecinos exigen» («townsmen urge, force») and so they sell, usually at prices lower than the Punata market. They are probably influenced also by the prospect of immediate payment, immediate satisfaction. The most glaring abuse of the system occurs in the case of peasants known as heavy drinkers who get in debt to their compañía partners during the course of the year. When the harvest arrives the partner demands his money on the spot. The peasant can pay his debt only by handing over his share of the crop at a price the townsman is willing to offer.

Yet the compañía system is a complex phenomenon perhaps best viewed in the context of increased market participation on the part of the peasants. Before the reform, haciendas like Palca were, from the point of view of towns in the region, almost perfect models of the autarchic latifundio sketched by Tannenbaum (1962:80-89). Local fairs were tiny. The campo stagnated [94] while produce concentrated in depots in the city and the patrones mainly profited from commerce there. The reform scattered this, diffusing wealth and commercial activity throughout the provincial towns (though always within the limits of the «plateau» discussed above). Townsmen as well as peasants now share the wealth which formerly went to the patrones; compañía, like the new market in consumer goods, chicha-selling, middleman trucking etc., is but an aspect of this. Indeed, several owners of chicherías in Punata and Tiraque work in compañía with the peasants and share ties of friendship with them. Middlemen truckers like Don Venustiano Villarroel also sharecrop with the campesinos.

Also, despite the abuses mentioned above, the peasants themselves see real value in the system. It allows them to sow more land than they could otherwise. In an area so full of risk from weather, price fluctuations, and disease, where formal credit sources are almost nonexistent, compañía offers them a means whereby they split the risk every time they plow. The portion of the harvest they hand over to their partners is, so to speak, their insurance bill, and if sometimes they complain that it is too high, they do not reject the idea of insurance for this. Without compañía it is possible some peasants would have had to leave Palca or starve. It is obviously to the partner's interest to supply quality seed and fertilizer, since he wants a good harvest as much as the peasant.[95] Just as the peasant plows his land each year

---

[94] Under the old regime townsmen worked to a degree in compañía with piqueros; the reform has allowed them to greatly expand their operations, working with ex-colonos who own many larger plots.

[95] The peasants farm in compañía only in potatoes, the main cash crop. It is

with a mixture of chemical and natural fertilizer, sacrificing some of the productivity he could attain with chemicals alone to keep the land fertile with manure (as they put it, if potatoes fail this year, they can «redeem» next year with wheat)—just as, on this technical level, some productivity is sacrificed to fertility in order to achieve security, so the peasant is willing to surrender part of his profit in compañía in order to minimize risk. It is his means of balancing both; it is his insurance; and it allows many peasants to keep more land under cultivation than they would otherwise be able to do.

ACCESS TO LAND, LAND DISTRIBUTION, INHERITANCE

Nuclear Palca consists of a total of 2,700 hectares,[96] of which roughly 900 are cultivable by the peasants at the moment and 700 more are usable as collective pasture without restriction on the size of individual peasants' flocks (see Peinado, 1969: 91-92, 95).

As can be seen from the map on pages 14-15,[97] the hacienda at present is divided up into plots which belong to individual peasants; the latter received title, in the case of the older *permanecidos* (those who stayed on the hacienda after the eviction of the thirty families, discussed in Chapter II), from the patrón. The sons of these men received title, in some cases, from their fathers, in others from the dirigente of the post-reform revolutionary sindicato. The thirty or so echados were granted titles on the hacienda by the present dirigente, Don Dionisio Guzmán. All but nine families hold full title to their plots, registered in La Paz at the office of the National Agrarian Reform Council.[98] Of these nine, four are the «dependents» expelled from other haciendas for various misdemeanors and granted land at Palca by the dirigente; one is Fortunato López, the first dirigente of the Palca sindicato, still scorned by many peasants for «favoring» the patrón; one was Andrés Lizzaraga, who died with no close kin; and another is Nicolás Murillo, a peasant evicted by the patrón who complains that, for reasons he does not understand, the present dirigente never delivered his full title to him.

---

significant that Don Venustiano Villarroel who, the peasants say, cheats in market dealings, works with many Palcans in compañía and does not cheat in this. He offers competitive prices also when he buys from them at their houses.

[96] A hectare is equal to 2.47 acres.

[97] It should be pointed out that this map was made by the topographer in 1955, approximately, after the return of the evicted peasants. Names have been changed; there have been shifts and consolidation of lands due to death and inheritance since then. It represents however, still a fairly accurate picture of land tenure on the hacienda; the inequities are apparent.

[98] When we visited the office of the council in La Paz, we were told that the *expediente,* the deed to Palca, was «missing.» We were never able to study it. This accounts for a certain confusion regarding the strictly legal status of the peasants' plots.

The rest are young men who only recently received land from their fathers or from the dirigente.

Indeed, it is hard for me also at this point to tell why these people have, so far, never received full title to their lands. When we first visited the hacienda, Don Dionisio told us that everyone in the community held full title. Only later did certain peasants inform us differently, and it was hard to cross-check this with Don Dionisio directly or with anyone close to him for fear of being accused of doubting his word. Land tenure is a subject one handles with delicacy among these peasants. For his part, Marcelo Peinado believed that these families have not received their land titles because they had not contributed to their sindicato's effort to obtain the titles (Peinado, 1969:92). This may be the explanation.[99] It appears that, de facto, although perhaps not strictly legally, any campesino can work a piece of land which does not belong to anyone else on the hacienda provided that this is approved by the officials of the sindicato. This places considerable power in the hands of the dirigente who is by far the most powerful figure in the sindicato. In the case of Andrés Lizzaraga, who was always helping Don Dionisio in jornal labor, and in the case of the dependent families particularly, I find it interesting that their insecurity of tenure favors the dirigente's interest.

Yet a certain insecurity of tenure hangs over the heads of all the peasants since, according to present Bolivian law, ex-peons hold their lands tax-free on condition that they work them in a manner which performs a «social function.»[100] According to Dr. Fausto Merida, attorney for the campesino Federation in Cochabamba, anyone strictly speaking could come upon a peasant's land and, if he could satisfy the National Agrarian Reform Council that the land was not being worked properly, not performing a «social function» (a sufficiently vague phrase), he could take it over. Even ex-patrones theoretically could do this, especially since they hold bonds in exchange for their lands (in accordance with the reform law) which have never been paid off.[101] At bottom land is legally the patrimony of the state (Flores Moncayo, 1956:102; Malloy, 1968:308). The fact of a certain insecurity of land tenure grants their leaders a degree of power over the peasants, as we shall see.

Indeed the whole issue of the legal status of the ex-colonos' land tenure lays bare certain basic dilemmas of this revolution, contradictions and problems we will return to again and again in these pages and

---

[99] López and Andrés Lizzaraga do not appear on the map for the simple reason they arrived on the hacienda and were granted lands after it was made up, i.e., late, after the struggle for lands was over.

[100] See Flores Moncayo, 1956: 102; 242-244; 271.

[101] I cite the opinion of Dr. Merida. See also Article 136 of the Agrarian Reform Law which explicitly indemnifies the ex-landowers with bonds payable in twenty-five years.

which are extremely hard to resolve within a Western liberal framework. If ever the importance of examining the kind of people relative to their institutions were demonstrated, if it were ever clearly shown, as Anderson (1967:9-15) long ago posited, that Western European institutions can accompany a modern exchange economy but are hardly adequate to create it, it is here.

The Bolivian revolution was a moderate one, again. The sociologist Arturo Urquidi, who helped formulate the agrarian reform law, called it «democratic-bourgeois» (1969:47). Reformers were trying to induce capitalism in the campo, but they knew the Indians were anything but modern capitalists. Hence the very core of the capitalistic revolution which occurred in the European countryside (Heilbroner, 1963; Polanyi, 1957; Wolf, 1969), which commoditized land and made it wholly alienable, never took place among these peasants. When land became the patrimony of the state, the latter replaced the patrón as the peasants' new guardian from whom they hold the land in usufruct on condition they work it.

This entailment deters economic speculation, but not political, and it keeps the peasant from using his property as collateral for credit, assuming such were available. Decommoditization of land is one of the strongest factors making for a closed corporateness difficult to change, as Wolf (1955:457-458) long ago pointed out. My purpose is not to criticize the Bolivian agrarian reformers. Total commoditization of land would doubtless have led to abuses and despoilment of many Indians and at least partial reconstitution of the latifundio. But present policy has led to other problems. One thing is certain: the dilemmas of Bolivian land tenure clearly dramatize the difficulty of revamping such a society by legal means building on existing structures and traditions. One can see what drives thinkers like García (1964) to call for a more radical change in institutions. In any case, a «democratic-bourgeois» solution for Bolivia (if it exists) depends on development of sectors other than the traditional campo itself.

As can be seen from the map, considerable variation exists in the amount of land held by the peasants. In the case of those peasants who were not evicted by the patrón, who by and large hold the bigger plots to the left on the map, away from the hacienda house, the majority hold approximately the same plots they held before the reform; the situation exists which Carter (1963:1965:65-88) described for the altiplano: the reform has simply given peasants legal title to lands they held before in usufruct. Yet even here the situation is complicated by the fact that many of those who stayed have received additional plots —often choice plots— which formerly belonged to the patrón. Ricardo Rodríguez and his brother Zenon have even acquired enough cash to buy land in Punata and the neighboring small hacienda of Paycko Mayo, respectively. Just before I left, I was told that Ricardo was planning to build a house in Punata.

As for the evicted peasants, a few returned to the plots they held
formerly, but most were awarded parcels in areas formerly held by the
patrón. Many of these peasants state they hold less land now than they
owned before the reform although, due to the greater freedom they
have now to dispose of their working time, they have as much or more
land under cultivation for their own use than they did before.

One thing is certain: the evicted peasants at the moment have in
general less land than those who stayed; they are poorer and, while not
forming in any sense a clear and separate class, are nonetheless looked
down upon by some of those who stayed. Why should this be?

The answer seems to lie in the dynamics of the reform as they
worked themselves out on the local level. Two factors appear involved
in the present imbalance which is not insignificant either absolutely—
in sheer gross numbers of square meters held by some peasants vis-à-vis
others—or relatively in the sense that certain individuals with small
families or even lacking dependents altogether own considerably more
and better land than others. One factor is certainly favoritism and/or
lack of foresight on the part of the dirigentes in granting of titles. Interacting with this was the structural imbalance created by accident of
inheritance and the eviction of the thirty families from the hacienda
seven years or so before the reform.

After eviction, the peons' houses were leveled and the patrón took
over their plots for his own use. Some of this land was parceled out
among the sons of peons who remained according to the ancient custom
in force at that time by which the patrón gave out plots to young men
upon their marriage in return for gratuitous services. It is significant,
I think, that the revolution never called these titles into question.
Despite a revolutionary ideology which held the legitimacy of the old
regime to be a hollow thing, on the local level the legitimacy of the
patrón's titles was never questioned. The dirigentes went on, so to
speak, seamlessly handing out titles to the sons of peons who had stayed
as the patrón had before him.

The evicted peasants, meanwhile, had increased in numbers, including several marriageable youths who normally would have inherited
land on the hacienda. When they returned they sought plots. Jealousy
and conflict arose as a surveyor was called out to aid in distribution of
the patrón's land. The echados had elected their own dirigente of their
own sindicato, the permanecidos had theirs. Neither could apparently
resolve the conflicts and bickering which arose among the peasants
themselves and between the patrón—still fighting to retain legal control
of the hacienda—and the peasants. Finally, a man appeared who seems
to have been able to unify the peasants, Don Dionisio Guzmán. This
man seems to have been acceptable to both factions within the community and to have acted firmly against the patrón and in the matter
of the allocation of land. The leaders of both factions gave up their
posts; nuclear Palca was merged in one rural union or sindicato under
the leadership of Don Dionisio (see Chapter VI).

Whether Don Dionisio acted with wisdom and fairness, however, in the distribution of land is another matter. There was probably no way he could have been perfectly equitable. The echados were seeking shares in a farm which had already been partially parceled out. It was doubtless impossible to reverse this process, to ask those who stayed on the hacienda to give up land they had already received. The echados and their sons in most cases were forced to accept different land and less land than they held in the old days. The fragmented plots near the hacienda house and around the tributaries of the Palca River (see map) were distributed among them. (See Appendix for the names of the evicted peasants.) This is, by and large, good land, much of it irrigateable and relatively sheltered from frost, which belonged to the patrón; however, the discrepancy in size between the holdings of men like Guillermo and Sinforiano Valdéz and Leandro Najera (15,000 to 30,000 square meters) and rich men like Ricardo Rodríguez and Francisco Cossío with nearly 60,000 square meters is considerable. Many of the echados have large families, but this was not always taken into account in the distribution of land. There can be no doubt that this skew in land distribution, which follows roughly the skew in income discussed earlier, is a strong factor behind the latter.

The truth is that Don Dionisio used the agrarian reform, and the return of the evicted peasants and subsequent factional dispute within the community to advance his interests and those of his allies. As one man put it to us, «Don Dionisio was *tonto* (not-too-bright) before, only a *hortelano* (peon detailed to care for the patrón's orchards), but when the reform came he got *zorro* (smart) and left his small plot in the lower part of the farm. He moved on up with the echados and grabbed up plenty of the patrón's land.» A simple glance at the map shows that the present dirigente indeed holds plenty of land,[102] and we have evidence which suggests that he owns de facto even more than the map shows—land which appears in the names of others.

Similarly, several peasants informed us that Don Dionisio «favors» his godchildren, and indeed it does seem that Sinforoso Najera and Angel Rojas—vigorous and able young men with small families whose marriage Don Dionisio sponsored—received considerable land from him in addition to that which they inherited as only sons. On the other hand, Nicolás Murillo, Jacinto Sánchez and Leandro Najera received very little land when they returned to the hacienda after being evicted by the patrón, although they have sizable families. Land distribution at Palca at present follows the contours neither of social justice—the ideal of the greatest good for the greatest number—nor of efficiency. There can be no doubt that, as far as the allocation of the hacienda's work force goes (considering such land as he kept under cultivation), the

---

[102] Carlos Camacho, in conversation, has told me that aggrandizement on the part of dirigentes has been common all through Bolivia; that everywhere they tend to hold considerably more land than most other peasants.

patrón distributed his labor more efficiently than the peasants as a whole are doing.

For example, Casimiro García, a divorced alcoholic with no dependents, owns approximately 70,000 square meters of land in the hacienda (see map), more than most peasants. He owns so much land he cannot work it all, renting a plot of 28,750 square meters to Daniel Parra for 600 pesos ($50) per year in direct violation of the law.[103] From observation I can say that two of his other plots suffer from lack of weeding. Casimiro works efficiently only on his field of choice land (10,000 square meters) directly behind the hacienda house where he lives. It is hard to account for the relatively large amount of land held by Don Casimiro on other than political grounds. He arrived at Palca under the aegis of José Rojas [104] whom he served as bodyguard, and held for a time a post of power in the Tiraque central; he speaks Spanish and is useful to the present dirigente of Palca on occasion (see Chapter VI).

Similarly, Saturnino Achá holds sizable lands in excess of his apparent ability or inclination to work; it is hard to account for this on grounds other than his friendship and usefulness to the dirigente. It would not be hard to find on the hacienda men who could make better use of the land than Achá and García. Such considerations must be kept in mind by those who would hold with Schultz (1964) to the «poor but efficient» hypothesis that no reallocation of traditional factors can improve peasant agriculture. Political favoritism and accidents of inheritance certainly interfere here with the working of Schultz's model. Whether more perfect adjustment of the man-land ratio at Palca would (granting other restraints) lead to significant change in living standards is, however, doubtful.

Inheritance at Palca normally proceeds from father to son: fathers parcel out portions of their land and flocks to sons as they come of age and marry; the youngest son comes into the paternal home [105] and ad-

---

[103] Luis Ramallo, another Palca peasant widely known as a drunkard, rented his land to townsmen from Tiraque before deserting his family. Significantly, the Palca dirigente learned about this only some time after it happened and flew into a rage but did nothing. Luis' family was living in the most abject poverty before I left.

[104] Noted revolutionary peasant leader who pioneered the revolt in the Cochabamba Valley and, according to the peasants, was a key figure in bringing it to the Tiraque region. He was elected to the Senate in 1956 (Patch, 1961: 129) but was brought low and imprisoned by the military junta in 1967.

According to the surveyor who measured Palca after the reform, Rojas was frequently present at the great hacienda and, along with Don Dionisio Guzmán, «showed me where the land of each peasant went,» i.e., made the de facto distribution of plots to the peasants which was later ratified by the National Agrarian Reform Council.

[105] Including its equipment, utensils, animals, etc. Such property is considered common within the household. Only clothing and consumer items such as

jacent lands—a form of ultimogeniture. Yet inheritance is anything but certain, for it depends on a number of variables. For example, formerly, when land was plentiful, fathers gave land to sons living in consensual unions and even, sometimes, to bachelors seeking to live apart from their family of orientation. Now they insist on legal marriage as a prerequisite for land—when, indeed, they have it to give.

Similarly, though it is a general rule that an only son inherits his father's land, implicit in this arrangement is the «duty,» as the dirigente phrased it to us, of the young man to care for his mother. Title passes to the latter until he comes of age; the widow may award a portion of land to her daughters, if she has them, which are worked by her sons-in-law and pass to these when she dies. In the case of Fortunato López, this has been the means by which he obtained the bit of land he now owns in the hacienda. Macedonio Najera similarly would be landless but for the plot he stands to inherit from his wife's mother, the widow of Agustín Claros. Macedonio and his wife live with the woman, a tough old crone, and must care for her in order to inherit.[106]

By the same token, a widow may favor a daughter over a son, depending on circumstances. The community knows that Antonia Lizzaraga, widow of Santos, will pass her land to her daughter rather than to her son Agustín, an ill-favored young drunkard, single, with whom she has quarreled. No one questions this. As one man said to me, «Agustín never helps his mother. He will receive nothing from her.»

Inheritance of a widow's land is one way an able, hard-working peasant may gain land for himself in addition to any he might obtain from his father.[107] Younger sons often end up with more land than their brothers, but not always. As Don Dionisio once told us, «If there are many sons or favorite sons, the younger may not end up with more.» If a father has limited land and many sons, the latter may petition the dirigente for land which once belonged to the patrón; as we have seen one factor behind the skewed land distribution is the fact that certain only sons who came into their father's land received land in addition from the dirigente, and there appears to be at present no mechanism of redistributing land in accord with fluctuations in family

---

bicycles, radios, etc. are thought of as personal and private, though freely borrowed by kin and friends.

There are no formally notarized wills among the peasants as there are in towns; matters are arranged informally among those concerned, and the dirigente adjudicates conflict. His decisions holds within the community.

[106] It is customary also for the youngest son to pay for the burial of his mother in order to inherit the paternal house and land.

[107] Another way is to buy land outside the hacienda on nearby piquerías where owners do have the legal right to sell. One man at Palca, Zenon Rodríguez, has done this, and Ricardo Rodríguez, Zenon's brother, was rumored to be buying a house in Punata, and Jacinto Sánchez had obtained a small house on San Miguel hill outside Cochabamba: an incipient «shantytown» where he was talking of moving, leaving his land at Palca to be divided among his landless sons.

size.[108] The dirigente at the moment is running out of land to distribute; more young men and their wives are being forced to live at home with their fathers either landless or with very little land at their disposal. Thus, as pointed out earlier, Palca stands face-to-face with a problem of land fragmentation unprecedented in its history.

For, before the reform, the patrón controlled the effects of inheritance on land distribution. He controlled population and the man-land ratio by regulating marriage and the distribution of land. Couples were forced to wait for the patrón's permission to marry; there were fewer consensual unions, illegitimacy was much rarer than now, and marriage took place only in church (see Chapter VI) after the patrón had given his consent and provided the young man with a plot of land. The peasants say this occurred only late, when a man was twenty-four or twenty-five, a full man ready for responsibility. This was the only means by which a man could obtain land. By the same token the patrón redistributed land when a family decreased in numbers or died out, and he moved people about on the hacienda whenever he chose; thus an efficient spatial allocation of man to land was maintained within the cultivated areas.

Youngest sons came into paternal house and land much as now. It was to the interest of peon as well as patrón to keep men home as long as possible since the extended family bore the burden of the hacienda's obligations more easily than families below a certain size. Inheritance through women seems not to have been permitted. With the advent of reform and distribution of land either by the dirigente or the fathers of families, families tended to become smaller. Young men built their houses usually near to their fathers and started their own families. (Though here, as elsewhere, there are variations, depending on circumstances such as inheritance of the wife's mother's land. When the latter has plenty of land and needs help, the couple may move in with her. Some couples say they live with the bride's mother simply because they get along better there.) It is only recently that, with the increase in number of landless youth living at home, Palca has experienced a trend once more back toward the extended family.

Conflict over land, finally, according to the dirigente, is not uncommon but appears less serious than might be expected in view of the imbalanced distribution described above. Don Dionisio says he is able to «fix up» disputes (e.g., between brothers) which are brought to him for adjudication; still, land is one of the most pervasive sources of tension on the hacienda. As Fortunato López put it:

---

[108] Short, perhaps, of total extinction of a family when the dirigente would redistribute its land. This is an unlikely occurence which I never witnessed. Some peasants say the dirigente would make such a redistribution if a man abandoned his family and stayed away a year, but I never saw this. In the one case of desertion I was privy to, kin, down to in-laws, worked the land for the wife and children.

Brothers most often fight due to envidia, especially about land. One brother may have more land than another, and for this they fight, especially when they are drunk. This is recent, only in the last six years, when there has been a scarcity of land. Before that there was plenty of land for all; the dirigente was able to give land to any young man who wanted it; and before the reform there was more respect, the patrón gave lands and the life of each family was the same. All were equal and there was no envidia like now.

To a degree, tension over land follows factional lines in the community. Shortly before my departure, when I mentioned to Nicolás Murillo and Jacinto Sánchez how the dirigente had planned to steal my jeep, they burst forth in anger concerning the amounts of land they had received, and I saw the not-fully-healed scar of the factional dispute in the community between those peasants who had stayed and those who had been evicted by the patrón.[109] Yet this is by no means a simple issue. Echados like Sinforiano Váldez, who might be expected also to resent the fact that they fared so poorly in the matter of land (considering the size of their families), manifest nothing but praise and love for Don Dionisio for the simple fact that he gave them land at all! At meetings the peasants on occasion speak in familial terms to the dirigente, calling him «*tatay*» and «*papasuy*» («my father» in Quechua), the same terms which were enjoined on them by the patrón. There is no doubt that the peasants tend to regard their leader as «compassionate» in the sense outlined by Bequiraj (1966:10-15). He is still seen as a dispenser of benefits, a kind of nurturant family figure or patrón.[110] And why should it be otherwise? The ability to effect change in their lives on their own initiative is not large for most of the peasants. Of them it could probably be said what John Stuart Mill wrote of the Irish cotter one hundred years ago:[111] «He can scarcely be either better or worse off by any act of his own.»

---

[109] Nicolás informed me at this point he was sending his oldest son to school in Tiraque to learn to read and write in the hope of obtaining redress eventually at the office of the Federation of campesino sindicatos in Cochabamba. Significantly, Nicolás felt he could not hope to accomplish much in this direction without educating his son and without 500 pesos (about $40) for bribes and fees.

[110] Structural factors, the alliances Don Dionisio has made within the community through sponsoring marriages, dispensing of land to favorites, etc., doubtless add to his power and the helpless feeling invoked in the poor who might oppose him. One suspects, further, that complicity in crime such as the selling of timber and even slaughter of political prisoners transported to Palca after the revolution (see Chapter VI) may reinforce the power the dirigente holds in the community.

[111] J. S. Mill, quoted *in* Parsons, Penn, and Raup, 1951:13.

Chapter VI

SOCIAL AND POLITICAL ORGANIZATION

Social organization on the hacienda is extremely simple. There are no permanent groupings beyond the nuclear or somewhat extended family living in the single mud house described in Chapter III and, since the reform, the sindicato which meets only irregularly. There are no clubs,[112] corporate lineages, secret societies or caste groups; there are no cooperatives. A sense of formal association is attenuated at Palca as elsewhere in Latin America (Díaz and Potter, 1967: 159) and works to block the peasants' potential for organization for change.

This is not to say that the community is totally formless or atomized, only that there is a relative lack of clear stable groupings which might serve as foci for community organization as well as training for leadership. As we have seen, the nuclear or extended family is supplemented on occasion in various types of work groups; ties of friendship, marriage, kinship or fictive kinship (compadrazgo and padrinazgo) crosscut the household on these and other occasions. The work group is often the informal friendship and drinking group (cf. Chapter VII), and there is a tendency for friends to be neighbors and rough economic equals. Thus, those evicted by the patrón, who by and large are poorer and live near one another on the hacienda, tend to associate more with each other than with those peasants who stayed.

Social coalitions, in short, are extremely contingent and depend on context like other aspects of the peasants' lives. Nicolás Murillo, for example, partakes of the dirigente's hospitality at a gran trilla and works in a festive fashion alongside Angel Rojas. Later, he complains to us bitterly how the dirigente «advanced» the boundaries of his ahijado Angel's land versus his own when the surveyor was measuring the hacienda.[113] Especially infuriating to Nicolás now seems to be the fact that Angel is able to graze his sheep on land Nicolás believes to be rightfully his.

Similarly, the dirigente, Don Dionisio Guzmán, will seek out Don Casimiro García, the hacienda's best Spanish-speaker, when he has

---

[112] In a very loose, informal sense, youths who play soccer more or less consistently each week might be considered an inchoate club.

[113] The dirigente, with apparent community support, showed the topographer the boundaries of the peasant's plots, and the latter made his map (see pp. 14-15). It is now on official record in the archives of the National Agrarian Reform Council in La Paz.

business to transact in town. Don Casimiro, or Saturnino Achá, Nicanor Sánchez—men whom Don Dionisio treats scornfully in other contexts—form part of the dirigente's party when he takes on the function of an «outward-facing chief» mainly because of their smattering of Spanish and formal schooling. The composition of a drinking-party depends in part on who has made or is selling chicha. The roster of a soccer game varies, though there are a number of youths who, more or less consistently, break and come together again, giving a sense of drift to life.

Yet rudimentary as social structure is at present, it is more developed than before the reform. Then, as now, there was no corporate grouping beyond the nuclear or extended family; but the peasants had much less time to develop ties of informal friendship and association. Voluntary work association was rare; the peasants had little time to simply sit around and drink chicha and chat; fiestas were much smaller and young men never thought of playing soccer among themselves or with youths of neighboring communities as they do now, two and sometimes three times a week. Soccer seems to be a means by which ties of friendship among young men are reinforced. Drinking enters here, since the same group of strong and likable young men who play soccer may be found together afterward in a chichería in Tiraque, Punata, Chaqo, wherever they happen to play if there is chicha available. The best players in the community (there are several of these, often brothers) are without exception good friends who help each other at work. Soccer, furthermore, provides the most noticeable occasion when the peasants give voice to a normally buried sense of community: Palca against the world. After a victory they return home singing, a bit drunk with arms about one another, over the long, flat, endless road yelling «Palca! Palca!» Soccer is a true new joy in their lives.[114]

The form of the hacienda, finally, strengthened the power of the patrón and the sense of sociocultural strippedness I have noted so often. Unlike haciendas elsewhere in Latin America[115] Palca did not draw on an intact Indian community for its labor, but the hacienda consisting

---

[114] This is perhaps the place to mention my impression, unprovable but nonetheless strong, that among these young men of eighteen to thirty are the strongest, most honest and potentially able men of the community. They were children or adolescent at the time of the revolution and escaped the worst aspects of life under the patrón; if anything, they seem almost pathetically childlike at times, malleable. The mixture of cunning and distrust which one senses, for example, in the present dirigente, is largely lacking among them, and they could, I feel, be trained as leaders if resources were available. Unfortunately, resources do not appear available in the foreseeable future, either at Palca or at similar haciendas in even more remote regions of Bolivia.

[115] A typology of haciendas, building on Mintz and Wolf's pioneering work (1957: 380-412), badly needs to be written. Preliminary evidence from Vicos (Fried, 1962: 773), Hualcan (Stein, 1961), the valley of Morelos (Maccoby, 1964) and elsewhere suggests the phenomena we lump under the term «hacienda» may be highly variable.

of scattered farmsteads itself *was* the community. Thus Palcans were deprived of the protection of what Fried has termed the «enclave society» of the indigenous community—the psychological security deriving from a certain autonomy of social control and communal action within one's own world even in the shadow of the hacienda. Vicos made economic use of the Indians but left their internal system of prestige and power, fiesta complex, etc., largely intact. On haciendas like Palca, however, common in Bolivia, the native community was totally subsumed by the patrón; the latter's «hand» reached deep into every aspect of the peon's life, and he was wholly open to the patrón economically (he could be evicted at any time) and politically (local power was implanted on the Indian from the outside).

Yet Palca was, and is, very different from the «open» peasant community outlined by Wolf (1955:462-467), with its permeable boundaries and qualitative social change. The patrón, through his control of labor, marriage and land distribution, effectively shut off the community from the outside. Similarly, today, despite the lack of extensive stable social structure, Palca's boundaries are clearly defined and hard to penetrate. No one joins the community without the sindicato's permission. Despite illegal practice in the matter of land, no one can buy or sell land in Palca, and marriage continues endogamous within the hacienda and adjacent farms.[116] The increased freedom and wealth brought by the reform have not qualitatively altered social relations at Palca —as they tend to do in the «open» society (Wolf, 1595:462)— but have merely expanded them. Thus marriage involves much the same ritual as before the reform and continues to link families through ties of affinal kinship and mutual aid as it did before, though the scope for mutual aid among the peasants has widened considerably. Also, marriage came later in the old days and depended on the patrón's permission and that of the couple's parents (chiefly the bride's) who usually do not oppose the wishes of young people. Before the reform, couples lived secretly in consensual unions —informants joke about how young men had to visit girls at their homes and slip out of bed early in the morning before the family awoke. Families were stricter; the work regime was tougher; there was simply less time for young people to go out «walking» in the evening as they do now at Palca.

Yet open concubinato did exist between young people. The young man might «rob» the girl from her father's house and take her to his own. After two or three days, the youth and his father went to the girl's family and entered into an agreement *(mañaco)* by which it was settled the girl would continue to live with her lover and his family.

---

[116] Now, as before the reform, women occasionally marry into Palca from nearby farms on the Tiraque plateau, never from higher altitudes which are viewed by the peasants as sharing a different way of life. I know of no case of outmarriage by men of the hacienda, either before or after the reform. One family evicted by the patrón, however, did not return.

Later, as a rule, the lovers would petition the patrón for permission to marry in church, which he usually granted, along with a plot of land. There was no civil marriage before the reform, and the marriage ceremony in church in Tiraque was a much less elaborate affair than now, since the peasants had so much less money to spend.

Today, couples live in concubinato after the mañaco agreement between families much as before, only now mañaco is somewhat more elaborate: the youth and his parents go together to the girl's parent's house bringing chicha and cigarettes, and agreement to the marriage is sealed in a small fiesta. Concubinato may last several years, until such time as the couple feel themselves financially or emotionally ready to formalize the union either legally or in church. In some cases, the marriage is sealed directly in church;[117] in others, it proceeds in stages: first the civil ceremony in Tiraque before the *registro civil,*[118] finally formal marriage before the priest. By then the girl usually has children, and one sees the (to a Westerner) mildly humorous spectacle of the bride dressed in her best and beautiful satiny pollera traipsing over the fields to church with a tot at her side and baby on her back bouncing up and down in a shawl.

Not infrequently, things do not reach this point, and the girl returns to her parents with or without children. Concubinato since the reform appears unstable and recapitulates the theme of drift or confusion I have noted so often at Palca, though the peasants do not think of it as experimental or «trial marriage». Small stigma seems to be attached to illegitimacy, though there are three or four young women in the community who are known to have had children by different men and who live at home with their family of orientation. The attitude of eligible bachelors toward these girls seem to be: plenty of good-natured willingness to «walk» with them in the evening, especially after chicha at a party, but they are not likely to marry them in church.

There are cases of mañaco agreements and concubinato where the young man moves in with his girl's family; this arrangement is, again, contingent, depending on amount of land available relative to manpower and personal relations within and between families. It may be seen as related to inheritance through widows described above, who would be hard pressed to work their land without the help of their son-in-law. For example, Guillermo Acuña, a landless young man, lives in concubinato with the daughter of old Saturnino Nájera and helps his incipient father-in-law, who otherwise would be sonless. Similarly Antonio Salazar, another landless youth from a neighboring hacienda, lives with the family of his concubinato wife, helps her father and stands to inherit. Julián Velardes has even left his own father's house after a quarrel and much

---

[117] Details of the wedding ceremony, expenses, etc., will be described in Chapter VII.

[118] A petty town official who performs much the same functions as a notary public or justice of the peace.

pain; he lives with his girl in the house of her brother, Julián Ramallo, a simple minded youth who might be hardpressed to manage alone. One can see here rather clearly the complex factors which may at any point shape residence and marriage.

Though most in the community proceed beyond concubinato to marriage in church or at least civil marriage, this is not true of everyone. There are several cases of concubinato between young people which have lasted at least four years, and two cases of mature men with sizable families—Calixto Lizzaraga and Saturnino Achà—who have never moved beyond that stage. The community tolerates this but does not respect it, and my impression during interviews with Lizzaraga and Achà was that they were at the very least reticent in talking about their marriage. Informants say that the attitudes of parents constitute the most important factor in determining length of concubinato. As Nicanor Sánchez put it, «Some parents are stricter than others and keep bothering people to marry fast; others are more easy in allowing a long time in concubinato. If there's no one around to make them do it, sometimes they'll never get married in church.»[119]

Another factor appears to be wealth, since there is no one among the richest peasants in the community who has not been married at least before the registro civil. Yet wealth cannot be a sufficient cause of legal marriage since many of the poorest peasants in the community have been married both in civil ceremony and in church, while Calixto Lizzaraga and Saturnino Achà are hardly poor. They are, however, great drunkards, living in what can only be described as muddy squalor in traditional houses lacking even those minor consumer items shared by most other peasants. Both roar and fight readily when in their cups, and the children hide. The pleasures of chicha seem more important to them than most other things, including official marriage.

Neither economic nor legal factors work against concubinato, since a girl who remains in that state risks little more than one officially married. If the consensual union dissolves, she returns to her family who live in much the same kind of house and eat the same food as her lover; she continues doing the same work—«la cocina y el pastoreo»—and her brother or father support her and her children as her lover had before. A woman who has lived at least two years in concubinato with a man has as full legal right of inheritance as one married in church, though if she marries later she renounces this. If a girl has lived even a short time with a man and he dies, even if there are no children she is entitled to a cash payment; the amount I saw change hands on one occasion was 400 pesos (a little over $33). Pressures of prestige and, in some people perhaps, a vague fear of religious retribution are more important in moving people out of consensual union and into legalized

---

[119] This seems to be true of both Calixto Lizzaraga and Saturnino Achá; their parents have long been dead.

marriage than the more material factors involved in specialized societies.

The fear of supernatural punishment, a «castigo de Dios» involving sickness and crop failure, provides a strong sanction supporting marriage once it has been legalized or consecrated in church. Community pressure also becomes more forceful here. It is a fact that although no stigma is attached to free and easy intercourse between the sexes before marriage, or to the break-up of concubinato relationships, the reverse is true after marriage. For example, Don Dionisio told us the reason Ignacio Claros' house is so poor («like the house of a dead man»), why he had never «had luck in his life» and his crops were always poor, was because he allowed his wife, Francisca, to commit adultery incessantly with Casimiro García—indeed, even collaborated in it:

for this adultery (Don Dionisio said) El Señor is not giving Ignacio any luck in his life, in his crops or in anything and his house appears like the house of a dead man. He said if they continue in their present manner, the peasants will have a meeting and enter into an agreement to kick both Casimiro and Francisca out of the community. He said, «Here at Palca we are very passive and Casimiro abused this.» He said that Justiniano (Najera) had complained to him that Casimiro had slept with his wife, and he had trouble calming Justiniano down. He said this situation of Don Casimiro is «bad» for the community, can be a bad example for other families.

Don Dionisio beat Casimiro with his fists in a Punata chichería and warned him to stop. Casimiro, bleeding, on his knees and weeping, promised to do so; yet he did not. When I left the hacienda two months later, the pathetic drunken trio were together as always, and Don Dionisio said nothing.

Also, it is worthwhile pointing out that it was not adultery alone which enraged the dirigente on this occasion but the fact that agents from the Alliance for Progress Experimental Farm above Palca were beginning to dun *him*, Don Dionisio, for the debt of nearly $100 which Casimiro owed. The dirigente was also furious because Casimiro tried to «lie,» to deny his liasion with Francisca Claros.

Yet barely over a month after the beating, Don Dionisio was calling Don Casimiro to his home to help him think out ways of stealing my jeep. «How can we get hold of the gringo's jeep?» Informants tell me he said. «Give me your ideas.» As a former minor revolutionary chieftain from Potosí (see pp. 95-106 and see Appendix for his life history), Casimiro was useful as the dirigente's «brains» on this occasion—a fine example of the shifting and contingent coalitions the peasants form, depending on context. There is little doubt that, with his knowledge of Spanish and acquaintance with peasant leaders on the provincial and departmental levels, Casimiro will continue to be useful to Don Dionisio when the latter leaves the hacienda, taking on functions of a cultural «broker» or «outward-facing chief.»

Still one cannot assume from this that all is expediency, that community regulation of marriage is lacking. It is, rather, explosive and informal like other aspects of social control. I learned of the case of a youth who was beaten to death with fists by the peasants during the fiesta of Santa Rosario for «forcing» the wife of a man from Paycko Mayu.[120] The peasants caught the young man at night by the wall of the Palca chapel and pounded him to death and buried him, I did not ask where. This was in the time of the MNR government of Paz Estenssoro when the peasant sindicatos and their Federation exercised more complete control in the countryside than they do at present.

Don Dionisio had some trouble calming Justiniano Najera down after his wife's slip with Casimiro García.[121] Adultery, especially on the part of a woman, runs the risk of violent retaliation on the part of the husband. When it is prolonged and flagrant, it runs the risk of community sanction. Adultery of this type is definitely rare, and divorce or separation are even rarer.[122]

Remarriage of a widow[123] or widower also appears rare: the peasants feel that step-parents are likely to favor their own children over those belonging to their partner, that they will not really love another person's children and this leads to conflict. Marriage in any case is not especially harmonious. Couples fight among themselves at Palca as elsewhere, especially when drunk; bruises, bites and scratches appear after a drinking bout and seem to be involved with a strange power in sexual relations. After drinking, couples often have not the slightest idea what they were fighting about but are enclosed in a mood Bequiraj has described as «diffuse suffering» (Bequiraj, 1966:11), dark, silent, shut in on themselves, walking along the road beneath the mountains.

Festive occasions—notably weddings—are moments when women may engage in explosive drunken weeping, baring on one hand the miseries of married life to the community at large, on the other warning the newlyweds that their life ahead is not a bed of roses but a way full of suffering, beatings and the death of children. At such times one sees

---

[120] Small hacienda bordering Palca, directly between the larger hacienda and the Santa Cruz-Cochabamba highway. It should be noted that this was a special case. The peasants' rage was directed as much against the rape as the adultery.

[121] The anguish and rage of Justiniano, a poor, strong, simple young peasant, somewhat alcoholic, was wrenching on this occasion. Like Wozzeck who murdered his errant mistress, he has «nothing else besides.»

[122] The only cases I know at Palca are Luis Ramallo, a young man who turned to drink after the death of his mother and ran away from his family to Santa Cruz, and the García-Claros triangle mentioned above. Casimiro García represents an anomaly (see Appendix). The Claros couple are unusual also in that, despite their relatively advanced age (forty and thirty-eight respectively for the man and woman) they are childless. Francisca especially is regarded with awe, fear and hatred by the community as a kind of *diabla* (devil) who unmanned her husband by giving him a «potion.» See p. 45.

[123] Sexual behavior, however, is another matter. Certain widows in the community, especially the lasciviousness of one, are a source of continual joking among unmarried young men. Widows are not expected to remain forever unsatisfied sexually.

the «extremism of response» Bequiraj has pointed to among peasants (Bequiraj, 1966:14)—a «one sidedness» and abandon which, in other contexts, can lend itself to acts of bewildering cruelty. At such times the weeping may take on an almost agonistic air, with one woman starting and others joining in as if to outdo one another in a fugue of woe.

Conflict between generations is not unknown.[124] Despite the stress ideally placed on paternal authority by the peasants, in reality most young people seek to set up their own independent household as soon as possible; as Pedro Najera, a «good son,» put it: «We feel more comfortable that way.» It is a source of some frustration in the community at the moment that so many young couples are forced to live with parents because of the shortage of land.

Conflict between families is also not uncommon, although Palca has hardly reached the state of «amoral familism» described by Banfield (1958). It would be more accurate to describe the situation here negatively, as weakness of identification with a range of humanity beyond the nuclear or extended family, or at most cliques formed by friendship and fictive kinship. The role of marriage—beyond its usual function of regulating sex and providing stable economic and socialization bases in the household—is to serve as one of the most vital mechanisms of extending that range of identification as far as it goes. It structures relationships beyond kinship,[125] notably of respect and mutual aid; the obligations of close affines can be as strong as kinship. For example, when Luis Ramallo deserted his family, the dirigente appointed José Rodríguez, husband of the sister of Luis wife, to help the abandoned woman even though the latter has a brother living in the community who could have helped. Again, contingency is shown: at that time Masica Flores, the wife, was at odds her brother Juan de Dios over a large perol for making chicha, which the latter had lent to his sister and which, he claimed, she had never returned. Juan de Dios did not want to help his sister because of this, so the dirigente chose José. (José further stated he would have helped anyway, as Doña Masica's brother-in-law, but it is interesting that when he told us about it, he said the dirigente «appointed» him. Possibly, he would have been less assiduous alone.)

Brothers-in-law help each other at work much as brothers do: marriage can be viewed as a mechanism for mobilizing resources like other customs (compadrazgo, the compañía system) discussed in these pages. Marriage can effect the fragmentation or consolidation of land. Whether, however, economic considerations in marriage are as important at Palca as Díaz and Potter (1967:156) claim they are elsewhere, whether the peasant «calculates assiduously how much certain matches will affect his gaining or losing this precious resource» (land) and «marriages are... arranged to consolidate holdings»—this is a moot point. Without excep-

---

[124] See the cases of Agustín Lizzaraga and Nicanor Sánchez, pp. 35, 107.
[125] At least ideally and roughly behaviorally.

tion in interviews the peasants say they marry «only for love.» Years of life under the patrón deprived them of the ability to control allocation of their land, and it is only recently that they have begun to do this. Analysis of Palca marriages implies that, while it is unlikely that economic considerations are totally lacking in most cases, they are not as conscious and intense as in the Díaz-Potter model. It is hard to isolate a purely material motive. For example, Angel Rojas married the dirigente's cousin and Don Dionisio is his padrino. Angel has certainly gained from this in the land distribution. But Angel and his wife—relatively sober and hard working both—appear also to share one of the stablest and happiest marriages in the community; from my observation, they share a bond of attraction which is deep and strong. I could not say that Angel married Cecilia Guzmán mainly to gain land.[126]

The same is true of Sinforoso Najera and of those peasants who stand to gain land through marrying the daughters of widows. The marriages I witnessed on the hacienda may have had some economic referent, but this could not have been the main thing since those involved were rough equals, holding approximately equal amounts of property. The same trend is evident in census data. Since, despite variations in ability and willingness to work, the peasants share similar life styles, and since marriage is largely endogamous within the community, a marked «climbing» impulse is not to be expected. Economic factors may be limiting in marriage, in that it is unlikely that youth from the very richest and very poorest families will wed, but that is the most one can say.

Marriage structures respect relations along the model of kinship. This is shown in the case of Agabito Linares, beaten by the community for allegedly sleeping with his mother-in-law. The peasants were, in a confused way, outraged by this; it was considered unseemly, vaguely like incest. The word they used over and over in talking about the case was «He showed a lack of respect *(respeto)* for his mother-in-law.»

Kinship and fictive kinship formally structure behavior and mobilize mutual aid and emotional support in time of need. Children owe obedience and respect to their parents and, as they grow older, the help of their hands. In return, parents protect their young and teach them the tasks of the farm. Following the map of kinship, people introduce a certain predictability to their lives; control is introduced; the stream of life is molded to the yearly work cycle on the farm. To the degree which people fulfill their roles in the family, it assumes its functions as a reproductive, socioeconomic and educational institution.

Kinship is reckoned bilaterally—an Eskimo terminology[127] (Murdock,

---

[126] Though it is possible at some level that lust for land, almost tangible in the big, strong, slow-moving Angel, is mixed up with lust for the woman. This must be at the feeling level, unconscious.

[127] With a slight paternal emphasis in that paternal parallel cousins are called by the same term as male siblings.

1948) reflects the lack of strong unilineal emphasis in residence; this in turn is related to the land situation already discussed. Obligations of respect and mutual aid impinge equally on paternal and maternal kin and weaken rapidly as they extended outward. Normally they do not extend beyond mother's and father's siblings and their children (first cousins) and the second ascending generation.

Yet even here a certain contingency enters. Though siblings are generally mutually supportive, Cirilo Guzmán rarely helps his brother, Don Dionisio; indeed, they barely speak. Don Dionisio told us straight out «I don't like him.» The dirigente has a more consistent source of aid in his dependents and ahijados than he has in his own brother.

Families vary, in short, at Palca as elsewhere. While the Najeras appear free and easy most of the time—a phalanx of strong men, brothers, cousins, fathers and uncles working and drinking together, playing soccer (in the case of the youngest), even lending each other money—Agustín Lizzaraga does not even help his widowed mother and the Guzmán brothers barely speak. How people really behave within the ideal web of kinship is, to a degree, an individual thing.

The importance of kinship in mobilizing (mainly) human resources is perhaps dramatized by its lack. Andrés Lizzaraga in effect was left to die like a dog because he had no close kin by descent or marriage in a community where there are no mechanisms for mutual aid in some situations beyond the bilateral family.

Friendship and fictive kinship,[128] finally, are mechanisms of association on the hacienda which perform some of the functions of kinship, although in attenuated form. As Erasmus (1950: 5, 51-52) writes, fictive kinship serves to extend bonds of security and assistance beyond the immediate family in peasant societies where the integrative and protective functions of truly massive kinship groups, e.g., in segmental societies, have been preempted by the state. Fictive kinship allows greater flexibility than lineage organization (Erasmus, 1950-51; Mintz and Wolf, 1967: 188) and yet preserves some of the latter's social insurance functions, its mobilizative power over resources in people.

Friendship does the same thing: Its «fit» with the Palca situation is obvious, and both friendship and compadrazgo have widened in scope since the reform. In the time of the patrón, such ties were confined mainly within the hacienda where the peons themselves were bound, and they were «horizontal» ties in Mintz and Wolf's (1967: 176) sense that they linked only the peasants; they made for social solidarity solely between people who were rough economic equals. The patrón never sought to enter into compadre relations with his peons (though the campesinos say he did so on occasion with the mayordomos), nor did the peons approach the patrón for this. The social distance between

---

[128] Between which there is not always a distinct difference but a kind of continuum. At Palca the word «compadre» is easily extended to good friends. Cf. Mintz and Wolf, 1967: 181.

them was too great; as Melchor Andia, a former curaca said, «We never thought of it.» From the patrón's point of view there was no need; [129] he was already getting all the traffic would bear out of a peasant bound to the farm by ignorance and lack of other economic alternatives. He was able to use the few favorites he needed as curacas without incurring a potential lien on himself by entering into compadre relations with them.

Since the reform, the range of fictive kinship has expanded to include neighboring haciendas, towns, and even people in the city of Cochabamba—a wide irregular web of varying strength and complexity, which may include anyone with whom the peasants have social dealings.[130] The web has taken on depth, so to speak, a third dimension which allows for «vertical» relations between individuals who are not economic or cultural equals. Fictive kinship at Palca also consists of several varieties.

Perhaps the strongest bond is that between married couples, who are ahijados, and the padrinos, who have sponsored their marriage. Marriage sponsorship also establishes or reinforces ties of friendship and respect between the padrinos themselves when, as sometimes happens, they are not married. Henceforth, such people address each other as «compadre,» as they do the parents of the bride and groom. The couple's parents address each other similarly.

But the strongest bond links the newlyweds with their padrino sponsors either in church marriage or marriage before the registro civil. Occasionally, the padrinos are parents of either bride or groom. Most often they are not. I have seen padrinos at a Palca wedding come from as far away as Cochabamba; the important thing for the peasant is that they be people of «respect,» which involves a certain stability and a certain amount of wealth. In return for sponsoring the wedding (i.e., defraying a considerable portion of the costs and standing with the bride and groom before the priest or registro civil), padrinos hold liens on the labor of their ahijados in time of need, and also gain the right or duty to instruct the couple in the proper conduct of their marriage, «to set things right if things go bad,» as Ricardo Rodríguez put it. They may scold the couple and make use of corporal punishment: «Parents

---

[129] As there was apparently in the Puerto Rican coffee community studied by Wolf (Mintz and Wolf, 1967:195) where landowners got free labor out of their compadres in return for small loans, use of tools, etc. We might hypothesize that for such «vertical» ties of fictive kinship to exist requires some leverage or bargaining power in the system, something lacking on the manorial hacienda we are describing. Put crudely, one does not need compadre relations with slaves. Yet the fact that the patrón never entered into such relations reduced the chance of competition among the peons.

[130] Significantly, Palcans form few if any fictive kin relations with people from the higher part of the hacienda, or from other haciendas 10,000 feet and above, whose clothing and diet are ruder than theirs, and with whom they do not intermarry.

don't have the right to beat young people, but padrinos do,» Ricardo told us. Allocation of this obligation to the padrinos of marriage and also (as we shall see) to the dirigente should work to reduce intergenerational conflict within the family. In practice some parents do in fact mix in their married children's affairs.

Padrinos from outside the hacienda seldom make use of the labor of their ahijados (though they may at times work in compañía with them); but the padrinos often own chicherías their ahijados frequent. (Indeed, this is how the relationship comes to fruition, the peasant dropping in, drinking, gradually getting friendly, until at last marriage comes up as a topic of conversation.) The town chicha-seller has a lien on the peasant in the sense that the latter would not feel right drinking in the chichería of another, or a least not visiting his padrino while in town. The town seller «gets his own» back from the peasant in business; marriage—being a padrino—is investment[131] from his point of view. The peasant in turn receives a source of refuge and help in trouble; a place to stay when he goes to town; a safe place to store belongings, especially money; and, sometimes, a loan. The peasant also gains a certain prestige in the community by having a town padrino, especially one from the city, sponsor his marriage.

Something of the complex factors involved is shown in this interview with Pedro Najera:

I asked Pedro how he came to have padrinos outside the community. He said that Don Marcelino of Punata is man with whom his father has sown many times in compañía and is a good man whom they (all the Najera family) like and for this he had sought him out as a padrino. Also, Marcelino has his chichería in Punata in which they sometimes drink, and when they all drink together this makes for friendship.

And Ambrosio Vargas:

He said—a bit proudly, I thought—that his madrina is from Tiraque but has lived a long time in Cochabamba and is married to a man from there. He said his madrina was a very good friend of his father, Fructuoso, who is dead, and for this he chose her as madrina (godmother)....

Fictive kinship at Palca consists also of compadrazgo or ritual co-parenthood related to the baptism and confirmation of children. Sharing in these rituals again establishes or reinforces relationships of trust and respect within generations—between the child's parents and the compadres they invite to serve as godparents—and a stronger bond between godparent and godchild. Again, the criteria of choice seems to be «respect» rather than wealth, «a good man,» as Francisco Cossío once told us, although, as Angel Rojas said, a compadre should have some

---

[131] These are, again, latent functions not necessarily seen or intended by the actors involved.

money «so he could lend it to you.» Sometimes a family[132] asks the same people who served as compadres of baptism to act as compadres of confirmation, sometimes not. Sometimes fictive kin are neighbors or kin, sometimes not. There seems to be no rigid rule, either, as to whether different godparents are chosen for successive children.

The important thing is that the compadres assume definite obligations toward the child which act as a kind of insurance for him. The child in turn owes his godparents respect and, as he grows older, help when they need it. At the same time the nodes in his life cycle—baptism, confirmation, first haircutting—act as detonators setting off a series of interactions among families on the parental level (visiting, exchange of food and drink, etc.; see Chapter VII for details) which, while not invoking precise obligations, reinforce already existing patterns of friendship and mutual aid. Compadrazgo is the idiom of this, in its ultimate religious sanction, it works to disarm the potential conflict in interaction. Again, it must be stressed that these are latent functions of which the peasants are not necessarily aware.

For example, if you ask them what the duties of a compadre of baptism or confirmation are, most peasants will say «To give clothes to the child only,» or «Clothes and a bit of money, 10 or 20 pesos.» One man told us that a padrino of baptism had the duty to instruct or advise the child, «to make Christians out of the children.» (I never saw this.) Only a few peasants seem aware that, if a child is orphaned, his godparents of baptism or confirmation have some obligation toward him.

But in practice such does seem to be the case. For example, Raymundo Sánchez was orphaned at fourteen and left alone with one sister; he says he could not have worked his father's fields without the aid of his father's compadres, Zenon and Ricardo Rodríguez, his own padrinos of baptism and confirmation respectively. They helped him a great deal «for nothing» and the neighbors helped in ayni. Raymundo says also that, if his padrinos had not done this, the community would not have respected them.[133]

Similarly, Don Dionisio Guzmán continues to help Torribia Cossío, widow of his padrino Emilio Ríos, at special occasions like the sowing of potatoes; he lends both his labor and the use of his oxen. It should be stressed that these labor obligations apply only within the hacienda or, at most, within closely adjacent farms. Godparents of baptism and

---

[132] It is most often the father of the child who seeks out others to be compadres (see Erasmus, 1950:6). He may give presents of chicha or a chicken to the prospective godparents, though this is not obligatory.

[133] At Palca, as elsewhere, it can be hard to define the limits of obligation. One pays some bills before others; the fear of loss, or hope of gain, in prestige may enter a relation a peasant speaks of as «voluntary.» I would not, however, want to regard all behavior as determined by such factors as prestige, community pressure, «the custom,» etc., to rule out more intangible factors like individual fondness and concern.

confirmation may be chosen from outside the hacienda, though this happens more rarely than is the case with padrinos of marriage nor are the peasants likely to invite people from the city of Cochabamba to participate in baptism of a child. Still, townsmen from Punata and Tiraque are sometimes asked to share in life cycle rites, and the relations of mutual respect, friendship and obligation on the parental level are much the same as that described for compadres of marriage.

Godparents have the additional obligation of buying the child's coffin and shroud if he dies before the age of seven. If there are separate padrinos for baptismal and confirmation rites, they may divide these purchases. If the padrino is the same throughout, he buys all. The obligations of padrinazgo can be onerous (I never heard a case of refusal of the role, however), and I heard at least one drunken outburst against the cash expense, but I found no evidence of the psychological cost Sayres (1965) found in Colombia where people felt highly ambivalent toward fictive kin who offer security but at the price of a kind of Orwellian Big-Brotherhood. There, as Sayres put it, «a man could not set out to do anything without having to deal with one ritual kinsman or another» and «so many people were delegated to watch, meddle and judge» that one informant «ended with a vigorous oath directed toward ahijados, padrinos and compadres anywhere and everywhere» (Sayres, 1965: SAY-3A). This kind of «negative affect» does not appear at Palca, perhaps because life style is so consistent, the work regime and series of alternatives before the people is so simple and well known, and because the spatial arrangement of homesteads scattered throughout the great farm works against the closer inspection and awareness of others' activities which Sayres found in his more compressed Mestizo communities. Just as an increasing shortage of land may lead over time to increased phenomena of «limited good,» it may also result in a drift toward Sayres' «negative affect» in ritual kinship. Only future research can determine this.

Yet fictive kinship can introduce tension in the community from a different direction. Just as it introduces formalized relationships and obligations resembling those of genuine kinship, it takes on some of the latter's taboos (Erasmus, 1950: 33). I know of a young man in the neighboring hacienda of Sancayani who was beaten to death with clubs by the men of the community for sleeping with his comadre. Significantly, it was not the single occurrence which offended the rather loosely organized community, but its repetition, the flouting of repeated warnings on the part of the dirigente. It seems the community cannot tolerate an extensive breakdown of the quasi-incest taboo here (or in the case of affines) because it would threaten the web of formalized relationships and obligations on which functions of social insurance and mutual aid depend.

Mere good friends, finally, may call themselves «compadre»: this is the kind of «fictive kinship» Don Dionisio has with Don Venustiano Villarroel of Punata. The peasants say of this relationship that it «involves respect only, not obligation like baptism»; but as we have seen in Chapter V, such relationships can be manipulated so as to take on economic importance. Compadres of this type do many of the same things for the peasants which genuine ritual compadres do: provide lodging and, in the city, guide the visitor to stores in places where he might otherwise get lost; store belongings and cash and even extend credit. The peasant, in turn, frequents his friend's or his compadres' chichería.

A man may share different types of fictive kinship with another, and compadrazgo bonds can be reduplicated. Thus, Sinforoso Najera told us how he has four compadres of baptism:

Don Dionisio (who is also his padrino of marriage) baptized two of his children, so he counts him as his compadre twice, and his mother, Marcella Merida, has baptized his two other children, so he counts her as his comadre twice.

In view of all this, it is not surprising to find Sinforoso so often drinking with the dirigente or helping the latter at work in his fields, or to learn that Sinforoso has fared rather well in the land distribution. Compadres of important life rites, it is worth noting, do not express overt conflict—at least I never saw or heard of an instance of this, though brothers, husbands and wives, and even fathers and sons may sometimes come to blows after drinking.

Finally, a townsman may sponsor an inanimate object in the community and thus, in a generalized way, validate and reinforce his bonds of friendship there. Justino Velardes of Tiraque is compadre of Palca's capilla, as well as compadre of baptism and good friendship with several peasants. He works in compañía with these and other peasants; he buys potatoes from them. Palcans in turn, when they are in Tiraque, frequent his chichería and hold weddings there and get drunk there during the long day when people are buried in the Tiraque cemetery. Justino's relations with the hacienda are so numerous and complex they would be hard to trace in detail; he admits he does a much greater business now than before the reform, both as chicha-seller and middleman in potatoes. Before, he could work in compañía only with the few piqueros in the region, and the peasants had only small amounts of money and time to spend in his chichería. Now, with the money the ex-peons have to spend, and with skillful manipulation of friendship and fictive kinship bonds to insure that a fair portion flows consistently in his direction, Justino has become relatively prosperous. There are others like him. In this way one can see, again, the role such ties play, not only in allocation of resources within the hacienda, but in contributing to the limited economic advance of the region as a whole.

POLITICAL ORGANIZATION, LEADERSHIP, THE SINDICATO

The hacienda's prereform political structure was simple: the patrón's work was law enforced through fist, whip and gun by means of two mayordomos[134] and two curacas chosen by the patrón from among the peons themselves. The curacas were responsible to the mayordomos, who in turn were directly responsible to the patrón. One of the mayordomos was, as the peasants put it, a «chief mayordomo,» the administrador or «second patrón» he lived in the hacienda house and the chain of authority passed through him. The curacas had the advantage of not having to farm in compañía with the patrón and, sometimes, they were given for food the patrón's animals that died of natural causes.

The prereform hacienda structure may be visualized as a broad-based pyramid (see fig. 6). The administrador and mayordomos were inevitably mestizos from Cochabamba or the valley towns, who spoke Spanish and possessed some schooling. The curacas were peasants who had the task of running the everyday work of the hacienda, seeing to it that their neighbors worked appropriately long and hard on the patrón's

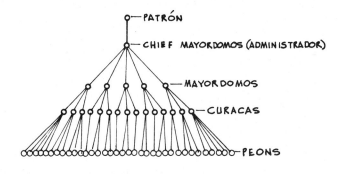

Figure 6

land, that his flocks were properly tended, etc. They carried out daily orders from the mayordomos and were selected, the peasants say, because of their physical strength and apparent devotion to the status quo. The patrón wanted men he could rely on. In this connection it is interesting that many peasants speak today of a rapid turnover among the curacas. The patrón apparently had difficulty finding men who would consistently extract from their neighbors the amount of work he wanted. Three curacas were among those peasants who «talked»

---

[134] This is at nuclear. Palca. All in all, the patrón hired five mayordomos to supervise the work in all regions of the hacienda (see Peinado, 1969:60). Other portions of the hacienda higher up (Palca Alto) had their own curacas also chosen from the peasants themselves.

against the patrón in the time of Villarroel and were evicted from the hacienda. Two of these live to this day in Palca, as popular as anyone as far as I could tell, though they hold no special post of power in the community. Only one man, Melchor Andia, an old man of seventy-four, is remembered by the peasants as a curaca who whipped them cruelly, took a fat sheep for the patrón at the slightest excuse and molested women. Melchor was once «very strong» and «rode about on a horse.» He lives to this day on his plot in Palca, grizzled, stripped of all power, afraid even to drink in the chicherías with his fellow peasants for fear that when they get drunk they will look at him and «remember.» Yet he is left alone mainly and takes part in the reciprocal work arrangements of the hacienda.

The mayordomos, on the other hand, are remembered as being brutal without exception. Through them the patrón's hand reached deep into the peasants' lives: their work, their marriages, their behavior in town. «All was the patrón,» they tell you today; as Jacinto Sánchez said, «We were all in the hand of the patrón.» The colonos had small chance to develop initiative or capacity for leadership; they were even more stripped and encapsulated politically than they were socially or economically. The hacienda was a taut, rigid, tyranny in miniature, reinforced by police and military and the attitudes of townspeople.[135]

The revolution destroyed this, destroyed the police and military who had supported the old regime and, in some cases, drove off certain of the townspeople of Tiraque who had supported the patrón or who were themselves patrones. Others were forced to accept the campesinos on a new basis and, despite the abuses they may have suffered in the beginning and the contempt in which they hold the «Indios», they have profited from the new situation.

In the wake of the hacienda structure came the sindicato, a rural league or union, which includes all adults of the farm[136] with officers elected by the male family heads. The sindicato movement is a nation-

---

[135] «Only local power counted,» Jean-Pierre Bernard writes of this time (Bernard, 1969:986), «because only local power was in contact with the peasants. Rural life was a kind of domain reserved for the landowners and their allies, clients and attendants.» Unlike revolutionary centers in the upper Cochabamba valley, where the decline of the latifundio system was accompanied by a process of «cholification» or «mestoization» (Bernard, 1969:986; Patch, 1956: 138), by increased education and a number of nonpeasant allies at various levels of influence who could mediate between the campesinos and the larger society, hacienda peasants usually lacked these. Hence on the rare occasions when they did rebel they were easily crushed. (See Bernard, 1969:996; Dandler-Hanhart, 1968:5-12.)

[136] Though the local peasant organizations called sindicatos include ex-haciendas they are not confined to these but may include groups of piqueros (independent peasants), arrenderos (peasants who rented hacienda plots), and indigenous Indian communities.

wide revolutionary phenomenon which shows great regional and intra-regional variation (Dandler-Hanhart, 1967; Heath, 1969; Malloy, 1968; Patch, 1956; 1960:120-124; Rickabaugh, 1966). At Palca, officers are elected democratically, informally, by raising of hands at a meeting; but as we have seen, the reasons peasants raise their hands one way or another may involve considerations which do not necessarily include Western ideas of democracy or justice. Once elected, certain officers—especially the secretary-general, or dirigente—exert considerable power. At Palca Don Dionisio wields power through the system of alliances he has built up in the community by means of compadrazgo and the distribution of land, and, barring some gross malfeasance on his part which threatens or embarrasses the community, it appears he can stay in office as long as he chooses.

The following is the formal structure of sindicato leadership:

Secretary-General (dirigente)	Dionisio Guzmán
Secretary of Relations	Eugenio Vargas
Secretary of Education	Nicanor Sánchez
Secretary of Roads	Ignacio Claros
Secretary of Justice	Luis Ramallo
Secretary of Acts	José Vargas
Secretary of Organization	Manuel Ochoa
Secretary of Sports	Sinforoso Najera
Secretary of Vinculation	Donato Claros
Secretary of Agriculture	Jacinto Sánchez
Secretary of Cooperation	Víctor Lizzaraga
Secretary of Hacienda	Daniel Vargas
Vocales	José Rodríguez
	Luciano Rojas

Most of these offices have no real function. When first questioned on this subject, Don Dionisio exploded with what appeared a trace of scorn: «They don't do anything, they're only titles.» He said that when he feels the need for a meeting of the sindicato he consults with his secretary of relations, Eugenio Vargas, and they announce it. He said also that when there is busness to be transacted outside the hacienda, he goes alone with Vargas, and when they return they «tell the others about it.»[137] The dirigente as head of the syndicate thus represents that body as a corporate group and has power to act in its name in the outside world (see Heath, 1969:194). It was the dirigente—Ricardo Rodríguez and, later, Don Dionisio—who pursued petitions for hacienda land under the reform law and collected money quotas from the peasants and traveled to La Paz for this. It is significant, however, that once the land titles were granted, the dirigente subsided more and more into the hacienda. We found Don Dionisio engaged in none of the ac-

---

[137] We found this to be generally true, except for the Spanish-speaking peasants, Casimiro García or Nicanor Sánchez, whom Don Dionisio often has accompany him to facilitate dealing with the outside world.

tive brokerage roles Heath, for example, has noted in the yungas (Heath, 1969:194): asking USAID for water-pipe, seeking a first-aid station, etc. As Bernard (1969: 1000, 10009, 1015) and Vellard (1963: 221) have shown, the peasant's political aspirations are often limited to attainment of his plot of land. I shall return later in detail to this point.

As for the other hacienda offices, again, at first Don Dionisio stated in an interview they were hollow titles. But when I asked for a little more detail, perhaps out of community pride, perhaps because he thought it was what I wanted to hear, he outlined the following official functions:

Secretary of Relations—assists the dirigente, is «right-hand man.» Acts in the dirigente's place when the latter is not present.
Secretary of Justice—resolves conflict or disputes between peasants.
Secretary of Roads—takes care of «roads» (i.e., the single dirt road leading from the highway into the hacienda).
Secretary of Sports—in charge of Palca's soccer team.
Secretary of Agriculture—«has charge of the farmer,» aids in sowing,» etc.
Secretary of Education—«tries to educate the peasants to support the school».
Secretary of Acts—writes what happens in meetings, calls the roli.
Secretary of Hacienda—«Controls quotas,» decides who pays how much in money or kind for community projects or when the community buys something.
Secretary of Organization—«organizes» (?).
Secretary of Cooperation—«looks for the lowest prices in the market for the peasants and tells them which prices are cheapest.»
Secretary of Vinculation—«watches over those who work. Sees that there are no loafers.»
Secretary-General—head of the syndicate.

Vocales—call people to sindicato meetings with the *pututu* (trumpet made of an ox-horn).

Thirteen months' fieldwork among these peasants failed to disclose evidence that occupants of the above posts do much of anything except for the dirigente and his secretary of relations and, perhaps, the secretaries of justice, education and sports. The secretary of justice, Luis Ramallo, was nominally charged with the adjudication of minor disputes, of minor breaches of customary law (e.g., small theft) within the community. Luis is a great drunkard who abandoned his family early during the course of my stay; conflict resolution and administration of customary law within the community at present lies in the hands of the dirigente and sporadic, ad hoc groupings of peasants.

By the same token Nicanor Sánchez, charged officially with promoting the interests of the school, did nothing in this direction that one could see. The Palca school was no nearer completion at the end of our stay than it was at the beginning, nor did Nicanor or any other peasant succeed in forcing the teachers assigned to the hacienda to fulfill their obligations (see Chapter VII). Further, Nicanor Sánchez, charged with cultivating land set apart for the benefit of the school, sold the products of that land and pocketed the proceeds—700 pesos (about $60). Just before our departure the dirigente was talking of forcing him to return the money to the school, of punishing him; but nothing happened. For his part, Nicanor, at meetings, whenever anything to do with the school came up, kept asking to be relieved of his post, saying he was «only very young, only a *wawa*» (Quechua: baby) and could do nothing.

The secretary of sports, Sinforoso Najera, is captain of the soccer team and, as such, fulfills the duties of his post. The dirigente performs the tasks of the other syndicate officers, such as deciding the amount each family head must contribute in money or kind for any community project and supervising community work on the road and on the Palca River. Certain of the posts articulate functions which are not performed by anyone in the community: no one, for example, calls the roll of family heads at a sindicato meeting (No one in the community can effectively read and write even in Quechua.) There is no one who «looks for the lowest prices in the market for the peasants.» Marketing, as we have seen, involves the individual family or at most ad hoc groups of friends and relatives in dealings with the outside; there are no cooperatives in either production or distribution.[138]

Formal syndicate leadership then, taken as a whole, is somewhat empty. It no longer includes men genuinely influential in the community such as Ricardo Rodríguez who, as dirigente, worked hard to expedite many of the peasants' land titles and who, in a crisis, would almost certainly be consulted. (The fact that he stood as padrino at the wedding of the present dirigente makes this even more probable.) On the other hand, the formal leadership structure does include people regarded with humor or indifference (Nicanor Sánchez, Ignacio Claros). Also, individuals very low in the prestige scale along certain dimensions—Casimiro García and Saturnino Achá—enter at surprising points into the decision-making process. Achá had even, before I left, been elected dirigente of the Tiraque central and, as such, was nominally Don Dionisio's superior; his usefulness in dealings with the outside has already been noted. As for García, I have already (p. 115) noted his intermittent function as the dirigente's «brains,» just as José Jiménez, one of his dependents, serves at times as his bodyguard, or «gun.»

There is a wide split, finally, between the avowed or ideal aims of the sindicato, and for that matter the entire pyramidal structure of syndicates in the Federación Nacional de Campesinos articulating upward through cantonal, provincial and departmental levels to the Ministry of Peasant Affairs in La Paz—there is a split between what these

---

[138] Nicanor Sánchez perhaps summarized the attitudes of Palcans toward cooperatives when, in answer to my question «Why don't you all chip in and buy a truck or two if you want one?,» he said, «If we do that, those who don't work or don't pay will want to use it just as much. It will not be fair and there will be fights about it.»

people say they do or hope to do and what they are at present doing. The structure does not function in accord with its rhetoric, and this has important implications for the political culture of the region. But before tackling this difficult and crucial problem, I shall outline the history of the formation of the Palca sindicato without which its present function can hardly be fully understood.

HISTORY OF THE SINDICATO

The history of the formation of sindicatos in the Tiraque region is of considerable importance theoretically (in what it has to suggest concerning the nature of revolutionary process and the role therein of peasant movements) and practically. (It shows how extremely various social process may prove in a country as fragmented as Bolivia.) On the most immediate theoretical or ideological level students are divided. Are peasant revolts spontaneous outbreaks on the part of the peasants themselves, a kind of «maturation,» as Bernard (1969:994) has written, an «internal evolution of the peasantry ... aggravation of imbalances which finally burst into the open?» Or are they largely the work of outside agitators? The first position grants initiative and organizational capacity to the peasant. The second implies an almost Marxian view that peasants are a passive mass, which moves only when pushed, that they «cannot represent themselves, they must be represented» (Marx, 1968:124).

On a broader yet related level the sindicato movement in the Tiraque region sheds light on the question whether revolution is likely among people who have been beaten down beyond endurance, or is more probable when, paradoxically, things start getting better. Is revolntion a function of exploitation or, rather, as Chalmers Johnson has posited, of «dissynchonization» of a people's values and their environment? (Johnson, 1966:33).

Our data definitely support the latter view, since it was in the upper Cochabamba valley proper—specifically around Ucureña (Patch, 1956; 1960; Dandler-Hanhart, 1967)—that the original revolutionary ferment began among the peasants, which only later spread to more marginal areas. «Dissynchronization» was much more striking in the valley than it was in more oppressed regions like Palca.

Further, the problem of inner versus outer causation of peasant revolts seems to me artificial since a mass without leadership is not likely to accomplish much, nor are leaders effective without a responsive mass. The evidence seems to show that, in Bolivia, due to varying factors of local history, peasants have shown varying degrees of initiative. One can see the data as forming a kind of continuum: organizational activity and demand for change began earlier in the upper

Cochabamba valley than it did elsewhere; [139] the peasants there seem to have been more open to change and to have produced more leaders than others; *but at every point there were followers and leaders—* cultural brokers mediating between the peasants and the larger world. To attempt to decide whether these were «inside» or «outside» the community, whether it was a «grass-roots» movement or not (Heath, 1969), seems hairsplitting.

For example, Dandler-Hanhart (1967) and Patch (1956, 1960) have explored the growth of the sindicato movement in the Upper Valley, showing, first, how the mass of peasantry was prepared for change by a longstanding process of mestoization, by the decline of latifundia, and and above all by the Chaco War which drew Bolivians of all classes into a war which must have been, for the individual soldier, one of the cruelest in history. After seeing the world for the first time outside his little hamlet, after such suffering, after above all taking defeat through the inefficiency of their officers, representatives of the old oligarchy (Klein, 1965, 1969), the Indians were less willing to sink back into their old mold of colono. As one veteran told Jorge Dandler (Dandler-Hanhart, 1967:53), «We wanted them to recognize what we were worth in the trenches.»

A «crisis of legitimacy» seized members of other classes also (Klein, 1965:25, 28); the old oligarchy resting on land and tin was irrevocably shaken. Dandler-Hanhart has shown how this crisis worked itself out on the local level in Ucureña in the formation of a school which worked in cooperation with the first sindicato in Boliva (dating from 1936) to attempt to rent land from the last surviving latifundio in the region. All these factors: a peasantry exposed to new ideas due to the Chaco War and the presence of a school; the survival of a latifundio «increasingly regarded as an anachronism» in the valley (Dandler-Hanhart, 1967:90) (dissynchronization of values and environment); the help of allies and «cultural brokers» in other classes—lawyers and teachers—men who had lost faith in the old dual society and sought to incorporate the Indian in a new Bolivia—all these factors were involved in the germinal revolutionary process in the upper valley. Subtract one variable and the situation might have worked out differently. Even a man like José Rojas, who became a powerful influence in the sindicato movement and who might be thought of as an autocthonous peasant leader, turns out on closer inspection to be an individual with much

---

[139] I am speaking here specifically of activity organized around the syndical movement and oriented toward structural change. Sporadic peasant revolt, on the other hand, directed against specific perceived injustice has been frequent in Bolivian history and widespread in the country (see Bernard, 1969:987-988). Mobilization of Indians in the nineteenth century had results which adumbrate the Chaco War (Morales, 1966), and the unrest during Villarroel's time doubtless put the idea of land reform in the heads of many peasants. But the formal syndical movement originated around Cochabamba (Dandler-Hanhart, 1967:14-17).

dissonant experience as the son of a peasant evicted from the latifundio who escaped to Argentina (Dandler-Hanhart, 1967:84, 96). The question of inside versus outside leaders, spontaneity versus artificiality of peasant revolts becomes moot.

What we can hypothesize is that there were present in Bolivia before the revolution peasants with more or less information about the outside world, more or less initiative, a greater or less image of themselves as people born to «work the land like a burro.» By the same token, some peasants had more allies outside their class than others (cf. Dandler-Hanhart, 1967). Information and allies nourish hope and the room to act. The data suggest that it is precisely peasants with such room, such leverage who are likely to start revolutions, not those who are most beaten down.

Thus all evidence points to the fact that the Tiraque region did not inaugurate the agrarian reform on its own but as a direct after-effect of events in the valley. The peasant syndicate at Ucureña, though formed in 1936, burst into prominence only in 1947 when José Rojas took over its leadership (Patch, 1960:121). At first this organization had modest aims: school-building and rental of land from the latifundio in the area (Dandler-Hanhart, 1967:53-57), but with attempts at suppression on the part of the landowners (along with Marxist influence on the leader, Rojas), the peasants grew more radical until finally, after the MNR assumed power in La Paz,[140] the Ucureña syndicate emerged as the base of the campesinos. Patch writes:

In 1949 members of the MNR began a new campaign in the rural areas, attempting to ... enlist their support against the vested power groups.... The early meetings of the *Sindicato Campesinos de Ucureña del Valle* organized task forces of campesinos and young MNR students from Cochabamba, dispatching them to the farthest reaches of Bolivia. Often these teams of organizers were the first to bring news of the revolution to Indian villages of remote valleys and ... plateaus. The syndicate groups showed the campesinos how to organize new syndicates of their own. Most of these later syndicates remain personally loyal today to Rojas, for they believe that he and no one else was responsible for their being established.... As the wild fire of revolt and hope raced through the villages, the entire campesino movement was completely outside the control of the national government or the MNR leaders. The only center it recognized was Ucureña. (Patch, 1960:121-122)

It is possible to trace, in the Tiraque region today, elements of this process as it worked itself out on the local level. There are peasants at

---

[140] Authorities agree that peasants played little part in the fighting in La Paz which brought the MNR to power in 1952 (Blasier, 1966:45). But peasants influenced the revolution later in regard to agrarian reform. The fact that the MNR dragged its heels on this issue, acting only when forced by the peasants and Trotskyite factions, is perhaps the main reason Malloy (1968:445) called them «reluctant revolutionaries» and Patch (1961), «restrained.» Most MNR were moderate, fearing a bloodbath in the campo and a ruin of production from agrarian reform. They need not have worried. As we have seen, for all their initial runaway power peasants are far from dominating present policy in Bolivia.

Palca today who remember that Rojas himself came to the hacienda during this time and addressed the campesinos, telling them they must not work any more for the patrón but should form a sindicato of their own and take over his land. Palca in particular seems to have had close ties with Ucureña. After 1953 Rojas is said to have stayed for a time in the hacienda house; Ucureña as the center (at that time) of the incipient Federación Nacional de Campesinos used Palca as a kind of «dumping ground» for undesirables from other sindicatos; Casimiro García, Rojas' former bodyguard, even settled permanently at Palca, as we have seen.

Sindicato formation on the hacienda, however, and in the Tiraque region as a whole, was not the work of Rojas directly but of local peasants («task forces») working under him. Specifically, Alejandro Vía, Martín Castellón and Demetrio Cisneros of the haciendas of Cruzani, Waca Wasi and Kaña Kota respectively «walked» at night, as they put it, to organize the peasants secretly against the patrones. It was a dangerous time; Alejandro says he was ambushed one night while «walking» and after this carried a rifle and took a group of campesinos with him. There is no better way to give a sense of it all than to let the man speak in his own voice, in his own place where we went to to talk to him:

Cruzani is a small green hamlet in bottomland about 10 km. off the highway surrounded by brown stony hills. You turn off the highway at Sak'abambilia and walk into greenness, stillness, under the willow trees. Hard to believe this land once swarmed with peasants, that there were shots.

We came at last to plowed fields and houses and found Vía's house without difficulty—of mud-brick, small and dark inside like the others, smaller than Palca. Vía greeted us warmly. Thin as a nail, full of nervous movement, in black, he fed us boiled eggs and *sara mut'i* and once started talking he was reliving his days of glory. He said that he and Sinforoso Rivas [141] formed the first sindicato in Punata in 1951. Later he helped organize sindicatos in Cruzani, Sak'abambilia and Wasqi Kocha; said he walked around from night to morning trying to make the peasants understand. He said he worked so hard to organize the peasants that he didn't have food in the house. He said it was often hard to make the peasants understand what the sindicatos were. This was before the departure of the patrones.

From Vía's account it appears that the course of the reform in this region roughly followed that in the valley: At first the sindicatos' aims were modest: to abolish pongueaje and reduce work for the patrón to three days per week; but attempts at suppression only made the peasants' demands more extreme. The patrones furthermore seem to have been confused and divided and, when the chips were down,

---

[141] Rivas, a more moderate leader than José Rojas, later became a power in the lower Cochabamba valley or the valley proper, as it is sometimes called (Dandler-Hanhart, 1967:17).

perhaps due to the mounting menace of the Ucureña syndicate (Patch, 1960:122-123), they were deserted by their old allies, the town authorities:

I questioned Alejandro closely about what the patrones were doing (while the sindicatos were forming). He said he spoke with many patrones: some agreed to the formation of the sindicatos and to their aims, others «got angry.» Hinojosa (patrón of Palca) was especially bad, he said. Vía said Hinojosa and Agustín Méndez called a meeting with the authorities in Punata «against the government of Paz Estenssoro.» He said that he, Vía, went disguised as a poor old peasant to hang around and overhear. He found that the patrones wanted to pay $180 to the Punata authorities to change the course of reform. The patrones didn't want to give up their lands to the peasants, and they wanted to hang Paz the way Villarroel was hung. About forty patrones attended the meeting, Alejandro said. He said he wrote a note directly after this to La Paz, to the government, and the government sent a writ *(manda)* directly to Ucureña which in turn wrote to Punata giving peasants there the right to arrest the patrones. The authorities in Punata who had been in league with the patrones disappeared, Vía said; if they returned to their houses the peasants had the legal right to arrest them. But the patrones did not return to their houses but fled. This broke their power in the Punata-Tiraque region.

Palca, as we have seen, proved something of an exception to this in that the patrón managed to stay on there two years or so longer than patrones on neighboring haciendas, until campesinos from these haciendas, under Vía's direction, surrounded the farm «on all sides» and forced the Palcans to act. According to Vía and other peasants we talked to, the patrón paid coima (bribery) to many peasants, including the first dirigente of the Palca sindicato, Fortunato López.[142] Hinojosa also apparently maintained alliances to the last with certain police units in Cochabamba and with diehard, last-ditch authorities in the region who opposed the reform and fought it to the end. But the patrones, as a group, seem to have been poorly organized. One further suspects,[143] though it is a taboo subject to even hint at now in an interview, that certain peasants whom the patrón had not evicted may even have favored the latter at this time over the echados who were trying to regain their lands. As long as the patrón's land had not been distributed, the permanecidos could hope to share in it. The arrival of the evicted peasants upset this. At all events the early revolutionary years at Palca, 1952-1956 or thereabouts, were chaotic, full of drift, conflict

---

[142] López, for his part, claims the mayordomos paid the peasants who stayed on the hacienda «salaries» during this time for a reduced work week.

[143] Ricardo Rodríguez and Cirilo Guzmán, for example, in unguarded moments, spoke scornfully of the evicted peasants, saying that *some* were not lazy or drunkards: words and intonations very like those used by the patrón when he referred to the same peasants in an interview. For his part, Donato Claros, another permanecido, said the evicted peasants «had not rendered such good service to the patrón, yet they got the patrón's good land.»

and lack of leadership[144]—a situation directly traceable to prereform conditions.

Thus conditions, far from mobilizing these peasants for revolt, tended to divide and paralyze them. The Tiraque region, where latifundia were far more prevalent than in the valleys, where the campesinos were deprived of both education and outside allies, received the revolution only after it had begun elsewhere, and Palca, the most oppressive hacienda, received it last of all. (Indeed, Palca can be viewed as almost a limiting case of peasants who «cannot represent themselves!») Our data do not support the view that revolution is a function of exploitation per se.

Further, prereform conditions have definitely influenced the shape of events down to the present. The lack of education and non-campesino links or «brokers» continues from their days of encapsulation under the old regime and leaves the peasants, as I shall show, even more deprived politically than they are economically.

Prerefom conditions have influenced leadership, as we have seen in the case of Fortunato López, first dirigente of the Palca sindicato (see p. 20).[145] Ricardo Rodríguez, who replaced López, managed to expedite many of the peasants' land titles, but he appears to have been unable to resolve the conflict which ensued when the echados returned and began to struggle for land. Don Dionisio Guzmán, the present dirigente, was chosen for the post mainly because he was able to resolve this conflict to the satisfaction (or at least acceptance) of most campesinos. For the rest, he fails totally as a modernizing «cultural broker» in dealings with the outside, although his structural position would seem to equip him ideally to play this role and dirigentes elsewhere have been active (Heath, 1969:194). He lingers on, gross, encogido, monolingual, totally unprepared by anything in his history to play a role in change; yet due to his resolution of the conflict resulting from eviction of thirty families from the hacienda (which was directly linked to brutal prereform conditions) he holds the gratitude of many peasants. Clever alliances cow the rest. We may summarize at this point briefly by stating that severity of past conditions is indeed an important

---

[144] A similar power vacuum affected the entire nation at this time, with the breakdown of the old police and army. See Malloy, 1968:ch. 13.

[145] López, again, was chosen for his ability to speak Spanish. Yet this skill, in this area, turns out to be a relatively minor consideration. Unlike the Aymara on the altiplano studied by Carter (1963:88), peasant leaders here do not need Spanish in order to navigate in the outside world since, due to the longstanding process of «cholification» discussed above, everyone they do business with at present (in the market, federation office, church) speaks Quechua. Criteria of leadership have not radically altered here as on the altiplano: ironically, «cholification» or mestoization, the greater cultural homogeneity of the Cochabamba area, works for conservatism in this aspect.

variable affecting the present, but in ways not fully anticipated at the outset of this study. This point will become clearer in our discussion of the function of the sindicato.

FUNCTIONS OF THE SINDICATO, LEADERSHIP

The Bolivian agrarian revolution from the beginning was inspired by two aims, not always congruent: social justice (to incorporate the Indian into the nation and appease his land hunger), and to maintain and improve economic development in the countryside (Bernard, 1969: 1012-1013; Patch, 1956:ch. 3, 1960:128). Within this context, Article 132 of the Agrarian Reform Law of 1953 states the function of the sindicato:

The campesino sindicato organization is recognized as a means of defense for the rights of its members and the preservation of their social conquests. The sindicatos shall intervene in the execution of the Agrarian Reform. They may be independent or affiliated to central.

An amendment to the law in 1962 expanded the ideal function of the sindicato to include:

press for new forms of production on the land, for the elimination of illiteracy, and for economic, social and cultural development. The sindicatos constitute schools of orientation and revolutionary training. (*Ley de Enmiendas,* November 1962).

Don Dionisio Guzmán, for his part, declared the aim of the Palca sindicato to be «to get a tractor, modern tools—to advance.» Our thesis briefly is that, at Palca as in other areas of Bolivia (Erasmus, 1967:359, 365), most of the above is rhetoric—ideal culture, perhaps —and that after the initial explosive drive to abolish services to the patrón and obtain land, the sindicato has pretty much subsided, remaining only a mechanism by which local leaders have been able to organize the community for occasional tasks, for local social control and defense, and a means by which certain leaders have aggrandized themselves. The departmental federation of sindicatos, articulating upward to La Paz, serves at present mainly as a means of mobilizing support for the government.

The following is a rough structure of the peasant sindicato movement. The departmental federations form part of the Confederación Nacional de Trabajadores Bolivianos and are represented at cabinet level by a Minister of Peasant Affairs (see fig. 7).

Demands, from my observation, were from time to time articulated *down* to the peasants; they were seldom articulated *up,* and as I have pointed out earlier, present government policy seems oriented toward bypassing these traditional peasants economically at the very moment they are being courted politically. Whether they are being «castrated,» as one old MNR partisan told me scathingly, whether policy could profitably be directed differently in view of limited resources and of the demonstrated capacity of these peasants to absorb resources only to reinforce traditional ways (see Chapter V; Reina, 1960:85; Stein,

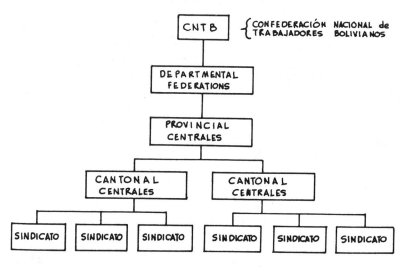

Figure 7

1961:18-21; Wagley, 1968:138), I cannot resolve. Suffice it to point out that marginality, again, is easy to come by in Bolivia. In this region only 64 kilometers from the city of Cochabamba, acknowledged by students to be one of the most active political and economic centers of the nation, conditions exist analogous to those described by Erasmus for the remote inaccessible south (Erasmus, 1967:363; see also p. 84). It is clear once again that simply because a structure is instituted, one cannot assume that behavior will follow; that installation of a health station, marketing system, or, in this case, a political structure modern in form guarantees participant behavior. People must still make a host of individual decisions within a structure which determine whether the avowed aims of that structure will be achieved. At best the ex-colonos of Palca have moved from a parochial to a subject political competence (Almond and Powell, 1966:305) despite their formal incorporation into the nation, and the sindicato movement has exerted almost no force for economic betterment.

This is the result of three interrelated factors:

1. Sheer lack of resources—money, trained men, material. The economic context in which the revolution occurred.

2. The social-structural context.

3. The local historical context in which the reform occurred in

the Tiraque region, which shaped the aspirations of the syndicate movement there as well as individual leaders like Don Dionisio who wield
power today in the campo.

This framework assumes the local syndicate and federation together
constitute a system of cultural brokerage linking the hacienda to the
larger society and, as with other structures such as the extension services and the bank, that attitudes and behavior of individuals both in
the larger organization and on the hacienda will influence how the total
system works. To anticipate, we can pose it as a likely hypothesis, building on the work of Bernard (1969: 1017), Landsberger, and Powell
(1964, 1969), that, as Landsberger writes, «peasant movements do not
begin ... to reach their goals until very slow-moving but profound
changes in the economic, power and value structure of the larger society take place» (Landsberger, quoted in Powell, 1969: 87-89). Bernard put it even more strongly when he wrote that the strength of peasant movements «depends more on the relative strength of the groups
that take it over than on the real nature of the crisis the peasants suffer
from» (Bernard, 1969: 1017). In Bolivia where such groups are weak,
lacking, or intent on mobilizing the peasants for their own political
aims, where the economic and value structure have only minimally
changed and where peasant leaders themselves, in spite of their structural position and ideology as «modernizing» brokers, seldom perform
that function, massive change is not to be expected.

Sheer lack of resources, to begin, marks the campesino federation's
activity in the campo as it does other agencies which articulate with
the peasants. Bolivia is still, as Osborne wrote long ago, *un país pobre*
—a poor country. The office of the sub-central at the cantonal level in
Tiraque lacked even a desk at the time I was there, and consisted of
a dank adobe building with mud floor like any peasant's hut; it is a
former (and still informal) chichería. The provincial office in Arani was
essentially the same, only with a few deal tables and chairs, and it
managed the occasional use of a jeep whose exact provenience I was
unable to trace. The federation office at the departmental level in
Cochabamba is somewhat more elaborate, though still located in a mudfloored house just off the market. The *jefe* at that level, Salvador Vásquez, shared a jeep with the prefect in which he traveled about the
department adjudicating disputes among the campesinos over land,
water, etc., which local dirigentes had been unable to resolve. The federation also prints handbills promoting, for example, a «Week of
Wheat» among the peasants. «If Cochabamba becomes the granary of
Bolivia,» reads one, «it's because the campesinos want it to.» Such
posters may be seen turning brown on the walls outside the federation
office, and in the sun, around the plaza in Tarata, Punata, Arani; but
none, as far as I know, reached Palca. Palca totally missed the «Week
of Wheat,» though they do, in fact, raise a lot of it, and they might
have obtained some of the superior seed which the government gave
away in small quantities at that time. But no one arrived to tell them

of this, nor do Palcans, except on rare occasions, visit their federation office in the city.

The federation publishes a newspaper in Spanish, *El Campo,* full of news about soccer games among peasants in areas around towns and cities and inspirational editorials and cartoons showing peasants conquering stumps and stones with tractors. I never saw this journal around Palca, and indeed how much it could mean to illiterate monolingual peasants using hand tools is obscure.

The federation finally has helped peasants build soccer fields in some areas; but this brief list about summarizes its functions beyond the political and quasi-military. It simply has not got the money to «press for new forms of production on the land, for the elimination of illiteracy,» etc.

A basic reason for this, of course, is that Bolivia herself lacks the money which oil, for example, gives Venezuela, which can be funneled into the campo in the form of all kinds of infrastructure (Erasmus, 1967: 369; Powell, 1964: iv, 21). Yet lack of material resource, crucial as it is, cannot be viewed as an independent variable but only as one among many—the background against which the long drama of Bolivian life has been played out. Even if great sums of money were to become avaliable, where would they go, now, in the countryside? How would they be distributed? The Bolivian sindicato movement has developed neither the links with credit extension or road agencies nor the complex skills among its leaders by which considerations of peasant voting support can be converted into pressures for economic improvement in the Venezuelan sindicatos (Powell, 1969: 76, 86-87). One suspects that even if money were made available under the present structure much of it would end in the pockets of political entrepreneurs. In other words, the revolution and the sindicato movement suddenly opened up avenues of political mobility to members of a larger range of classes; the revolutionary ideology and formation of peasant masses who could be manipulated widened the field of exploitable political resources; but economic differentiation has been slow. There is no reason to expect a shift in political culture, a change from the opportunistic, personalistic, caudillo-style politics Kling long ago identified in those Latin American societies which had not significantly altered their economic base (Kling, 1956; see also Anderson, 1967: 24).

I have alluded earlier to the great power which such caciques exercised locally in the years immediately following 1953, when destruction of the old police and army left a vacuum in the campo which the sindicatos rushed to fill. This is dramatized by the rise of José Rojas, who carried on an epic feud with Miguel Veizaga in the upper Cochabamba valley, each with his private army of campesinos raiding and counter-raiding one another, killing and pillaging (Malloy, 1968: ch. 14). It is shown by disorders in the mines (Malloy, 1968: 420); by the rise of great caudillos in the steamy forests of the east (Malloy, 1968: 389); by the formation everywhere of peasant militias beyond the control of the MNR government. Even today you hear echoes of this period in Tiraque when the townspeople tell you how the campesino central imposed a curfew on the town «in the time of Victor Paz,» and if they saw a light on after ten o'clock at night, gangs of drunken peasants led by García and others would break down doors and smash jars of chicha. It is implicit in the stories of Casimiro García abusing Tiraque women; in Don Dionisio Guzmán thinking drunkenly he could intercept my jeep even on the highway and my assistant saying: «He must know you can't do that anymore»; in the informal execution of the sex offender described on page 116. The campo was «Indianized,» as Malloy puts it. The peasant movement was largely autonomous. As late as 1960, the sindicatos and the baronies of various personalist bosses constituted such law as existed outside the cities (Malloy, 1968: 320, 457). At Palca this is reflected in the ease with which José Rojas simply ordered various criminals transported there as from one part of his domain to another, and in the fact that several Palcans were drafted into the militia (By then—the early 60s—Rojas had thrown in his lot with the Paz faction of the MNR) which moved to break the great caudillo of Santa Cruz, Sandoval Morón.

For the militias were courted by the central government and drawn into conflict regionally (as in the case of Morón), sectorally (against miners and railway workers; see Lord, 1965:61), and the internecine factionalism within the MNR itself.[146] Revolution never ended the old Klingian job politics *(empleocracia)* but merely continued it, exacerbated by sectoral and ideological differences (Malloy, 1968:ch. 13, 14). In these struggles the peasantry was turned into a weapon serving the interests of various leaders rather than its own economic development (Lord, 1965:56). Support was mobilized through bribery, paternalism, and personalist charisma[147] rather than through internalization of a set of values (Easton, 1953). A «transition,» as Lord (1965:62) puts it, was never made «from the concept of the campesino syndicate as a weapon» to one «as an element in education, production and orderly political development.»

Several points are crucial here:

1. From the viewpoint of both peasants and their leaders the factors of time and the cultural and economic distance the ex-colonos had to cross to enter national life are important. The very backwardness of the peasants lent explosive force to the revolution, since it led to intense focus on the abolition of anachronistic services and distribution of land. But it meant also that the peasant tended to feel the job was done once he had received his land, to opt out of national concern and

---

[146] Thus Rojas and Veizaga were personal rivals but were coopted by rival factions of the MNR (Malloy, 1968:chs. 13-14). Veizaga's defeat marked also the decline of the faction he represented at the national level, the conservative Guevarist wing.

[147] More accurately, «hypnotic» or «inspirational» leaders. See Friedrich, 1961.

revert to localism. This gave the revolution a much narrower base than the nonrevolutionary land reform in Venezuela which took years to develop and had time to engender a broad program of economic development (Erasmus, 1967: 369-370). The suddenness of the revolution meant also that there was small chance for training and political socialization of either mass or leaders—again compared to Venezuela (Powell, 1964; 1969). Force, bribery, personalism, mobility according to the Kling model—these become the rule, rather than brokerage for the peasant's interests. Further, why should peasant leaders, these (structurally but hardly behaviorally) modern brokers, act to change the base from which they are profiting any more than the economic middlemen cited in Chapter V?

2. The peasant movement was never well fused with a general labor movement as it was in Venezuela, nor to intellectuals and bureaus concerned with economic development. This means not only that the Bolivian syndicates have never had the avenues open to pressure for credit, extension, etc., which have been present in Venezuela, but also that links with the larger society have been lacking, which could help integrate the peasants culturally into the nation. Forces working for change in political culture—so noticeable in Venezuela (Powell, 1969: 62-63)—have been much slower in Bolivia.

3. Manipulation of a politically unaware peasantry by ambitious local leaders who have been coopted by the national level means that such leaders can, as Lord (1965: 54) puts it, «bargain this *campesino* support to the highest bidder among those competing for power at the national level.» It follows that those leaders with the most following, or with the most accessible following (such as in the highly populated areas around cities)[148] will be able to pull more weight than those in more marginal areas. This may be a factor behind the political apathy I found at Palca. To anticipate, we can posit that Palca may be caught on a kind of plateau politically as well as economically.

4. The fact that Bolivian sindicatos have been largely «captives» of a one-party system, rather than being tied to competing political parties, means that the party in power can afford to ignore peasant demands more easily than under a more competitive system (Erasmus, 1967: 370).

Recent events in Bolivia show some effort on the part of the central government to control or «nationalize» the chaos in the interest of development. Reconstitution of the Security Police and a national army with United States aid was an attempt in this direction; in the

---

[148] Jorge Dandler-Hanhart informs me that it is not always peasants around cities who pack political wallop, since many peasants, mobilized as militia, and who are valuable for this reason, come from the *serranías* (highland areas). By now these militia are well organized; there are relatively well-trained groups who, time and again, are mobilized. But the Tiraque region is marginal from this point of view, as well as from the point of view of sheer numbers.

early 60s Paz used the army to help crush certain bosses (Veizaga, Morón) and to «nationalize» the rest (Malloy, 1968:462). The military junta which took power in 1964 continued this policy; by the time I arrived in Bolivia in 1967 the peasant movement had been pretty well coopted by the government, at least around Cochabamba. Rojas was in jail,[149] and Salvador Vásquez, his protegé and former cohort, was head of the peasant federation at the departmental level and in the pay of the government. Reduction of the centrales at the cantonal and provincial levels was probably a reflection of this policy, since it weakened peasant autonomy at the local level and freed energy for production.

But if conflict had abated to the point of ending outright war in the countryside, it does not follow that the government was secure or that the sindicato movement had become more effective as a force for modernization. No links whatever had been set up by the latter with extension services or bank. «In» versus «out» politics continued on the national level, with uncertainty as to how factions in the army would behave; plots and counterplots by exiled or disaffected elements of both left and right, MNR elements, Lechinistas,[150] Falangistas,[151] etc. Peasant militias were mobilized as always for political purposes. Disaffected elements—MNRistas, Lechinistas, along with the middle class and partly counter-revolutionary Falange and a general in the army[152]— were accused of conspiring against the government, and peasant militias were mobilized with machine guns in trucks to move into Cochabamba to «show support» for the government. At Palca this meant visits by Salvador Vásquez in order to reorganize the sub-central of Tiraque and threats by the leader to the peasants of dire consequences if they did not stay «united» behind the government (see pp. 102-103).

---

[149] Rojas was out of power in 1967 and jailed in 1968. Always a Paz supporter in MNR days, he swung to the junta in 1964 along with other Cochabamba leaders; this sounded the death knell for the MNR at that time (Malloy, 1968: 460, 488). Later, Rojas lost out in a power struggle with two rising leaders, Jorge Solíz of Ucureña and Gregorio López of Punata; the exact cause of his jailing and fall from power is obscure. (I owe this last information to personal conversation with Jorge Dandler-Hanhart.)

[150] Followers of ex-Vice-President Juan Lechín, mining leader who lead armed miners to help defeat the old regime in 1952. Lechín later formed a leftist sector of the MNR in 1960 and his own party, broke with Paz and was exiled. His decline coincided with the decline of the miners and the rise of the peasant bloc and the Oriente in the struggle for power in the country (Hennessey, 1964: 205-207).

[151] Members of the FSB (Falange Socialista Boliviana), strong among the middle class in La Paz, represents elements of the old oligarchy. It is characteristic of this «restrained» revolution that it permits these elements to persist in their professions, businesses, etc., in their power bases in the cities, and to continue to work against any government but their own.

[152] Significant of the spoils-struggle aspect of Bolivian politics: one cannot imagine what program this motley crew would have devised had they succeeded to power. Yet they were willing to come together in this venture.

The status of the peasants' land tenure, along with the survival of elements of the old landowning class in the cities (a direct result of the moderate or «restrained» quality of the revolution) might be calculated to give a certain credence to these words. Significantly, Vásquez at no point tried to mobilize these peasants for direct action as he had others; at most, he seemed to be preparing the ground for such a move should it seem necessary. Nor did he make use of more complex and tangible strategies of support-mobilization through demand-satisfaction in use elsewhere in Bolivia[153] (Easton, 1953). He asked less of these peasants and gave less; yet psychologically mobilization methods were like those in use elsewhere: stick-and-carrot, force and demand-satisfaction, rather than development of affective commitment to the system through the growth of increasing consciousness. Leaders still manipulate the peasants' ignorance, greed, and fear.

For this reason, I have referred to politicization among these peasants as revolving around a «subject competence» (Almond and Powell, 1966:59, 305). It follows that when writers refer to the Bolivian peasant as being «now the locus of considerable political power» (Wagley, 1968:136; see also Patch, 1960:108-176) or «standing on top of a mountain» (Antezana, 1955: 18), it needs to be specified which particular peasants (in a nation as highly varied regionally as Bolivia); who has the power, leaders or followers; what kind or level of political socialization the peasant has undergone. I hold that, in the Tiraque area in general and at Palca in particular, in everyday orientations toward politics the rank-and-file has developed little beyond a «subject-participant orientation» in that they know they must be active, be participants, but the party and other groups afford the average peasant little opportunity for sharing in decisions (Almond and Powell, 1966:59). The aims of their participation, further, are rudimentary. Their political socialization, knowledge of politics and their aspirations are rudimentary in the extreme, like other aspects of their culture, amounting to little more than a desire to be left alone with security of land tenure.

In other words, even though a political structure—the sindicato and federation—has been set up to link the peasants to the larger society, it scarcely functions, or functions only one way, partly because of the peasants' political culture and that of their leaders (Almond and Powell, 1966:50). And even «subject-participant orientation» is none too strong among these peasants perhaps because, on one hand, they

---

[153] Jorge Dandler-Hanhart, who has worked extensively in the upper Cochabamba valley, tells me such techniques include provision of chicha to the peasants, trucks, gasoline, etc. A most interesting question for future research are the linkages, if any, between provincial economic entrepreneurs of the type discussed in Chapter V and political entrepreneurship, and links between peasant leaders and town officials such as the alcalde. Evidence of this kind is hard to come by, but not wholly absent; there is some indication, for example, that the Punata central collects a rake-off on taxes collected from peasants in the market.

are marginal to the government's concerns in the distribution of benefits and know it, and on the other because of encogido attitudes deriving from a general sense of cultural separateness and inferiority. Palca
probably knows they don't pull as much weight with the federation as
more populous areas in the valley; they are as shy, as out of place in
the city on political errands as they are on economic. They have minimal personal linkage to federation leaders; the result is apathy and
withdrawal which I can dramatize in no better fashion than directly
from my notes:

It was early in the morning (June 8) when Don Dionisio received by foot
messenger an order from Guillermo Cossío, Secretary-General of the Tiraque
central, to come to Tiraque «with all his base,» (i.e., all members of the sindicato) at noon that very day to hear their jefe, «compañero Vásquez.» This was
the first contact I know which the Federation has had with Palca since February
of this year when Vásquez also came to Tiraque collecting quotas of food from
the peasants to aid victims of the February flood in Cochabamba.[154] Fortunately,
as it turned out, Palca's soccer team had a game scheduled in Tiraque that afternoon; otherwise the only Palcans who would have come to listen to Vásquez
would have been Don Dionisio, his Secretary of Relations, Eugenio Vargas, and,
significantly, Casimiro García.
We drove these peasants into Tiraque about 1 P.M., and it was 3 before
Vásquez arrived in a white taxi from Cochabamba, accompanied by a tall husky
young man with curly hair who gave me an impression of sternly posing, like
Mussolini. Vásquez also doesn't seem wholly real with his stern military face,
moustache, and rumpled suit and pot belly. He rode into town and vanished in
a side street to eat. Meanwhile, Don Dionisio, Eugenio and Casimiro had vanished into a chichería along with Guillermo Cossío, and the youths of the soccer
team played a scrub game with the Tiraqueños which, it was apparent to me,
they were impatient to continue as soon as the meeting was over. Finally, Vásquez
emerged with his friend, climbed in the taxi and drove to the soccer field on the
outskirts of the small hamlet. They debouched from their cab and strode to a
big eucalyptus on the edge of the field; the peasants followed and formed a rough
circle on both sides of them. There (after preliminary speeches by Guillermo
Cossío and the alcalde of Tiraque) Vásquez began, speaking totally in Quechua.
«Hermanos campesinos, compañeros,» he began. He said he was very unhappy
that so few peasants had come to this meeting. He said there are 5,000 peasants
in the Tiraque sub-central with 32 haciendas, but at most 1,000 shown up. (The
Palca delegation, soccer players, young and apparently uninterested in the proceedings, were waiting patiently on the fringe for it all to end to get on with
their game.) Vásquez said the dirigentes who had failed to mobilize their peasants
were betraying the revolution; that they—the campesinos—had no unity among
themselves. «You peasants believe that you are masters of your lands and forget
that your government is in danger,» he cried. Yesterday, he said, a plot was discovered in Cochabamba against the government. «If the Rosca comes back, the
last hair on your head won't be enough to pay them—they will exact great ven-
geance *(bastante venganza)*. All you poor dirigentes are marked and will go to
jail. For this reason, you must find a new unity. The government is fighting for
you so that the Rosca can't return.» But with such a small turnout he can't orga-

---

[154] The city of Cochabamba suffered greatly from floods during the rainy
season of 1968. Mud houses, farms, etc. on the outskirts particularly suffered,
and many agencies, including the campesino federation, were called on to provide
relief.

nize anything, Vásquez said. «I came in vain, I contracted a taxi for 100 pesos in vain.» He said that neither the people of Tiraque nor the campesinos of this region will get any help from the Federation or from the prefect in Cochabamba.

Vásquez went on to say he would talk to the prefect in Cochabamba. In effect, he was threatening the peasants, because a campesino might well need such aid from the prefect or his federation if he got in trouble in the city. Vásquez said that people from other communities «who are united» would receive such aid; but not people from here.

Vásquez ended here; whereupon the dirigentes crowded around him, urging him to finish reorganizing the central that day because «We cant' always be coming into Tiraque.» Then came a brief comic speech by Don Dionisio who emerged from the crowd and jumped up beside Vásquez and Cossío. The Palca dirigente, obviously tipsy, said he had only received the memorandum that morning and that «they» (the peasants) «aren't our sons that we can tie them up and deliver them in Tiraque.» The crowd roared at this, whereupon Vásquez strode off with an order that the dirigentes come to Tiraque with all their base next Sunday, with any peasant who did not come to be fined 10 pesos.

Vásquez did not return the next week, however, but sent an aide who arrived even later than his boss, after many peasants were well into chicha, and he interrupted another soccer game. The turnout was only slightly larger; but no one, at Palca at any rate, ever paid a fine, and the aide, a short fat man with a red face, spittle forming at his mouth corners, made an excited speech about the status of the peasants' land, the threat of the Rosca etc.; applause was lukewarm. At the end he ordered the Tiraque sub-central to hold elections to choose four dirigentes, two of whom—a Secretary-General and Secretary of Relations—would man an office in Tiraque and come frequently there. Four men were chosen from member sindicatos of the central, including Don Dionisio Guzmán of Palca as Secretary of Relations. Soon after this, Don Dionisio rejected the post, saying: «I have no sons to work my fields for me.» The other dirigentes, hearing this, followed suit, with the result that a very small turnout of campesinos the week following elected a new roster of candidates, including Saturnino Achá of Palca as Secretary-General (who soon devoted himself as assiduously as possible to the collection of fines and bribes) and Encarnación Orellana of Tiraque, a piquero said by some to have been a partisan of the patrones. (I can attest to his flat refusal to treat—with the passing knowledge of veterinary medicine he possesses—a sick ox belonging to a peasant from Palca.) Many were displeased at the election. There were mutterings about Achá: «Perro de Hinojosa,» the peasants called him. («Dog of the patrón,» referring to the fact that once, as curaca, Achá had cared for the patrón's animals.) «Crooked one» (*moqo* in Quechua, referring to his slightly hunched back), «He runs around like a sick dog.» New elections were called for. People said a larger turnout would never have elected these two; but the fact is still before my departure five months later nothing had been done. Attitudes of drift and apathy toward politics tinged with cynicism,[155] along with a strong inward focus on traditional agriculture, have, I think, been well documented.

Yet a festive air can be mixed with politics, as with so many things. If the syndical movement has been associated elsewhere with a decline in alcoholic intake, as Heath (1965:290) claims, this is not true at Palca. Rather the opposite: a summons from the federation on the occasions of a visit from a «bigshot» can trigger an informal fiesta. These peasants not only «know they must be active politically,» they can sometimes love it as a break in routine, a chance for change, color, the wildness of hope. Thus when President Barrientos visited Arani in 1967 on the anniversary of the founding of the provincial capital, Palca responded vigorously to the federation's call to appear. Barrientos descended in his helicopter and was borne into town on the shoulders of the campesinos. Parades, churchbells: The president lunched with the alcalde and then, in the sun, from a balcony on the alcaldía, addressed the crowd in the plaza. He spoke of his government's developmental aims, the threats of extremists, etc., and pulled rolls of pesos from his pocket and handed them to local officials to repair Arani's electric plant and build a small clinic and basketball court. A handsome man, Barrientos bought the town financially and charismatically; but the Palcans did not see it, they were in the chicherías. On the way back Don Dionisio talked drunkenly of getting the president to visit Palca, saying that two years ago Barrientos passed through Tiraque and promised to come to the hacienda but never did. In short, the magnetism of distant figures modeled on a good patrón (the president, El Señor) is not tarnished; the peasants still believe, as Patch (1960:141) wrote, that «their problems will be resolved ... if they can only set them before «Don Hernan» (Siles) or «Don Victor» (Paz Estenssoro) or, implicitly, General Barrientos.[156] As long as such figures command the personalistic loyalty of these peasants, they can probably be mobil-

---

[155] Don Dionisio complained, for example, that Salvador Vásquez «almost never comes here,» i.e., to the Tiraque region, and he said he has «lost respect» for Vásquez because the latter once promised to come to Palca and never came. It is true that, during my thirteen months on the hacienda, the peasants were visited a total of three times by representatives of their federation. Nobody from other branches of government, no congressional deputy or representative of the prefect, came to Tiraque officially. Out of a random sample of thirteen heads of families queried, only one knew the vice-president's name.

[156] This attitude is not confined to the peasantry, since I frequently heard officials of the town of Tiraque, for example, speak of getting the president to «spend a whole day in Tiraque to learn about the place» in the hope that, if he didn't spend some money now, «he would later in order to help the town.» Pervasive everywhere, due to perennial poverty perhaps, is the idea that change can only be effected through the intervention of outside powers who must be placated and manipulated (see Chapter VII).

ized in a crisis to support the government, no matter what cynicism[157] they feel toward local officials and issues.

Still, defensiveness, indifference, a desire just not to be bothered marks Palca's attitude toward most political demands articulated down toward it, and the peasants are equally diffident about expressing upward in the system needs or desires which they themselves feel. There is variation here (see Chapter X). Not all peasants of the region or even within the hacienda are equally encogido, as Erasmus puts it. Yet there are structural factors working for this behavior; the region, taken as a whole, is doubtless marginal to the central government's concerns compared with certain others. Psychological factors are significant also, since it is here, as in their interaction with Don Venustiano Villarroel of Punata, that Palcans show clearly the effects of specially tough prereform conditions, their timidity, passivity, and feeling of being lost in the outside world.

For example, on one occasion Don Dionisio went with us to Cochabamba, along with his secretary of relations; they wanted information concerning the proposed change in the tax law which would have allowed them to pay taxes on their land [158] and presumably increase security of tenure. The peasants had not the slightest idea where their federation office was located; my assistant and I found it for them. They followed us single file in the streets, at a distance, and hung back when we arrived at the office: my assistant spoke for them. The same held true at the office of the federation lawyer. Dr. Fausto Merida, where we were referred. Here they would hardly have entered had not my assistant and myself urged them on, and they could not wait to leave. Don Dionisio, in his best black coat, wrinkled and much too short for him; Don Eugenio Vargas, all but lost in a big double-breasted suit with baggy pants—they were even more conspicuous in the city than in Punata, and were safe inside a chichería by four P.M. My assistant and I agreed that, if we had not accompanied them, they would probably have sunk into it sooner and never found the office.

To sum up, no better illustration could be offered of the inability of the present Palca leadership to function as a modernizing broker between the hacienda and the outside world. Don Dionisio was able to resolve the schism on the farm inherited from the past, which was a direct result of brutal prereform conditions. He appeared at least an

---

[157] Thus when General Ovando, the second member of the ruling junta, was announced as planning to visit Tiraque in 1968, and the central wanted to assess each peasant 5 pesos for the general's food, Don Dionisio said: «They don't need that much. It's only a chance for the central to sneak a bit in its pocket.» A certain hostility between the peasants and the town of Tiraque has already been shown; it will become more manifest in future pages.

[158] Miss Katherine Barnes of the Land Tenure Center of the University of Wisconsin, who returned from Bolivia in April 1970, informed me this tax law has been «permanently shelved» by the Congress.

adequate leader for his occasion—giver of land, resolver of conflict, the
«compassionate» peasant leader outlined by Bequiraj (1966:13). He is
firmly entrenched in the affection of most Palcans for this reason, as
well as in the phalanx of allies he has subtly built up.[159]

But to effect change, to deal with the outside, more is needed
which nothing in Don Dionisio's history has prepared him for. In this
arena, his heritage from the old regime leaves him postively handicapped.

And the sindicato movement, the federation and its leaders are,
for the complex reasons sketched above, either disinclined or unable
to extend a modernizing thrust down to these peasants. Thus there is
even less impetus toward change either from the «grass-roots» up or
from the top down in the political sphere than there is in the economic.
The federation remains, in this marginal geographic area, a mechanism
by which the government can manipulate a moderate anxiety concerning
land litles for political and incipiently military purposes.

OTHER FUNCTIONS, DEFENSE, SOCIAL CONTROL, TOWN-COUNTRY ATTITUDES

Within the community, the syndicate performs minor economic and
festive functions such as communal labor on the road and on the Palca
River when necessary, and voting the amount of money each family
must contribute to pay for the fiesta of the patron saint of Santa Rosario (see Chapter VII). Latently, the sindicato works on these occasions as a mechanism of tension release, of reinforcement of community solidarity and security. The syndicate also meets and votes on
matters of community interest, such as whether or not to accept the
offer of the organization cited in Chapter IV to set up a health station
on the hacienda. On these occasions the dirigente appears fairly detached, tolerant; he makes small attempt to persuade, and the voting
I observed took place in a democratic fashion. In view of his behavior
in other contexts, however, this probably reflects Don Dionisio's relative indifference rather than internalization of any democratic norm.

Here is perhaps the place to mention the fact that the dirigente's
easygoing tolerance at sindicato meetings results in lack of organization.
(The peasants' ineffectiveness in getting together to complete their

---

[159] One might, of course, well ask who at Palca could serve better than Don
Dionisio: that is indeed problematical. The point is, though, that leadership
decisions were made under pressures that were internal and no longer exist but
which still affect the present. Further, potential leaders I interviewed don't want
the post of dirigente, (1) because they fear retribution from the patrones; (2) because, they say, Don Dionisio has milked the post already for all the traffic can
bear, and there is nothing in it for them.

school has already been described.) Several peasants commented to us how the dirigente had changed; how he had been «different,» tough and decisive when Palca's land was being parceled out, but since then had become easygoing. «Since he hasn't sons himself, he lacks incentive to do anything,» the schoolteacher told us, speaking of the school. Another informant, a peasant, went so far as to say: «He's doing all right, he doesn't care about the other campesinos.»

The sindicato functioned defensively in rejecting the health station; this is surely one aspect of its main function at present: to act as a sheath protecting the peasant from the very real threat of outside exploitation by serving as a mechanism of social control on the local level. This preserves a degree of order within the community at the same time that it keeps community affairs from coming to the attention of town authorities.

For the peasants, at present, are forced to share power with these. Such was not always the case (see p. 140). There was a time when the sindicatos and their centrales ruled supreme, and with a kind of dizziness, in the countryside. They were a law unto themselves both internally and in their relations versus the outside (Heath, 1959; Patch, 1960:123). But with the advent of the military junta to power in 1964 and with reconstitution of a national army and police, the centrales were reduced; the peasants have been forced to share administration of social control on the local level with police who have been installed, for example, in the town of Tiraque. This does not mean that under certain conditions the peasants cannot still take the law into their own hands, or that, certainly—despite the social and economic relations which many peasants have built up with Tiraqueños—hostility has been wholly overcome between town and country. But for most purposes, as a rule, law such as it is is shared between peasant leadership on the local level and authorities of the town, and these act roughly as a check on one another.

For example, under normal conditions on the hacienda minor disputes between neighbors, between inheritors over land or husband and wife would be handled by the secretary of justice of the syndicate; if he could not solve the problem, it went to the dirigente. The same is true of minor offenses such as small theft or assault: the great aim among these peasants is always to have trouble handled on the hacienda, away from the town where the police are regarded as on the qui vive to throw a man in jail and extract a fine. Palcans would rather suffer a beating from their dirigente any day than pay money to the police «who are always thinking of *multa* (fines).»

And at Palca, of course, where the secretary of justice is an absconded alcoholic, it was the dirigente who handled all such cases. For example, Jacinto Najera told us how, when he was first married, he got drunk and fought his wife, and Don Dionisio punished him:

Don Dionisio, who was not only dirigente but their padrino as well, hit them both, but he hit Jacinto harder. Jacinto said that, as padrino, Don Dionisio has the right to do that; normally, as dirigente, he gives the order to punish to the vocales of the sindicato and the vocales do the actual administering of punishment, always during meetings of the campesinos. Jacinto said that Don Dionisio whipped him on this occasion, but normally the punishment doesn't consist only of hitting a man but of a *castigo de chancho* (a «pig's punishment»)—i.e., the man to be punished is supported on his hands with his feet about two meters off the ground propped against a wall while he is beaten with a whip.

Whipping for theft, also, seems common—I was told of at least three cases involving peasants from both inside and outside the community. The dirigente again administered the «castigo de chancho» after the culprit had been captured and taken to his house. In general, the community looks to Don Dionisio before making a decision even in a crisis, as when Sinforiano Vargas went berserk, and tried to smash his wife's head with a pickax. The peasants did not immediately go after him but let the man wander for hours on the edge of the community until Don Dionisio ordered a group to got out and capture him.

Yet the peasants under the influence of liquor and inflamed by outrage (usually by offenses of a sexual and desecratory nature) are capable of erupting explosively. A case of impromptu punishment for rape has already been described; this took place, to be sure, «in the time of Paz» when the peasants were more autonomous at present. Still, the sudden, savage beating of Agabito Linares by the women of the community, without warning and totally ad hoc, has overtones of the same thing and gives a sense of Palca life, the drift, crudity and potential violence:

There was a fiesta in the house of Leandro Najera for his son Luis (just out of the army, one of the growing number of landless youths). We went there, and moving from the sun into the dark bare mudfloored room where the fiesta was in progress was like entering hell. A phonograph was playing *cuecas* and raw loud *huayños*. Drunken peasants danced in the dust; Agabito Linares, drunk and weaving, tried to embrace me; Macedonio Najera stood unsteadily by the door, drooling. All seemed drunk except for Luis and his brother Pedro.... Don Dionisio had just fallen in the courtyard and had a bloody nose and Eusebio (my assistant) and several women helped him with care and respect into an inner room to lie down. Pablo Flores was crawling on his hands and kness across the floor.... A fight broke out between Agabito and his wife, both drunk and in rags, in a corner—he tore her blouse, baring her floppy breasts. The wife's mother intervened and they moiled around shouting and tearing one another in the dark. «I'm your mother! Hit me! Hit me!» The mother-in-law kept screeching; they fell in a heap in the corner. Finally, other women intervened and threw the mother-in-law out, and then Agabito and his wife fought. «Without shame! Without shame!» The wife kept screaming—referring to the fact that Agabito is widely believed to sleep with his wife's mother; suddenly the women ganged up on Agabito, hitting him and banging his head against the mud wall. They were all over him—Leona Najera, Juana Anivar, wife of Pedro Flores (who got in cruel and telling blows making the head sound like sodden sand against cement); the wife of Felipe Rodríguez was nursing a baby, but this didn't keep her from giving it to Agabito. The latter finally escaped and urinated in the yard.

Doña Juana told us later that they beat Agabito up «because he has no respect for his mother-in-law»; but that also, while the mother-in-law was there, he tried to beat his wife, and this triggered it. The women of the community felt it was simply too much humiliation for his wife on this occasion, «in front of everybody.» The community is still capable of acting on occasion spontaneously and en masse, especially if the dirigente is, as in this and other instances, indisposed through drink.

Yet even if the Palcans had carried the punishment all the way with Agabito, it is probable that, in the last analysis, they would have had to deal with outside authorities. They could not have simply buried the body and forgotten it, as in the case of the rapist described earlier or, as is rumored, with the political prisoners José Rojas had transported to the hacienda during the revolution, who were summarily executed.

The very presence of police in the towns means that, as Don Dionisio told us, if something serious occurs like a murder or suicide, it is his «duty» to notify the town authorities according to law, otherwise «neighbors would gossip» and «everyone would get in trouble.» Thus when Daniel Claros hung himself after a long history of conflict within his family, Don Dionisio went into Tiraque and contacted officials there—the *Juez Instructor* (roughly analogous to our justice of the peace), an employee of the alcaldía, and the doctor—and brought them back to the scene. The town authorities questioned the peasants and even considered arresting Daniel's domineering old mother on «suspicion» because the young man's first wife had hung herself in a similar fashion; but Don Dionisio talked them out of this. The officials also tried to charge the dead man's family 300 pesos ($25) for their «inspection,» and the doctor sought 600 pesos for an autopsy, claiming he needed to «open up the man's stomach to see if he had suffered blows.» A vigorous protest by Palca's dirigente quashed this, and the 300-peso «inspection» was reduced to 200. Daniel was buried at dusk the following day without ceremony in the Tiraque cemetery by his neighbors who had been drinking all day.

This case shows (beyond the dirigente's efficiency in defense—again, in a traditional role) the present mutually limiting powers of the sindicato and the town. Before 1964, the sindicato would have buried Daniel with no questions asked. The abuse implicit in a totally autonomous peasant movement is obvious. By the same token, the town has a long history of exploitation of the peasants, and the evidence shows that the townspeople will still try to «take advantage» of a situation if they get the chance. This is not moralistic criticism. The fact is that, despite the spur to economic activity granted by the reform, a town like Tiraque is still stagnant. Officials such as the Juez Instructor have small chance to better their lot except through petty political entrepreneurship. The sindicato is curbed by the town and vice versa.

This tendency is reinforced by the economic symbiosis between town and country outlined in Chapter V, by the vecinos' memory of peasants' depredations against the town and by political considerations: Town officials know that large peasant turnouts on the occasion of politicians' visits increase their importance to the latter and hence their chances of receiving patronage. Thus, though there is ample evidence of continuing contempt and hostility on both sides,[160] the peasants of Palca and the vecinos (particularly of Tiraque) have reached a stand-off. The latter would not—for the reasons above adumbrated—want to insist on a 600-peso autopsy, for example. Don Nemesio would not risk hiding a suicide.[161] A balance of power exists, but peasants and townspeople are hardly unified in a cultural or emotional sense.

There can be, finally, at times, a religious overtone to conflict resolution on the hacienda—the dirigente or, sometimes, his wife makes the sign of the Cross over the forehead of a kneeling peasant after punishment is administered or conflict resolved; it is as if to say «You are forgiven. Go and sin no more.» This occurs only occasionally, a trace element, so to speak, but it hints at the religiosity hovering over the peasants' lives and entering at many points into it, despite their lack of education and despite the rarity of visits by a priest.

---

[160] Townspeople informally, especially after a few drinks, will refer to the peasants as «Indios,» «barbaros,» etc., who, after the reform, «want to make themselves equal to us» *(igualarse)*. Don Dionisio, for his part, refers to Tiraqueños, including the priest, as «*suwas*» (Quechua: «thieves»). Some peasants told us of the rape, by town louts, of peasant women after drinking and the beating of their husbands.

[161] My notes contain evidence of the arrest of peasants on other haciendas by Tiraque police for offenses committed both on and of the hacienda.

Chapter VII

CEREMONIAL AND RELIGION—VALUES

For ceremonial and religion are, conceived broadly, perhaps the richest aspects of culture on the hacienda. A festive element pervades many activities, as we have seen, from politics to marketing; the peasants are formally Catholics and go to mass in Tiraque or pray to God and the saints in their chapel when weather conditions—notably lack of rain—menace the crops. I myself have witnessed a peasant inside a neighbor's house fall to his kness during a sudden hailstorm and pray to El Señor to stop the hail and make a cross afterwards with ashes from the fire on the bare earth floor.

The simplest curse involves God and the saints. On two occasions when drought grew really severe, the peasants carried the statue of their patron saint into Tiraque and held special masses, praying for rain. Ancient Incaic ritual is present vestigially in the burning of c'oa to the Pachamama (Earth Mother) before the sowing of potatoes and in the pouring of a few drops of chicha on the earth every time one drinks as a libation to the latter. If the word «fiesta» is extended to include any gathering for ritual or recreational purposes marked by drinking and a generally excited mood, then fiesta or fiesta-related activity uses up a large portion of the peasants' time, though formal fiestas involving the entire community are few and rudimentary compared to those of the upper Cochabamba valley proper (Goins, 1954).

Using this broad definition, we can distinguish three types of fiesta at Palca:

1. Formal communal fiestas, religious or with religious overtones.
2. Fiestas assciated with the individual's life cycle.
3. Informal fiestas.

FORMAL COMMUNAL FIESTAS

Formal fiestas are but four in number, and of these only two —Todos Santos and the fiesta of the patron saint, Santa Rosario, involve special preparation on the part of the community. Christmas and Carnaval early in February serve as occasions for relaxation and visiting and drinking among friends and neighbors both on and off the hacienda; but since this type of activity may occur at any time, it is hard to conceive of these occasions as formal fiestas. However, the peasants frequently jour-

ney to neighboring farms and the town of Tiraque to take part in local
festivities, and Easter is the occasion of an Easter mass.

By far the greatest fiesta of the year, focus of anticipation and preparation for weeks in advance, is the fiesta of Santa Rosario which takes
place on October 7. By this date most if not all the work of sowing
potatoes is completed; the peasants have finished most of the year's
heavy work and ahead lies mainly hoeing and weeding and hoping for
the harvest; it is the time of year when many weddings occur.

Preparation for Santa Rosario begins weeks in advance. At a meeting
of the sindicato the peasants decide how much they are going to «chip
in» for quotas to pay for the band and the visit of the priest —about
20 pesos (a little less than $2) per family head plus quantities of food.
At this meeting the peasants also decide at whose house chicha is to be
brewed for the fiesta; as in the days of the patrón, two places are selected for this, one high up near the hacienda house, one lower down
near the highway, and each peasant brings his quota of grain and helps
brew chicha from time immemorial. The dirigente meanwhile is traveling
to and from Punata to hire the band and buy candles and special food
for the priest, and to Tiraque in order to hire the latter. The price is not
cheap —600 pesos ($50) for two masses— and the peasants themselves
recognize this.

Those peasants also, who are sponsoring their own private devotions
to the patron saint, who are serving as pasante, meanwhile make their
own preparations: brewing chicha, hiring their own private band. A
wealthy peasant may sometimes make chicha and hire a band for a private party without religious considerations. The point to be stressed is
that the peasants spend a fair portion of money relative to their income
in this fiesta, and piety, superstition, and a sheer desire to blow off
steam, to dance and get drunk, are all involved. They are so closely inter-
woven it is sometimes hard to separate them.

By October 6 all is furor. The diablado dancers who will go into action after the mass practice in the dust in a field near the chapel, pounding the hard dry earth with their feet, in gaudy uniforms that creak, in
ghastly masks some students believe represent the Indians' view of the
Spanish. The hacienda swarms with visitors and sellers from Punata
who squat in their polleras on the ground in front of the chapel and
peddle bread, sweet cakes, bananas and chicha. Everywhere bits of color,
blue sky.

The day reaches its peak in the visit of the priest during the afternoon to hold the Vesper Mass *(Misa de Las Vísperas)* after which it falls
off in drunkenness. Santa Rosario provides the one occasion besides
Easter during the year when the priest visits Palca; by serving as his
chauffeur I was close to him all through his visit and can present something of the quality of Palca religion:

We rode to Palca with the priest, his sacristan, and organist—this last poor
and old and wheezy, with a bulbous nose and wing-tipped collar out of the last
century. His small shabby organ fits him perfectly, and it was touching to observe

the great concern he showed for the poor old thing when we lifted it into the jeep. We finally assured him that it wouldn't get broken in driving the 8 kilometers to Palca from Tiraque, that I would drive with care, etc. The priest, who had invited us for several glasses of chicha in his house played the accordion for us and complained in English to me of his bad stomach. His name is José Muñoz Villarroel. He has very soft hands and bad breath and keeps calling me «Mi querido» and putting his hot soft hand on my shoulder; I keep remembering as we ride that he is rumored in Tiraque to be the father of the unmarried telephone operator's baby and how Don Dionisio keeps calling him «Suwa kura» («thieving priest» in Quechua), but never to his face and he apparently would never think of not inviting him....[162]

At Palca mass was said about 1:30 P.M. It was the only time I had been inside the little chapel with its tarnished brass altar and plaster saints along the walls. The church had always been locked before and probably will be again until next year at Easter. The mass was exactly like others I had attended in Tiraque: the peasants kneeling and praying (there is pathos in the backs of the peasant's shoes: the abarcas with soles of old rubber tires showing, the cheap plastic affairs of the women), the priest alternately singing and intoning in Latin with the organist playing and intoning in turn. This time the latter did not go astray in the middle of Beethoven's Minuet in G, but he still did not hit one true note in his singing. I could not believe it possible for a man to sing for an hour offkey all the time—chance alone should dictate one true note. But this *viejito* in wingtipped collar and runny nose and spotted suit missed them all. Again, I had a sense of ironic contrast between the meaning of the mass, of noble sacrifice, and this reality. The peasants have no idea what the Latin means, only that it is somehow impressive; and the priest looked as if he knew this. He seemed bored and hurried, and when it was over and time for the women to carry the plaster Virgin on their shoulders out of the church, he berated the community for dressing her up in gaudy ill-fitting clothes to which money had been pinned. He said the Virgin had enough clothes already and did not need any more, and he had the people take off all her rags.[163]

It should be stressed that at another level irony fades: The peasants may not know Latin, but their dream of redemption is very real, though mute, and is linked to the genuine pain of their condition. Significantly, they hope to obtain favorable attention from the supernatural through propitiation, manipulation, bribery, methods with which they are familiar in other aspects of their lives. Always the Virgin or patrón saint is conceived as something external, «out there», and powerful like the weather or market changes. One seeks her protection like that of any patrón one does not necessarily love. Religion as a matter of internal ethical concern is alien to these peasants.

One seeks a bargain in religion just as one goes after a bargain in the market. What matters is not the substance of a ritual but the fact

---

[162] Note the cynicism here; the advisability of having the Virgin's earthly representative on your side is, however, never doubted. The cynicism seems well merited. Priests are expensive. In some areas before the reform priests were said to take Indian girls in for a night of «instruction» before their marriage. Professor Ronald Clark told me of a priest on the altiplano who sold land in heaven to peasant families in exchange for favors from their women.

[163] This lesson did not stay with the people. The following year (1968 a new priest came to Tiraque, and the peasants went on as before.

that it is performed; further, Catholic ritual can be applied syncretically to vestigial Inca belief. Thus when a young Spanish Jesuit came out from Cochabamba during a teacher's strike (see Chapter VIII) and stayed at the hacienda house and held classes for the children, Guillermo Flores got him to bless his new oven «to keep a pachamama from living there.» He said he would not want to bring out the priest from Tiraque for this purpose—it would cost too much—but since Padre Esteban was staying at our house he wanted to «take advantage» of this situation and have the young priest do it for nothing.

Finally, nothing has changed in these attitudes with the reform—which is to be expected since the peasants' existential situation, their control over crucial aspects of the environment, has hardly altered. The Bolivian Catholic Church (as distinguished from foreign orders such as certain Jesuits, the Maryknoll and Franciscan fathers) has wholly detached itself from reform in the campo, at least around Cochabamba.[164] Its representatives interact with the peasants in a traditional manner which betrays, in subtle ways, the same attitude tward the «Indios» as other townspeople. In view of all this, it is not surprising that the Bolivian revolution lacks the strain of chiliasm traceable, for example, in Mexico from Hidalgo to Madero and Zapata, that there has been small effort to change consummatory values.

After emerging from the chapel, the women carry the Virgin of Santa Rosario about the yard stopping at each of its four corners. The priest, his organist, and the little old wheezy organ closely follow; at each corner they stop, the organ plays and the organist sings, and the priest says a few words in Latin. Then skyrockets are set off in the middle of the yard, and the procession moves on, driving ahead of it the diablado[165] dancers who cavort and reel wildly, kicking up dust. By now many of these are drunk, and fights can occur. Once, Agustín Lizzaraga and his brother Calixto went at it with fists even while the priest was speaking and had to be separated before the latter could finish. Calixto later could not remember what it as all about: «We were drunk, that's all.»

When all four stations have been visited and the Virgin restored to her perch in the chapel, the band hired by the community (young men from Pucara or the valley towns) resumes playing in the yard, and all is dancing and drinking. The boom of the drum and the raw blare of

---

[164] Palcans even identify the priests in Tiraque before the reform as friends of the patrón. It should be mentioned, further, that the Maryknoll fathers, for example, who are working around the city of Cochabamba, forming cooperatives, etc., have not as yet penetrated very far into the campo; they are also gradualists, like good North Americans, and hope to change values and attitudes only over the long haul.

[165] By serving as diablado dancers, men are exempted from contributing to the quotas to pay for the band and priest. As mentioned earlier, young men may also earn 10 pesos or so plus food and chicha by serving as diablado dancers at fiestas in neighboring farms.

horns last deep into the night. Before the reform, the peasants say, the fiesta was much smaller; the patrón controlled it: there were fewer visitors and bands were smaller, consisting only of *quenas* and *zamponas*. But now they play modern instruments and some bands have a wider repertory: the *cumbia* from Colombia, the *taqirari* from Santa Cruz along with the perennial *huaynos* and *cuecas* of the mountains. They dance until breathless and drink chicha and dance again. There are bands and chicha in the houses of the pasantes. Some peasants along with townspeople are selling chicha; chicha is everywhere. Sexual freedom between the unattached can be open at this time.

The next day consists of more of the same, interrupted only by the mass which is similar to the Vesper mass except that the pasantes appear with their gaudy flags and garlands and parade around in front of the church before the service. At the conclusion of the latter, the standards (*banderas* and *guías de flor*) are left in the church, and those who are to serve as pasantes the following year pick them up and take them to their houses. The peasants refer to this as «passing the guía or bandera»: «I have passed the guía to my brother Sinforiano,» and it is tantamount to a pledge on the part of Sinforiano to make a *devoto* to the Virgin the following year. The pledge is made directly to the Virgin; the community takes no part in it, exerts no pressure. As we shall see, however, the pledge is no less binding for this.

Sometimes the same man who carries a standard into the church carries it out again, signaling by this the repetition of his vow to serve as pasante. A peasant generally feels he has not completed his devoto until he has served as pasante at least twice: Cesario Zapata, for example, was convinced that his ox had died as a «castigo» from the Virgin because he had served one year as pasante and then delayed in doing it again. For this reason he assumed the obligation of the office the last year I was on the hacienda.

Duties of a pasante consist of «paying for the bandera» (or guía de flor) either by pinning money to the vestments of the Virgin or, sometimes, by purchase of a new standard in Punata; of hiring a band and paying for food and drink for friends and neighbors. Costs of the office are not inconsiderable in both cash and kind. For example, Demetrio Rodríguez, a poor young man who is landless except for property belonging to his mother-in-law which he works and expects eventually to inherit, paid 350 pesos to hire a band from Pucara for his private fiesta and bartered his entire production of lima beans—eight arrobas—for eight arrobas of maize in order to make chicha. Since the price per arroba he could have obtained in the market was 25 pesos, he spent roughly 400 pesos for the chicha which also included in its composition [166] eight arrobas of barley—half his year's production. Since

---

[166] In the Cochabamba valleys proper, chicha is usually made with maize only, and is considered quite fine. It is advertised in the city according to the

the market price of barley was 10 pesos per arroba, the total cost of chicha in kind was 480 pesos, and Demetrio also slaughtered two sheep for the fiesta—market price 60 to 80 pesos. He pinned 30 pesos to the vestments of the virgin. Thus we have the following total expenses of serving as pasante:

> 350 pesos — band
> 480 pesos — chicha
> 120 pesos — meat (lamb)
> 30 pesos — Virgin
> ____
>
> Total: 980 pesos ($82)

When one realizes that Demetrio's total cash income above subsistence amounts to about $396 according to my calculations, one can see why Demetrio says «Yes, to be pasante is hard» (though, «We don't think about this because you never lose anything with the Virgin»). According to my reckoning, he spent a little less than one-fourth of his cash income during the year 1968 in making the devotion.

Alejandro Muriel, a sickly young man whose total cash income for 1968 was even less than Demetrio's (about $242), spent a smaller percentage of that income on his pasante service (about 14 percent), mainly because he hired an old-fashioned band consisting of only three men playing traditional reed flutes (qenas and zampoñas). Angel Rojas, a more prosperus peasant, paid out 18 percent; Cirilo Guzmán, still more prosperous, with an income in 1968 of roughly $417 above subsistence needs, spent about 15 percent for his pasante duties. While the cost of making a devoto to the saints is not as great as that noted by Erasmus (1967; see also p. 74) for the south, it is nonetheless considerable. Particularly expensive sometimes for the poor is the purchase of new clothes, which Palcans feel they must obtain in order to serve as pasante if they do not already own them.

Palcans also stand as pasante at the fiestas of neighboring farms where, besides the expenses above cited, one pays an additional 30 pesos or so to the priest for the mass.[167] People often complain of the cost of being pasante which, as mentioned above, consists of a dyadic contract between the individual and the supernatural but is no less binding for this. Thus:

Demetrio (Rodríguez) said this is the second time he has been pasante. He was pasante before in 1966 and with this second time, he said, he will have completed his duty. Eusebio (my assistant) asked him where they get this idea that they have to be pasante twice in order to fulfill their duty, and Demetrio said he didn't know, it is just the «custom.» It would appear the community does not force a man to do this.

_____

names of the provincial towns, e.g., «Chicha Punateña» (Punata), «Chicha Cliceña» (Cliza), etc. But in the Tiraque area chicha is brewed from a mixture of maize and wheat or barley grain and tastes like a wet dog smells.

[167] I was unable to discover a reason for this beyond minor difference in custom.

I asked: What would happen if, instead of receiving good things from the Virgin, he gets all bad things. He said only that he just doesn't think about receiving bad things from the Virgin. He did say, however, that if he doesn't fulfill his promise to the Virgin to be pasante; if once he promises and doesn't follow through all the way—i.e., be pasante two times—in this case the Virgin might indeed punish him and he might receive bad luck.

Cirilo Guzmán went so far as to say he would really rather not have spent money on his second devoto to the Virgin, but he feared a punishment if he did not. He said also that it is «bad luck» to «think too much» about how much money you are going to pin to the Virgin's robes before you do it—again, for fear of a «castigo.»

Finally, Alejandro Muriel, with great gaunt eyes, feverish, a figure out of Goya, said that «Yes, it is hard, but I have never had luck in my life, never felt well, always sick.» He thought that if he had made his devoto the Virgin will give him better health so he can work better; that «suddenly» he will receive aid from the Virgin—a miracle. He too said that he «never thinks» of receiving anything but good from the Virgin in return for his service as pasante.

To sum up, there are perhaps five main points to be stressed in connection with the fiesta of Santa Rosario:

1. The fiesta is much the same in form as it was before the reform when the patrón gave grain for chicha and hired the priest; it has only expanded in force and size. This fits with evidence elsewehere, e.g., Vicos (Mangin, 1961:86), where change in structure of the hacienda organization left the form of the fiesta system relatively intact. The evidence again seems to suggest that, without mechanisms to break down the cultural insularity of peasants, increased prosperity below a certain threshold is likely to intensify traditional ways.

2. Formal fiesta offices are rudimentary like the rest of Palca's culture. The office of pasante is voluntary as far as the community is concerned. One does not need to have served as pasante to hold political office; there is no community censure of a man who does not serve.[168] Obligation enters only between the individual and the supernatural. Thus the office may act as a leveling mechanism for individual families but not as far as the community is concerned. It is possible that the office acts to increase internal economic differentiation, since poor or average-income peasants take it on more often than the very richest, and the office tends to cost a higher percentage of a poor man's income than that of one relatively well-to-do.

3. The lack of obligatoriness to the post of pasante and its lack of interdigitation with political office is a consequence of, and a contributing factor to, the fact that the fiesta does not integrate Palca as strongly as, again, Vicos (Mangin, 1961:86-87). This situation is related

---

[168] Ricardo Rodríguez, Francisco Cossío, and Mariano Alvarez, three of the wealthiest peasants at Palca, have never been pasante and seem no less respected for this.

to the structural and historical factors discussed earlier: the fact that
Palca consisted, not of an enclave with its own politico-religious hierarchy upon which the hacienda drew for labor, but of scattered farmsteads lacking such leadership, with such leaders as did exist adventiti-
ously imposed by the patrón. The fiesta was never a mechanism to
reinforce community sentiment inchoately against the outside (patrón
or other); the patrón in fact largely sponsored it. The fiesta does,
however, reinforce ties both within and without the community and
functions in a minor way to underline the boundaries, the corporate
sense of the community.

4.   Religious office (the post of pasante) may be seen as a form
of insurance—like compadre and sharecropping arrangements. In an
environment so full of risk from weather and disease, it is advisable to
have the Virgin on your side, or at least not against you, just as it
is a good idea to build resources in people: friends you can rely on,
compañía relations, etc. Religion can thus be seen as another way of
building resources, intangible yet adaptive (from the peasants' point
of view) at the level they are living on, which helps keep them at that
level (see pp. 79, 91). Using the scarcity postulate in its broadest sense
we might say that it is hard to have it both ways, to build resources of
this type and still save money for tractors and trucks.

5.   Psychologically, ceremonial is analogous to a projective area
where those suffering anxiety or bad luck engage in attempts at exorcization. It is entirely possible, as Mangin (1961:90) suggests, the ritual
acts themselves have anxiety-reducing value regardless of whether one's
luck actually improves after serving as pasante. But it is also possible
that, over the long haul, the office may have the latent function of
increasing anxiety due to its negative effects on material income. Over
the long haul, too, even the strongest might be expected to take on
the post, since there are no outright skeptics or Protestants in the community, and suffering in time catches up with most. But over a range
shorter than this, the fiesta makes for minor economic differentiation.

After the mass on October 7, Santa Rosario once more dissolves
in dancing and drinking. The priest leaves, and money pinned to the
Virgin is placed in a box to be used for the mass the coming Easter.[169]
Dancing and eating and drinking continue until night, when some of the
bands leave, and through the next day; when the last band leaves, the
peasants keep on drinking in their houses, moving here and there,
wherever the chicha lasts, until three or four days after the fiesta. Serving as pasante or simply throwing a party thus turns one's house into
an informal center where friends and neighbors gather and reinforce

---

[169] This box is kept in the dirigente's house. A few people told us, just before we left, that Don Dionisio had appropriated some of this money on occasion,
as well as other fiesta monies entrusted to his care, for his own use. As can be
imagined, it was hard to prove this. Anyone, moreover, not only the pasantes,
may pin 10 pesos or so to the vestments of the Virgin, hoping for her favor.

relationships. A pasante may be said, unwittingly or not, to make an investment in people as well as in the grace of the supernatural. The mutual aid involved in brewing chicha (as well as in drinking it) adds to this.

And the fiesta as a whole reinforces ties throughout the community, since it is the only occasion during the year when everyone no matter how far apart he lives on the large hacienda is certain of having at least minimal interaction with everyone else, when the whole community gathers on the spot for a purpose. One renews contact also with friends and compadres from nearby farms and from the towns. (Many of the latter do a brisk business in chicha and food.) Fights occur, but follow no pattern of intra- or inter-community hostility, and rarely does one care the next morning. Grudges are uncommon: «We were drunk, that's all.» Guilt or shame is not attached to the man who gives his wife a black eye, vomits or fouls himself, falls asleep in the road. Anyone over sixteen may drink with anyone else, and there are no solitary drunkards. The main thing is to drink and dance a lot and «visit a lot of people, the houses of the pasantes.» [170]

The second formal fiesta on the hacienda, Todos Santos on November 1 and 2, is much smaller and quieter than Santa Rosario, since it involves intimately only those who have suffered a loss through death within the family within the past year—sibling, spouse, son or daughter or parent—and there is no religious mass or violent celebration. Only those who have suffered such a death collect food [171] (including special items such as bananas and papayas for which it is necessary to pay cash in Punata), and brew chicha for the occasion and build altars in their houses—frames of wood draped with alizo [172] leaves on which food is placed as provision for the souls of the dead who are believed to return at midday to eat. Chicha is set out as well, along with dolls made of bread called *urpus,* representing all kinds of shapes of children and animals.

It is thought necessary to do all this lest the spirits of the dead get angry and bring a «castigo» on one. Nor would one want to be niggardly for the same reason. For example, the altar of Daniel Vargas, a fairly well-to-do peasant, had (for Palca) a truly Lucullan air:

Over a wooden table covered with colored cloth was arched a wooden frame woven with alizo leaves.... The urpus were hung on strings on the frame; it reminded me of nothing so much as a row of slippers hanging in a closet. Also,

---

[170] It is hard to account for this relative lack of violence connected with drinking which has been found elsewhere (Bunzel, 1940; Viqueira and Palerm, 1954). Possible explanations may be the lack of factionalism in the community (or the impregnability of the dirigente and his supporters), the spatial looseness of the community, and its cultural homogeneity.

[171] Anyone with a death in the family may erect a small altar and put out food for the dead; but only the people I am describing put out provision in any quantity and go through the Todos Santos rituals.

[172] A local tree very similar to the beech tree of the northern hemisphere.

there were all kinds of fruit hanging from the strings: papaya, bananas, pineapples, green beans; on the table beneath were plates stuffed with chicken, *chuñu* and potatoes: the idea, again, is that the souls of the dead come to eat at noon. Also hanging from the frame were two plucked chickens with locotos in their mouths, and a rabbit.

There appears also some community pressure on a man to do his best on this occasion. Other altars we visited were only slightly less well stocked. Like other fiestas, Todos Santos provides the occasion for visiting and mutual aid between friends and neighbors, first in the making of chicha and preparing the altar, later in drinking the brew and consumption of the food. Those who build the altar share the food. There is a strong religious strain mixed with the social and alimentary: for example, while we were sitting drinking chicha in Daniel's house:

Felicidad (his wife) began to pray to the altar, answered in a kind of counterpoint by a youth who was sitting on the other side of the room—I was unable to get his name; Daniel said he was from Waca Wasi. I asked Eusebio (my field assistant) what they were saying; it sounded almost Oriental, they did not sing or speak but it emerged as a kind of singsong which reminded me of an Arab market. Eusebio said they were saying three Ave Marías. He said there are also *alabanzas* (literally, «praises») and choruses which can be sung—first the alabanza and then the chorus.

Praying and consumption of chicha continue until noon of the next day, November 2, when the altar and table are carried out of the house and food is shared in the open by those who have helped. Anyone passing may be invited to eat, though the bread, fruit, chickens and rabbits are reserved for the altar-builders. After this, family and friends visit the cemetery in Tiraque where the adult dead are buried; they sit by and on the graves (upraised mounds of earth marked by wooden crosses), drink chicha, eat bread and fruit and pray. After this they return home and the small and quiet fiesta ends, though the chicha may last for a day or so after.

During these two days, also, the young men of the community play a lot of soccer and a game called *rayolas,* where the aim is to pitch a coin from a distance of about 20 feet into a small hole. The functions of Todos Santos appear, like those of Santa Rosario, recreational and largely integrative: reinforcement of bonds between kin and neighbors and friends, ritual exorcization of anxiety caused by recent death. Like Santa Rosario, Todos Santos has increased in size since the revolution within the traditional form. Like Santa Rosario also, (see p. 160) the fiesta is a knife that cuts two ways. If on one hand mobilization of friends and neighbors and ritual work to reduce anxiety, on the other, the fiesta adds to the expenses of death which are considerable and may, over time, actually increase anxiety. It would not be the first time that human institutions set up to make people secure (cf. the expenses of advanced nations on nuclear warheads, etc. in the interest of «national security») had a somewhat opposite effect.

FIESTAS ASSOCIATED WITH THE LIFE CYCLE

An individual's progress through life is marked by ceremonial at various points—in part biological, in part determined by purely cultural selection—along the continuum from birth to death. A person passes through ritual at baptism, first haircutting, confirmation, when he marries in church and after he dies. Civil marriage is occasion for a fiesta, though not a religious ritual, as are, frequently, birthdays.

Babies are baptized when very young—three days to a week after birth—and this is the occasion for a small fiesta involving the immediate family, the padrinos of the infant (who become through the baptism compadres of its parents) and perhaps a few close friends and neighbors. Baptism takes place in the church in Tiraque; the parents and padrinos go together to town to accomplish this, and the fiesta occurs afterward. As mentioned earlier (p. 122), ritual recognition of nodes in the life cycle can act to reinforce patterns of friendship and mutual aid.

The baptism of Nicolás Murillo's new baby illustrates this:

I asked how much it cost. Nicolás said 10 pesos for the priest, 10 pesos to the registro civil for the certificate. (He produced this.) He said that very few go to the baptism; it is for the family and padrinos only. The padrino buys new clothes for the baby for the baptism, and Nicolás said he killed a sheep, which they roasted in the padrino's house. He said he also bought plenty of chicha in Tiraque which they drank in Ponce's (the padrino's) house; he said such is an obligation of the father in the circumstances.

Other life cycle fiestas perform much the same function, only on a wider scale involving more people and greater expenditure. The fiestas may widen the bonds of padrinazgo and compadrazgo or simply reinforce those already existing. For example, the widow Torribia Cossío complained how much these bonds cost her:

She said she was madrina of baptism, confirmation and first haircutting to Angel Vargas' little son. She said the first haircutting cost her in all 200 pesos to buy new clothes for the child (of two or three years) and also to give a bit of money to the child. She said the haircutting lasts two days—the first day they cut part of the hair, in front, the second day the back half. She said you also have to give a lamb, a very young sheep, to the child; that the haircutting costs more than baptism and confirmation where you only give new clothes: about 8 pesos apiece there because the baby is much smaller and the clothes cost less.

The widow was a bit drunk (see p. 123) and complained bitterly about the cost of it all; yet when I asked her why she served as madrina when she obviously didn't like it, she said simply that she «couldn't» refuse the honor, that Angel Vargas «would never forgive» her and at Palca it is not the custom to refuse such a request. Very real cultural constraints underlie the system of fiestas and perpetuate it, and its «fit» with the peasants' total ecological situation has already been analyzed (Chapters V and VI).

After the hair is cut, which is done by friends and neighbors in turn, each giving a bit of money (2 to 5 pesos) to the child for each piece of hair they cut (beginning with the madrina), the child's father serves all the guests plenty of food and chicha. Later, the compadres invite the family to their house for a «bit of chicha» and food, and after this it is not unusual for families to remember their compadres, the padrinos of their child at first-haircutting or baptism, to invite them to a dinner of roast lamb on their birthday, though this is strictly optional. The extensive reciprocity involved here is apparent.

Confirmation, which occurs when a child is anywhere from six to eleven years of age, involves much the same process, besides another payment to the priest. Marriage makes for a larger fiesta than any of these. Besides building human resources involved in reciprocity and reinforcing liens, weddings take on multiple functions like the fiesta of Santa Rosario itself: recreation, tension and aggression release—people really blow off steam.

A civil wedding, however, is simple; the one I witnessed involved only the bride and groom, close kin and neighbors and padrinos who, in this case, were also the bride's parents. We all rode into Tiraque; the padrino paid 80 pesos to the registro civil for a marriage license plus 20 pesos apiece to legitimize the two children of the bride, after which everyone adjourned to a chichería to drink chicha, eat boiled potatoes and dance to huayños from a phonograph. Everyone got high, to be sure, and the party was still going on the next day in the house of the newlyweds. But it is nothing like a church wedding.

There, preparations are much more extensive, involving considerable interaction and mutual aid—purchase of clothing, preparation of quantities of chicha and food. Many more peasants, dressed in their best, attend, and after the marriage ceremony about noon, the couple, padrinos, friends and relatives, vecinos, and just about anyone who happens along adjourn to a chichería. A band, hired for the occasion, plays; it is a wild time yet with a certain structure:

We emerged in the sun (in Tiraque after the mass) in the still bright blazing mountain town, uncannily blue and green, pure and still, and we followed the band through the cobbled streets, and I thought «Great, we're waking them up, the band, like New Orleans, brassy and bright like the sun, the women in their polleras.» The town cholos stared as if an eland had come into their lives, and then we were in the chichería all swept and breezy, with walls of baby blue and a door leading into a courtyard. We were seated and served chicha, and later lamb and chuñu and rice. There seemed to be a subtle but definite structure to the whole thing. The largest and choicest pieces of lamb appeared to be reserved for the padrinos, Remejo Najera and Emiliana Parra, and for the bridal couple (Felipe Rodríguez, Adriana Guzmán). These last shared an entire leg of lamb. The bridal couple sat together on a bench along the wall, draped in confetti and a golden ribbon which united them both, and they ate together with their fingers and a spoon from a large pot from which the leg of lamb protruded. A similar choice portion was served to the padrinos.... After this, everyone was served pretty much what we were: bits of lamb, chuñu, rice and potatoes.

After this, the pitchers of chicha go round, the band starts up, and the bridal couple goes out into the center of the floor dancing the *cueca* with a handkerchief; then the padrinos—for some time it is only the novios and their padrinos, stately in their best clothes, whirling in the old colonial dance; finally more people join in and the band becomes deafening in the blue room—huayños, cuecas, the *taqirari* from Santa Cruz, loud and brassy—the dancers kick up dust. In the three church weddings I attended, the peasants danced in the chichería in Tiraque through the afternoon and then returned to the house of the groom's father, along with the band, people from town, anyone, and dancing, drinking and feasting continued far into the night. The band stayed until late the following day; the fiesta continued as long as the chicha lasted, much like the fiesta of Santa Rosario; two and three days later a remnant may be seen sitting around the yard drinking chicha, quite drunk and urging you to join them.

Weddings can provide the context for a subtle structuring of drunken behavior, also, notably agonistic contrapuntal weeping on the part of women remembering their own youth. On one occasion a drunken woman took on the role of Cassandra, railing at the bride that her wedded life ahead was not happy, but consisted of hard work, fights, and beatings by one's husband. Some women appear sexually aroused by dancing with various men, and sexual freedom between the young and unattached is common at night in the dark fields.

The mass and band are paid for by the padrinos; the groom or his father pays for the food and drink. A wedding is not cheap: Felipe Rodríguez' marriage, for example, cost 1,500 pesos $125)—100 and 500 pesos for the mass and band respectively, the rest on food and drink and expensive new clothes for the newlyweds. Weddings, like Todos Santos and Santa Rosario particularly, have grown longer and more elaborate since the reform. José Rodríguez, Felipe's father, sold almost all his potatoes to pay for the wedding and had to farm in compañía the following year largely because of it (see p. 99); yet he would not have had it otherwise. As he put it, people «would not respect me» if he had not given his son a good wedding.

Death is the final place in the life cycle ceremonially recognized by the peasants, and, in the case of an adult,[173] it is one of the most expensive. Palcans have a saying: «A dead man is an ox,» meaning that most peasants have to sell an ox to cover the death of a close relative (1,200 to 1,500 pesos, $100 to $125). One must buy a coffin in Punata, a plot in the cemetery in Tiraque, and pay sundry fees to the priest, doctor, and registro civil. One must kill sheep and buy a lot of chicha to treat friends and neighbors who accompany the body to the cemetery. (There is no formal funeral: the body is buried as soon as pos-

---

[173] Children below the age of five are buried without ceremony either in Tiraque or in a cemetery above the hacienda in Ucuchi Kancha; the cost, in money, is the small coffin only.

sible without ceremony except for a wake the night after death, when people sit around the body laid out in his house on a table, smoking cigarettes and chewing coca and waving their hats from time to time formally over the deceased in a gesture of goodbye.) One must pay the incidental expenses involved in the wake—candles, coca, cigarettes— and for masses for the dead at nine days, six months, and one year after death at the rate of 100 pesos per mass. Besides this, there is Todos Santos. In view of all this, it is easy to see how death can be a true calamity for a peasant, especially when a productive man or woman is struck down.

The quality of one's relations have nothing to do with it. Fortunato Ramallo quarreled incessantly and bitterly with his daughter, yet had to sell an ox to bury her and pay for masses for fear, on one level, of the community's criticism, on another, of supernatural punishment. As Fortunato López put it,

If you fulfill the masses, God will forgive the sins of the dead. But if you don't, God will not pardon the dead, and they can get angry and bring bad luck to their families, their animals and crops.

Juan de Dios Flores said the community would «criticize anyone very strongly» who tried to avoid paying masses for the dead—in fact, he never knew of anyone who had done this, it was just about unthinkable. The masses, wakes and drinking may be seen as efforts by the community to repair itself, to recover after the blow which, each man knows, can strike him or his family at any time. People gather together; the wake and later drinking particularly are occasions for talking about the dead and explosive weeping, along with the playing of games by the young men and their feeling almost as at a child's party, staying up all night. Whether, as with Todos Santos or Santa Rosario, the effort to banish anxiety does not in some ways work to increase it through expenditure of income on the part of the bereaved—this is a moot point.

Finally, a birthday or, indeed, any day may be the occasion of an informal fiesta—the killing of a pig and making chicharrón of its chopped roasted flesh; inviting friends and neighbors for chicha and boiled potatoes. An animal who dies a natural death will similarly be roasted and eaten; the festive aspects of labor, marketing, and political meetings in town have already been discussed.

To sum up, (1) Fiestas are important in Palcan life. (2) They have not changed in form or content since the reform, only become more extensive and elaborate. Increased income below a threshold hard to define may lead to intensification of the traditional rather than modernization. (3) Though the fiestas function as mechanisms to release and control tension and anxiety and reduce these through building solidarity among people, they have perhaps the opposite function of increasing anxiety through reduction of income in cash and kind. The fact that the peasants persist in their fiestas, however, and have elaborated them suggests that they do not perceive this latter effect, or that if they do, the pleasures of eating and drinking and renewing bonds with people outweigh it. Further, in the isolation in which they still live, resorces in people mobilized by traditional methods still constitute their strongest security.

VALUES

Implicit in all that has been presented up to now is a certain consistency of world view held by the peasants, a certain set of values. Most campesinos are not articulate about this—one must infer it largely from what they say and do in their everyday lives. Further, the consistency is limited. If there is one thing which impresses the student at Palca after he has been there a period of time, it is the remarkable degree of variation among the peasants as people despite the crudity and stripped quality of their culture and the similarity of their way of life. There is Angel Rojas, big, strong, stolid, rooted in the earth: he has a land hunger, he lusts for it, smells of it almost tangibly. Luis Ramallo, on the other hand, cares so little for land relative to chicha that he is willing to rent it out illegally and leave his children in rags in order to follow his passion. Felix Villarroel probably represents the old, grizzled, childless peasants living alone in traditional huts with their wives when he says, in answer to the question «What do you value most in life?» «Work. I have no other hope.» Zenon Rodríguez, for his part, though poor in material terms, lives surrounded and respected by his many sons and is remembered by the community for having rather bravely favored the peasants' cause when he served as curaca. He relates his idea of a good man with a certain elegance: «A good man was my friend, Santos Lizzaraga. He was strong and you could believe what he said.»

There are overtones here of the ancient Incaic maxim «Ama suwa, ama lulla» («Don't be a liar, don't be a thief»). Somewhere in this old man the Inca lives, however rude and inchoate. At the other extreme lie men like José Rodríguez and José Jiménez who show most clearly that exploitation is but the obverse of colonial dependence (Mannoni, 1964: 39-47), who will, in the words of a Tiraqueño I once spoke to, «do anything.»

Yet despite this variety there are definite foci of interest which engage every Palcan. Everyone is concerned about good health and good crops, as is evident without exception in people's motivation to make a devoto to the patron saint. If you inquire further and ask a man why crops fail, he will most likely reply «the weather,» although some quite pragmatically recognize «neglect of the fields» as a factor. If you go beyond this to ask what causes the weather, a wide range of replies appears. Some believe crop failure is caused by a «castigo de

Dios,» which may be the result of the guilt of a person or persons. Most often guilt is attributed to people outside the community, «in the towns» or «afar,» and I never heard of scapegoating in the community attached to this. Other peasants declare they don't know what causes the weather, whether it is a «castigo» or not—«I don't think about it.» Yet it is significant that Luis Flores, for example, an old man who was most adamant about not believing in other causes for crop failure besides the weather, nonetheless goes to church to pray to God and Santa Rosario for rain in a dry year. He has also served as pasante. The peasant does not, so to speak, miss any bets.

The propitiating, manipulatory aspect of peasant religion has been touched on. What we can safely say is the peasant cannot afford to miss any bets, for he lives in a world of anxiety, from new ovens and «far places» where pachamamas may lurk, to the sky with its weather changes. The individual tries to manage this anxiety by whatever techniques lie at hand: As in the case of his clothing (pp. 30, 32), whatever methods the peasant appropriates depend on context, ad hoc, opportunistic. A truck overturns at night on the highway; the driver dies slowly, untended; the cargo of lumber is gone by the morning. A peasant uses the accidental presence of a priest to gain a bargain blessing of his new oven. The presence of my jeep is similarly exploited.

The menace, furthermore, of the world is real, from market and weather to deceptive outside agencies. The peasant has small capital and few allies. He lives with death constantly. In his situation it is not surprising that he should often turn out instrumental, nonempathic, opportunistic, maximizing security rather than innovative risk; that, as Katz put it: «In the end, only the family can be trusted, and everybody else is a fair target for exploitation (if one gets the chance)» (1967:99).

CHAPTER VIII

EDUCATION

EDUCATION OF the illiterate peasant masses, who make up most of the estimated 75 percent of the population which is illiterate (Urquidi, 1969:106), was, as mentioned earlier (p. 5), a major stated aim of the MNR revolutionary elite. The modernizers knew that universal suffrage would remain ineffective as an integrating mechanism and economic progress limited as long as the peasants remained illiterate and monolingual, and in 1955 they implemented a code of laws applying to education which made the Ministry of Peasant Affairs directly responsible for education of the rural sector (Comitas, 1968:641-642).

Certain courageous rural teachers, moreover, were involved with the agrarian revolution years earlier at its inception, and nurtured and protected it at certain crucial junctures. As Dandler-Hanhart (1967) has shown, it was these teachers who, after the Chaco War had effectively discredited the old regime, became modernizing cultural brokers for the peasants around Ucureña. They saw the newly formed sindicato as an instrument of change; they fought for it and helped it through several crises. They were among the most important allies the peasants possessed, and without them the revolution in the Cochabamba region would surely have taken a different course. As mentioned earlier (Chapters V and VI), the peasants of the highland latifundia, who lacked such allies, not only received the revolution later but in many ways preserve to this day elements of the sociocultural isolation they endured during the days of the patrones.

In part, this is the aftermath of deliberate policy on the part of the patrones. The latter knew, as Comitas (1968:634) and Weeks (1947) have pointed out, that they only stood to lose by educating the Indians; that maintenance of their docile labor pool could only be menaced by opening up skills and alternatives not needed on the paleotechnic hacienda. Preservation of the stratified conquest state, which Bolivia essentially was, depended on the preservation of ignorance as much as on the use of force, and it was not until 1929 that any significant effort was made to extend education outside the cities and downward in the social order. In that year, the government decreed that haciendas with more than twenty-five workers were required to set up primary schools on their property, and that these should be under the supervision of the Ministry of Public Instruction and the Rector of the University in the departmental capital (Comitas, 1968:637).

This law was never enforced—a result which is not surprising in view of the fact that local power lay wholly in the hand of the patrones and that in La Paz only slightly less so. In 1931 came the founding, at Warisata on the Altiplano, of the first *núcleo* or nuclear peasant school, which was, as Comitas (1968:638) points out, a radical innovation in the campo that was to persist and spread. The núcleo consists of a central school, set up in a town or hacienda, which acts as a supervising focus for smaller «sectional» schools established in surrounding hamlets and haciendas. In 1935, the government decreed the establishment of sixteen such nuclear schools in Bolivia; the Chaco War (1932-1936), which stoked so many fires in Bolivia, stimulated education also; yet school expansion in the countryside was very limited prior to 1952 (Comitas, 1968:639).

Since that time, if one looks at structural change, the facts and figures, progress has been impressive. By 1965 a total of 5,250 public and private schools had been set up in the campo, an increase of over 500 percent from 1946 (Comitas, 1968:643). In 1964 there were 286 núcleos in the countryside. By 1967 this figure had risen to 381, while the number of new rural teachers turned out each year had risen from 453 to 500 (Fortún, 1968:1066-1067). This appears particularly impressive when one realizes that the population of Bolivia has risen slowly, from 3,597,000 in 1963 to 3,801,000 in 1967, an annual rate of increase of 1.4 percent.[174]

The percentage of the population of rural school-age children registered in school increased 250 percent between 1951 and 1965 (Comitas, 1968:643). Many writers have been impressed by the willingness of peasants to build schools, often on their own initiative without state aid (Comitas, 1968:644; Schweng, 1966:54; Urquidi, 1969:107). One cannot travel in Bolivia without being struck by the fact that peasant communities, even the most poverty stricken and remote have, as a rule, completed a school. Leonard (1966:54) has gone so far as to state that «improvement in their educational system has been one of the most significant accomplishments of (peasant) communities during the last decade» and Carter (1964:87-88) posited formal education as «one of the most basic» factors pushing peasants of the altiplano into «full integration with Bolivian national life and economy.»

Yet in this mellifluous symphony one can hear, without straining too hard, a few sour notes. Urquidi (1969:107) has referred to the formal educational apparatus in Bolivia as «an alarmingly sterile bureaucracy, skillfully disguised by showy propaganda,» and he cites figures from the Ministry of Peasant Affairs for 1966 (indicating that illiteracy rose in Bolivia in the years 1950-1965 from 1,615,567 to 2,209, 566) as «the best proof» of such «administrative inefficiency.» Comitas (1968:639, 645-647) analyzes at some length the shortcomings of Bolivian rural education as it is actually carried on: the short-

---

[174] From United Nations Statistical Yearbook, 1969. The Yearbook of 1970 posits a slightly higher annual rate of increase: 2.6.

ages of equipment; the meager training of teachers who are also poorly paid and whose attendance to duty is often hindered by the need to work at other jobs; the political power of the teachers union, which makes it almost impossible to fire a man; the endless national and religious holidays and so on. He concludes (1968:648), striking directly at the theme of this work:

> In an abstract sense, the very extension of educational services to the rural masses can be considered a revolutionary act.
> Analysis of the structure and content of rural education however, leads us to diametrically opposite conclusions.

Basically, Comitas criticizes rural education on the tactical level for the reasons above adumbrated. Strategically, on the level of policy, he objects to the setting-up of different goals for peasant children as against those from the city, to the forming of different kinds of education in city and country which, he feels, can only perpetuate the old class divisions. He attacks the stress on Spanish as the language of instruction in country schools, which he feels serves to alienate the peasant from his surroundings, and in any case, is rapidly forgotten within a few years (see p. 94). All these conclusions, with the exception of the problem of separate, vocational education in the campo, which never, as far as I could see, was tried at Palca, are supported by my data.

Palca, first of all, like so many latifundia, had no school to speak of under the patrón. Immediately after the reform, during the years 1954-1956 or thereabouts, when Ricardo Rodríguez was dirigente of the sindicato and the peasants were in the process of gaining titles to their land, the fathers of families paid men privately to come out from Arani and Tiraque and teach in a now-abandoned house on the hacienda. One ex-teacher I interviewed said he left Palca in 1956 because the peasants petitioned the government for a public school «with teachers paid by the government»; it was around this time that the núcleo was founded at Boqueron Khasa above Palca to which the hacienda's present sectional school now belongs. Since then, Palca's school has been located in a room in the old hacienda house, and, up until 1967, there had been four teachers working there, none of whom are remembered by the peasants as especially competent. The last, Daniel Fernández, who was on the spot when I arrived, was roundly despised by the peasants for playing with the children «like a child himself,» and for spending much of his time brewing chicha to sell; he called on the help of his pupils to haul the wood necessary to make the fire. Often I would see the children—first- and second-graders—walking down the road or over the stubbly fields around the hacienda house with bundles of twigs on their backs, as much as they could carry. School attendance dropped from twenty-seven to fifteen during 1967 and finally to eight in 1968. The peasants' general attitude was that they believed in education, but not of this type; they felt the children could be more help at at home.

Adding to the problem were incessant teachers' strikes (motivated by salary considerations interlarded with political opposition to the Barrientos government) and holidays, civil service parades, etc. in Cochabamba which Sr. Fernández never failed to attend. The peasants, finally, disgusted, petitioned the núcleo at Boqueron Khasa for a change, and in 1968 they received the teacher who had been stationed at Sancayani above Palca while Sr. Fernández took the latter's place. Sr. Elidoro Torrico, who was still at Palca when I left, departed from Sancayani under even a greater cloud than Sr. Fernández' at Palca. Although married,[175] he cajoled peasant girls into intercourse and then dropped them. He was literally forced to leave. He is an intelligent man, unfortunately alcoholic and, as the peasants say, «lazy»; classes under his regime were held hardly more often than under his predecessor. The gulf between formal aim and actual function is as evident in rural education as it is in other bureaucratic structures we have studied.

For the teachers well know that their mission in the campo is more than to teach first- and second-graders the rudiments of reading and writing. Even a man like Daniel Fernández realizes that his aim, as he put it, is to be a «local leader» working for change; more than once he said to us apologetically that the peasants had promised to give him potatoes after the harvest but never did, and this was why he had to sell chicha to make extra money. Sr. Torrico—who seems positively Chekhovian with his combination of intelligent understanding of peasant problems, good intentions, and total inability to get up in the morning—outlined the aims of the rural teachers as taught in the normal schools:

To act as the «guide» (orientador) of the community; specifically: (1) To teach basic health and hygiene—i.e., washing with soap and water—to both parents and children, but especially to the children. (2) To teach young people the basic principles of home economy: how to manage sums of money; how to find good seed and store it; how to sell their goods in «proper» markets and invest what they earn in «productive outlets» (presumably not in chicha). (3) Educate little girls for the home—how to cook and wash the house, spin and weave cloth. «There are schoolbooks which teach this,» Don Elidoro said. (4) Recreation: to teach sports, music, songs, dances, national hymns.

Sr. Torrico did teach the children to wash themselves in the irrigation ditch which flows from the mountains by the hacienda house; but for much of 1968 the teachers were on strike, or Torrico was hung over or engaged in strife with his wife—school was held so seldom in short, that the children scarcely had time for enough continuity to learn to wash

---

[175] See Appendix for the life history of this man, another example of an unstable «marginal man» who all too often, it sems, falls into brokerage roles in the countryside.

themselves. I never saw them doing it outside of class on their own. The other aims, except for soccer which both teachers played with the peasants, were wholly unachieved. The model of one teacher, who sold so much chicha, and the other who drank it, could hardly be expected to change the peasants' habits in this matter.

The failure of the teacher as a modernizing broker interacts with and reinforces in the kind of feedback the peasants' own ambiguous attitude toward education as reflected for example, in the difficulty in organizing to complete their school. Thus out of a sample of seventeen families queried on this subject, in which I included peasants from all income levels; peasants like Fortunato López who had spent considerable time away from the hacienda; the little «oldtimer,» Luis Flores, and the innovator, Jacinto Sánchez—in short, a roughly representative sample [176] of the community—only five said definitely they wanted their sons to work in an occupation outside agriculture such as that of mechanic or tailor. Six said they hoped their sons would become farmers. The others said it should be «up to the boy,» or according to what his abilities were, what occupation he chose. But all wanted their sons to attend some school and learn to read and write Spanish.

Yet many feel that they are giving up something to send a child to school, who might otherwise be helping at various agricultural chores. The psychology involved is similar to that involved in Chayanov's (1966) consumer-labor balance described earlier (see Chapter V): the peasants in general have faith in, and respect for, the idea of education; they want to have hope for their sons; but when they see the school floundering before their eyes, they are loath to make even the minor sacrifice of their children's time for it.

When it comes to education, also, each man tends to think of his own children and not of his neighbor's. Community responsibility for the school as a felt need is poorly developed at Palca. These attitudes—scorn for the school plus a certain «amoral familism»— are well illustrated in this interview Ricardo Rodríguez:

I asked him his opinion of the school here at Palca. He said his sons go to Tiraque (to the third and fourth grade, as far as schooling is carried in this region), and for this reason he hasn't got much interest in the school here. He said also that he doesn't respect the teachers here, «They don't teach much,» and for this reason too the school doesn't interest him.

Ricardo was able to expand his allegiance to the whole community when he served as dirigente expediting land titles. (Perhaps this was

---

[176] Attitudes toward education do not seem to correlate with any of the variables according to which I selected my sample: wealth, age, innovation, whether a person had stayed on the hacienda or been evicted by the patrón. Also, importantly, behavior did not always fit with answers to my formal questionaire, e.g., Jacinto Sánchez showed himself more or less indifferent to his children on the latter, but has sent all his children through the fourth grade.

not wholly selfless. The power he subtly wields in the community today suggests that the resources he was building at this time in goodwill were no less real for being intangible.) But to champion community education apparently offers a leader much less, which is perhaps one reason why the present dirigente of the sindicato and his Secretary of Education have done so little to even push for the completion of Palca's school. The size and richness of the fields, which require the peasants to work longer than elsewhere and provides them with more money for fiestas, may be another factor. But by far most crucial in the failure of Palca education so far are: (1) The quality of teachers offered up by the larger society who have failed in the rudiments of their job, let alone served as «orientadores» of the community. I have observed also that the rural teachers at their meetings never seem to tire of pointing out what inferior material peasant children are compared to children of the towns, how rural education is a joke compared to the towns, etc. The teachers—themselves usually natives of the provincial towns—share the town attitudes toward the peasants discussed earlier. (2) The sindicato leadership itself, notably the secretario-general who has no sons himself and for this reason has not put himself out to complete the school, and the Secretary of Education, a feckless and none-too-honest young man. It is probable that to effect even minimal change in formal education at Palca, the combined force of several leaders would be needed—the schoolteacher, along with influential peasants.

The people are ready for education. The willingness of a Nicolás Murillo or a Jacinto Sánchez to send their boys [177] to school in Tiraque day after day, long after they have grown large enough to help in the fields, shows this. It is disconcerting to see bright, healthy, open young children turned back just when they have begun to grow, to realize that, within a few years, the openness of a boy of ten or so will be lost, bleared with chicha, with a certain dullness, suspiciousness. The impoverishment of Palca's culture—symbolized perhaps most clearly by the fact that a boy's only toy is a stripped bicycle rim, which he runs with a stick is hardly being relieved by the present formal educational system. Nor does there seem, in Bolivia, any easy way out of the situation. Vocational education of the kind Comitas (1968) is opposed to, on the grounds that it perpetuates the class structure, had not even been tried in the Tiraque area, nor does it seem that there is talent available to launch such a program within the foreseeable future. Palcans are probably doing close to as well as they can with what they have, and serious capital infusions do not appear likely. As against Comitas, I would hold that it is not the teaching of Spanish per se

---

[177] In general, boys are sent to school ahead of girls and kept there longer. Six men on the hacienda speak a smattering of Spanish, but there is not a single woman who does so. Those six: Victor and Casimiro García, Nicanor Sánchez, Luis Najera, Francisco López and Saturnino Achá, are also slightly literate; no woman is.

which has so little effect, or a negative effect, but the fact that the educational program is so poorly carried out. Spanish is a very helpful skill to acquire against the day when young men may be forced off the hacienda, either to the colonization projects to the east or into the cities. In either eventuality—trying to learn a trade in the city or inter-acting with people from all over Bolivia in the colonization projects—Spanish would seem useful as unitary means of communication. If the peasants spoke fluent Spanish, they would in all probability be treated better by the townspeople; information would be harder to conceal from the peasants; their self-image vis-à-vis the townspeople would alter. Hickman (1968: 395) has adduced evidence, not only of the high percentage of Spanish-speakers who already populate the growing coloni-zation projects, but of the tremendous advange such ability provides in that environment.

To mean anything, however, Spanish must be incorporated into a program of agricultural vocational education in the countryside (see above, p. 94). It must be intimately linked with material relevant to the peasants' life reality, so they will be strongly motivated, granted their pragmatic orientation, to learn it. Despite technological and capital lim-itations, the peasants could be taught much relevant to their business, notably in regard to market dealings and technical details of seed and fertilizer. The saving of cash capital and increased cooperation might be gradually inculcated and, in time, a breakthrough into the neo-technic attempted, though such a policy should be undertaken only with cautious regard for the Tiraque region's long-term position in the overall development of Bolivian agriculture (see p. 73). In line with this, Palca and neighboring farms could be incorporated into the gov-ernment-sponsored community development program (Dirección Nacio-nal de Desarrollo de Comunidades) where young men selected by the community as potential leaders are sent outside the local community for training and then back in as educational and change agents (Fortún, 1968: 1062-1063). Such a program involves risk, in that if underpaid and inadequately supervised it might (like other bureaucracies described here) result in abuses. It might also result in conflict with the present leadership structure at Palca; but change in that area could hardly be for the worse. Such agents might prove useful if and when the time comes to persuade the peasants of the advisability of large-scale migra-tion to the east, or of a fundamental change from the raising of grain and potatoes to sheep.[178] They could also stimulate Spanish, basic hy-giene, etc.

A program of vocational education in various trades, conducted on a paid or voluntary basis by city unions, might also be a useful innova-

---

[178] Certain Palcans I spoke with just before I left accepted this possibility with surprising equanimity. It should be clear by now that they are, by and large, anything but stupid. Another option they consider possible is more intensive specialization in wheat.

tion in the campo. I am assuming, again, that with rare exceptions, and in opposition to Antezana (quoted in Heath, 1969: 207), peasants are more likely to pick up manual skills connected with urban life, rather than leap to the university in one generation. Semi-skilled white-collar work would also seem relatively inaccessible, at first. The fact that they know absolutely nothing about manual urban skills might make the peasant even easier to teach, since they have nothing to unlearn (Foster, 1967: 346).

On the other hand this ignorance, which is but an aspect of the rudimentariness and strippedness of the hacienda which I have noted (see especially Chapter III), could well serve as a block to industrialization, as Salz (1955: 61-64) has suggested for similar hacienda Indians in Ecuador, because there is so little preexisting technical and mechanical knowledge on which to build, so little which can be, as she puts it, «transferred.» The peasants' crude hand tools, which they do not even embellish, hardly prepare them for city skills. Even their body movements appear awkward in the city. For these reasons, a program of vocational education could be valuable to help preadapt the peasants to city life.

But the basic problem remains lack of economic alternatives in Bolivia. In a city like Cochabamba, which is still so little industrialized (though more so than anywhere else outside of La Paz), which has such a high rate of unemployment among its artisans, who needs an influx of peasants? By dint of investment of considerable money and time, they might be taught trades; but what would one be preparing them for? [179]

In the last analysis much depends on the development of resources —oil and gas, agriculture, cattle— in the tropic lowlands.

Educational reform, finally, on higher levels, could hope to change over time the gente decente attitudes of bureaucrats and townspeople toward the peasants, the scorn and lack of empathy which are factors in the poor functioning of organizations set up to articulate with the campo. More stress in the universities on «dirty shirt» subjects—business, engineering, scientific agriculture—could spark a shift away from the traditional humanism. But as McCord (1965-134) has shown, such education, to be effective, must be correlated with a program of economic development. There is no point in creating a business and technical elite if there is no place to use it. That Bolivia possesses a kind of entrepreneurial potential seems to me obvious from the activity which has sprung up more or less spontaneously in the Cochabamba valleys since the reform (Chapter V), in Santa Cruz (Patch, 1963), and on the altiplano cited by Clark (1968). The practical, flexible, opportunistic orientation of many peasants implies that, if openings are created, the

---

[179] Indications are that education in a vacuum is not only neutral but can lead to positive harm (see p. 94; also McCord, 1965: 134).

younger men, at least, may—under certain conditions—move into them. Political entrepreneurship is in plentiful supply; a widening of the economic base might redirect this into channels more suitable for development of the country. By definition, the old, Klingian, empleocracía mentality survives mainly in the absence of such.

CHAPTER IX

PUCARA

IN LIGHT OF the earlier discussion, the differences between Palca and its neighbor, Pucara, appear minor. Both haciendas labor within bonds which severely limit them. To recapitulate, my original hypothesis was that the person—the quality of the living individual as shown in everyday life—is an important factor in change; that, as Eric Wolf has put it (1966: 19), «complex societies ... differ less in the formal organization of their economic or legal or political systems than in the character of their supplementary interpersonal sets.» I posited that Bolivian peasants would show many vestiges of prerevolutionary interaction patterns, learned attitudes and behavior poorly adapted for economic innovation or political incorporation, and that these vestiges would appear more strongly where preform conditions had been most severe.

To test this proposition, work was carried out at Palca, the large brutalized ex-hacienda, and at the smaller neighboring farm of Pucara where conditions under the patrón had been easier. Everything except size and preform conditions (which tend to co-vary) was, with minor exceptions, held constant: material culture, language, crops, ceremonial and sociopolitical organization. Pucara is smaller than nuclear Palca in the amount of land which is cultivable; individual plots are smaller, stonier and less productive. Pucara lacks the timber resources found at Palca. The richest peasant there produces in a year roughly the same as a middle-income man at Palca.

A rich Palcan like Ricardo Rodríguez, Mariano Alvarez or Francisco Cossío may produce twice the amount of potatoes which anyone from Pucara can produce. Since the total population of Pucara is sixty families as opposed to eighty-six in nuclear Palca, I estimate the total production of the latter to be at least one-third greater in most years.

HISTORY

Pucara, which consists today of two small sindicatos (Pucara Alto and Pucara Bajo) of twenty-two and thirty-eight family heads respectively, forms a single community for some purposes and acts separately for others; it corresponds to two separate haciendas before the reform which labored under different patrones. The shape of preform conditions was similar to Palca—work on the patrones' land, diezmos, compañía, pongueaje, etc. The authority structure of the haciendas was similar to that of Palca, only smaller, with one mayordomo and one curaca each for Pucara Alto and Bajo, and the peasants say the patrones visited the region much less frequently than the patrón at Palca. The work regime was easier with, much of the time, five days of work per week for the hacienda (four during the time of Villarroel), and the colonos were whipped less than at Palca. (The peasants attribute this to organizational factors and to Pucara's smaller fields: the fact that the patrones were almost always absent and there was simply less work to do, the colonos had to work less hard.) There was no mass eviction at Pucara as there was at Palca. According to the best information I could obtain, only four families were thrown out, two in each hacienda, and of these only the two sons of one man from Pucara Alto returned after the reform to claim land. Pucara never experienced the factional dispute, with its impact on land distribution and the course of leadership, which occurred at Palca.

Income levels were roughly equal among Pucara's peasants before the reform. They never knew doctors. As at Palca, the peons had very little money to spend at the local fairs; the small amount of free time they had which Palca lacked did not mean significant larger participation in markets in the provincial towns or at fiestas. Their own fiesta for the patron saint, San Miguel, in September, was a tiny affair run by the patrón. As at Palca, the patrones' employees supervised who came and went on the hacienda, even down to the peasants' friends. The colonos were isolated politically, socially, economically, ceremonially.

As at Palca also, they received the revolution later than the Cochabamba Valley proper and as a result of outside organizers working under the direction of Ucureña. Syndicates were formed with identical offices and with similar formal functions to the Palca sindicato. Since the reform, Pucara has undergone the same general trends as Palca: production increase after initial decline; population increase, which the peasants attribute to relaxed discipline within the family mainly and secondarily to the fact that they visit doctors now as well as curanderos; economic differentiation (though not to the same degree as at Palca); and increased involvement in the Punata market. Social relations of friendship and compadrazgo have also expanded; Pucarans farm in compañía with each other and with townspeople, though to nowhere near the extent as at Palca. Medical beliefs and beliefs concerning the supernatural show no significant variation on the haciendas, implying that Pucarans as well as Palcans feel themselves open to external forces which must be propitiated, manipulated, appeased. Both communities endure the same vagaries of weather and of market.

Yet there are differences. Pucara never had the timber or the expanse of land available to which undesirables from other haciendas could be transported and turned into political and economic capital by the dirigente. While there was some imbalance in land distribution, in that some peasants are said to have «advanced» their properties at the expense of others, this never assumed the proportions found at Palca. There are no persistent rumors connected with Pucara concerning the murder of political prisoners. Pucara's hacienda houses were totally destroyed, leaving no ruin which, at Palca, in its sprawling decayed grandeur, could be used as a haven for political leaders. For these reasons, Pucara never developed Palca's ties with the revolutionary center at Ucureña which influenced distribution of land on the larger hacienda (see Chapter V). It is likely that Palca's connection with Ucureña is a factor, along with its relative prosperity, in the prestige it holds in the region, and in the fact that Don Dionisio Guzmán, Palca's dirigente, is more prominent than the dirigentes of Pucara in any council of local leaders (see Chapter VI). But both communities are limited in the power they can exert politically outside the region.

PUCARA TODAY—THE HACIENDAS COMPARED

If you climb over the ridge, dry and brown during every season but that of the rains, which separates Palca from its neighbor, and move down into Pucara across the riverbed of the same name, you have no special feeling of change. Houses are of the same type as Palca, with here and there a roof of corrugated iron. There are the same rows of potato plants; a peasant hoeing the furrows will be using the same pointed lampa, his homespun pants rolled to his knees. A bicycle leans against the wall of a house; a radio sounds inside the black open door.

Only gradually you note differences. A large L-shaped building on the right, with iron roof and water spigot in the yard, is Pucara's school to which children from both Pucara Alto and Bajo are sent. It is finished, unlike Palca's, and possesses windows of glass. Cement lies in a wheelbarrow and bricks are piled in the yard which, you learn, are being used to construct wash basins and showers for the children. A latrine is also planned. A field full of crosses on a hill straight ahead is a cemetery which the peasants have made themselves; you climb up past this and come to a lake— creation of the peasants who, under the patrones, dammed up several springs for irrigation purposes. Pucara Bajo —more brown fields interspersed with eucalyptus and mud houses— lies on the far side of the lake. Only gradually you notice the houses in Pucara are smaller than at Palca, with more stones in their composition; that iron and tile roofs are rarer, and there is no chapel in the community. Looms, radios, phonographs, accordions, etc., are in the houses, but they are scarcer, and there are fewer animals. You learn that Punata is the only market Pucarans attend, since they are nearer to that town than Palca and further from Tiraque, and further as well from the fairs on the highway. Two trucks visit Pucara Alto and Bajo respectively on Tuesday, Punata fair day; they pick up peasants and deposit them in the marketplace. Pucara trades in the open market in Punata, very little with middlemen like Don Venustiano Villarroel, and certainly never with the latter. As Patricio Linares of Pucara Bajo put it:

Venustiano comes once in a while to Pucara at harvest time to buy *papas mishkas* (new potatoes), but not often. Patricio said they think—at Pucara—that Don Venustiano and his wife bully and cheat the peasants from Palca plenty, not so much Venustiano but his wife who really is a huge fat thing, and for this those from Pucara don't want to go to Venustiano. Patricio said he heard the wife cheats more than Venustiano because she stands near the scale and never lets Venustiano near it.»

There seems to be no explanation for this difference in marketing methods between the haciendas—the fact that Palca deals with a middleman and Pucara does not—beyond sheer historical accident. Venustiano simply arrived at Palca after the reform rather than on other haciendas (perhaps because it is the most lucrative farm in the region) and entered into economic and social relations with the peasants there which, over time, were self-reinforcing. Pucara's peasants trade in the market and in general are less shy and slavish in their human dealings than Palca; yet they too have a diffuse orientation to the fair: they drink chicha, go to have fun, to build up friendship, compañía relations, etc., though on a smaller scale than at Palca. Pucara needs, in effect, less credit from the townspeople because its fields are smaller and also, I am convinced, because its alcohol consumption is much lower.

It will be recalled that, at Palca, it is the poorest, unlucky, or least efficient peasant who works most in sharecropping arrangements. Sharecropping correlates along other dimensions with a past history of eviction from the hacienda by the patrón, with a history of transplantation from elsewhere after the reform, and with alcoholism. While any peasant, in a given year, may work part of his fields in compañía, it is the echado, the «undesirable,» the tomador who engages in it perennially. Pucara (except for one or two borderline problem drinkers) lacks these types at the moment. Yet it would be hard to prove this greater individual openness or stability gives the smaller community any economic advantage over Palca. The limitations involved in the open market have been noted (see p. 88). The amount a peasant may earn there over what he makes dealing with a private middleman like Don Venustiano is minor, and Palca's larger, richer fields provide its people with considerably more income than its neighbor. As noted, the level of prosperity Palca has achieved has worked to expand and intensify traditional activities, rather than for modernization.

Pucarans, again, share a material and socioeconomic culture which is in every way as stripped as Palca; yet it lacks the sense of drift and confusion of the larger hacienda, and Pucarans are different as people from many Palcans. This fact is understood by the peasants themselves as well as by townspeople. The music of human interaction is different. There is no one on the smaller hacienda like José Rodríguez who, if he wants a ride, will fall on your neck, kissing it and imploring with tears in his eyes. There is no one like Saturnino Achá, who kisses your hand, hopping around «like a sick dog» saying «Mi jefe, mi jefe,» half slavish, half mocking, who one month later will be in a plot to rob you. There is no one at Pucara who is so grateful to the dirigente for giving him land that he bows to him at a meeting and calls him «tatay.»

Pucara possesses at most one or two men as shut up and shy as Cirilo Guzmán or his brother, Don Dionisio, and it totally lacks men as far gone in drink as Martin and Agabo Claros, Casimiro García, Luis Ramallo—men definitely stigmatized by the community as tomadores. There are a few heavy drinkers, but far fewer than at Palca, and there is no man who speaks more than a few words of Spanish, no «marginal» men like Achá. These considerations raise important issues in connection with my original hypothesis. It is a fact that, at Palca, with the exception of two individuals, all drunkards or «problem drinkers» are echados or the sons of echados; peasants brought in from elsewhere after the reform; or «marginal» men. While everyone in those categories is not, by a far sight, either alcoholic or unstable, on a statistical basis such a history makes these outcomes more probable. It is generally a poor echado (like José above) who is most fawning. This implies that history—prereform conditions—does indeed influence behavior in the present, but in a much more complicated and indirect manner than originally supposed. It is not simply a matter of early learning,[180] of perpetuation of slavish or encogido patterns learned under the patrón, but of many factors, a complex chain of events which introduce elements wholly unanticipated at the outset of this study: eviction of thirty families from the hacienda with subsequent hardship and increased dependency; wandering, uprooted families implanted on the hacienda from elsewhere; marginality resulting from minor talent (in the case of García and Achá) which finds no productive outlet in the present situation. It is almost as if a process of historical selection were at work to deposit, at Palca, a sizable percentage of unstable people; since the patrón doubtless knew his men, he would not in all probability, have evicted his best workers. A streak of weakness or instability could well have existed to begin with in at least some echado families which was exacerbated by years of wandering. The «undesirables,» for their part, had been thrown out by their own sindicatos for definite malfeasance. If anything, it is those peasants who stayed at Palca and suffered the patrón longest who are, in general, most like Pucara, though several of these are extremely shy and hard to talk to. These considerations suggest:

1.   The original hypothesis is supported in some cases. Encogido and dependent patterns learned under the patrón persist in some peasants who have never traveled and are stronger among such at Palca than at Pucara.

---

[180] I was unable to establish any significant differences in the texture of attitudes and behavior toward children on the haciendas now or before the reform.

2. The behavioral heritage of the old regime is more complex than anticipated. Shy, suspicious, «shut up» (callado) persons may show alcoholic, unstable[181] or dependent traits in some cases, in some cases not. The alcoholic, however, tends to swing between shyness and bombast, mixed with obsequiousness, and often simply passes out.

3. Uprootedness, rather than early learning or differential severity of prereform hacienda conditions per se, seems the crucial variable to explain the differences beteen Palca and Pucara. The eviction of the echados at the larger hacienda (itself a reflection, to be sure, of tougher conditions) worked for instability and dependent attitudes toward the «compassionate» (Bequiraj, 1966: 13) dirigente who, like a good patrón, gave them land. This historical-structural factor is probably more important in the greater patronization of Palca relative to Pucara than psychological orientations; more likely, it reinforced such orientations among the echados, especially after their years of dependency and hardship.

4. Similar considerations apply to the «undesirables» from other haciendas who work for the dirigente at Palca; the «marginals,» García and Achá, can be said to be uprooted from a different point of view. Availability of land at Palca was a factor here, since the Peasant Federation could hardly have sent these people here if there had been no land to give them. Pucara escaped these whims of history.

5. Other factors involved in the greater callado quality of Palca peasants may be guilt and fear connected with abuses in land distribution (granted the insecurities of land tenure discussed earlier), and the fact that, literally, they have a number of buried skeletons they fear may be uncovered. Unfortunately I was unable to verify the persistent rumors we heard in Tiraque and elsewhere that Palca served as a «dumping-ground» for political prisoners after the revolution.

Pucarans not only seem more open than Palcans, they show it clearly in action. Pucara labors under the same limitations as the larger hacienda—lack of credit and extension facilities, political manipulation of the Peasant Federation and so on; agencies set up ostensibly to help the peasants have cheated them (see p. 97). Yet Pucara moves out much more efficiently than Palca to take advantage of whatever is available in the larger society. In general we may say that the smaller community, with less to work with, makes better use of what it has. The completed school has been noted. Pucara has not only created an artificial lake, it has built a number of sluices and, since the reform, pools to control and distribute irrigation. Unfortunately, most of Pucara's land consists of nonirrigateable fields wholly at the mercy of vagaries of the weather. Even with relatively better irrigation, Pucara cannot come close to the production of Palca's larger, richer, flatter lands.

---

[181] Criminality sems to vary independently of any of these. For example, José Jiménez, driven from another hacienda for theft, who serves today as Don Dionisio's bodyguard, shows none of these traits.

Just before I left, Pucara, under the influence of its schoolteacher working in cooperation with the dirigentes, had established a consumer's cooperative whereby the peasants contribute quotas to buy staples which are stored in the schoolbuilding—rice, sugar, salt, alcohol—and which the peasants can purchase when they choose without going to the fair. Pucara also has a band which plays at fiestas in communities roundabout and provides a fair supplementary income to those who play in it. Construction of their own cemetery on noncultivable land means the community saves money on death expenses: they do not need to pay for plots in the Tiraque cemetery or pay fees for papers to town officials. While Pucara lacks the outstanding individual innovations found at Palca (Chapter III), there is convincing evidence that it works better as a community than the big farm.

A comparison of the haciendas' relations with the city of Cochabamba is also instructive. While the Palca leadership appeared lost in the city and could not even locate the office of its federation (pp. 147-148), Pucara's leaders—both Secretary-Generals, the Secretaries of Relations and Education—went together with the schoolteacher to the prefect of Cochabamba and asked for and received 3,000 bricks, ten bags of lime and ten of cement for their school improvements at very low prices. They also obtained twenty steel plows at a considerable reduction over retail price and free powdered milk for the children. This project was initiated by Pucara's schoolteacher, Isidoro Parra, an energetic and intelligent young man, but, as Isidoro puts it, the peasant leaders «entered into agreement» with him and went with him and between them they obtained the material.

Pucara acts differently in town than Palca. My assistant, who accompanied the peasants on their expedition, said of them, «They walked in the street like men» and never walked single file or showed fear in entering an office.

The prefect promised them pipe, also, to build a sewer for their school latrine, but he was replaced by the La Paz government before he could deliver. The Pucara peasants heard of this and went to the city again to make sure the official did not forget his pledge; I went with them:

I entered the prefectura with the Pucara peasants. I couldn't help but notice the difference between them and the Palca peasants: they were quite well dressed in store clothes, and they did not walk behind me as Don Dionisio and Eugenio Vargas (of Palca) had when we went to the city with them; they walked erect and quietly and did not seem afraid. They inquired in the prefectura for the prefect. The clerk said he was not there but was probably at his house in the Calle 25 de Mayo. The peasants set off—they had gone with Isidoro before, they told us—they knew where the prefect's house was and went there. The peasants talked with his wife, as far as I could see without fear; she said to wait, the prefect would be home about midday and would talk to them.

As it happened, the prefect left his post without obtaining the pipe for them, though he did give a gaudy Bolivian flag to the school with

Pucara's name on it; he felt, doubtless, that he had discharged his promise with this, and the peasants were very proud of it. But they did not give up trying to obtain pipe; the schoolteacher particularly importuned me to take them here and there in the valley to find a reasonable price, trying, finally, also, through hints and direct requests to get money out of me. Before I left, the peasants had begun building a stone drainage ditch from their school to the Pucara River.

A crucial factor in fomenting this initiative was the teacher, Isidoro Parra, who seemed to take seriously his formal function as cultural broker and «orientador» of the community. A greater contrast with the teachers at Palca could hardly be imagined: Isidoro and his wife continued to hold classes for fifty-three children from Pucara Alto and Bajo through 1968,[182] through strikes when they were not paid (they lived on quotas of food the peasants contributed for them), through feelings of conflict when Isidoro—who did not love the government—felt that he was betraying his Federation and his fellow-workers by continuing to teach. But his primary loyalty was to Pucara, to the children.

One can say, again, sheer chance plays a role here: Palca gets one kind of teacher, Pucara another. There is perhaps truth in this. But it is also true that Isidoro Parra was sent first to the larger hacienda and found the *ambiente* there nothing he could stomach. As he puts it, when he first went to Palca,

There was a peasant meeting—Don Dionisio was dirigente—and the peasants promised to send their children, plenty of children for three classes to teach on the part of his wife (also a teacher) and himself. But three or four days later, «There were no kids.» Isidoro said that he had plenty of difficulty in obtaining kids for their classes; that parents wanted to send little children of four or five to school but didn't want to send older ones of seven or eight years because they wanted to keep them home to work in the house or to care for the flocks. «They preferred to make them work to sending them to school.» He said the peasants also expressed a desire to finish their school and that he personally stirred them up to do this and climbed personally on the roof to work with them. But then Achá arrived «with his big mouth» and began to say that the teachers were cheating the peasants; and that finally he, Isidoro, got angry and said he wasn't a «*niñero*» to be caring for little kids that young and he told them all to go to the devil and asked to be transferred.

Isidoro's testimony suggests another variable which must be considered: the likelihood that child labor is somewhat more economically important at Palca, with its larger flocks and fields, than it is at Pucara, and hence more likely to conflict with formal education. The fact that a man like Achá, further, would be opposed to a teacher who is willing to work with his hands, implies he has absorbed certain gente decente

---

[182] This figure was quoted to me by the teacher and the dirigente; I am not sure it is literally true day in and day out. But many more children attend classes in Pucara than at Palca.

attitudes not shared by other peasants. In this case, at this level of analysis, his «big mouth» was a factor in Palca's losing a good teacher. Palca's heterogeneous population probably makes it harder for a teacher to please everybody in the community than the smaller, more stable population in Pucara.

Another factor may simply be the presence of the old hacienda house at Palca, which Pucara lacks and which —though Palcans recognize it verbally as inadequate for their school— nonetheless does serve as such; as long as it functions, the peasants may lack a certain incentive to take time away from their large fields to build a new one.

In any case, the evidence is that the schoolteacher can be a significant cultural broker and change-agent in the community. There can be no doubt Pucara's teacher played a genuine role of leadership in encouraging the community to finish its school and make improvements on it. That Isidoro Parra gave some thought to his role as «orientador» is shown by the following:

I asked him how it was he managed to get so much cooperation from the peasants. He said: «Little by little. I had to convince the dirigentes little by little. Also, get them to finish each thing as fast as possible, because if you don't do this, they forget it and nothing gets finished. Isidoro said that when the peasants see that the teacher finishes what he sets out to do, that he delivers, the peasants also follow through.»

That leadership, finally, is an important element in Pucara's more efficient organization and more open stance toward the world is suggested by several things. Though Pucara's syndicate prossesses the same offices as Palca's, and though most of these offices, like Palca's, have only minimal function, there is a much more straightforward, one-to-one correlation of power and formal office on the smaller hacienda. Pucara does not have people like Casimiro García, Saturnino Achá, Ricardo Rodríguez, who can exert power behind the scenes; it lacks the subtle, half-buried cliques and factions which reflect Palca's heterogeneous population and its more complicated history, *and which act to aggrandize their own personal interests more than the formal aims of the sindicato.* In other words, Pucara has a higher percentage of leaders acting in the «community interest» relative to its smaller population: two dirigentes, two secretaries of relations, and two secretaries of Education —the last of which are much more active than the man at Palca. Thus Isidoro Parra had more allies when he went to the city from Pucara than he would have had from Palca.

The criteria of choice of Pucara leaders were different from those at Palca. Don Gregorio Camacho of Pucara Alto was chosen dirigente, the peasants say, because he is «strong» and «commands respect», and the people felt he would be able to obtain things from the outside and also get things done within the community —as indeed he has, within limits. The reasons why Teófilo Méndez was chosen dirigente of Pucara Bajo are interesting: his father, Severino, was a dynamic leader during the early days of the reform until he became ill with lung trouble. The peasants say they chose Teófilo as dirigente because he was «very passive» and they picked him in order to make him «finish things like his father» and learn what the dirigente's role is. As far as I could observe, he worked well with Don Gregorio within the limits imposed on both men. Both are more effective as «outward-facing chiefs» than Don Dionisio Guzmán of Palca who was picked for his post mainly for internal reasons having to do with a factional dispute within the community—criteria no longer relevant to the hacienda's situation in the world, its need for cultural brokerage. Both of Pucara's leaders have sizable families of their own, unlike Don Dionisio who «has no sons of his own» and for this reason seems to lack incentive to promote Palca's school. In a sense, we might say that Pucara's leadership lies much less in the hand of the past than Palca's, and its dirigentes are coping in a more realistic and straightforward manner with community problems. Sindicato meetings are held a good deal more often on the smaller hacienda and are better attended, perhaps because distances to be covered are much shorter than at Palca.

But in the last analysis, after granting the reality of all these differences between the haciendas, we must, I think, hold that they are minor in view of the limitations imposed on both communities (and the entire Tiraque region, for that matter). The variable of prereform conditions is minor. Both haciendas are marginal politically, in the sense that both are of limited value to leaders on higher levels, hence limited in the amount of «muscle» they can exert. Both suffer from the lack of structural links between their federation and credit and extension agencies; from the general lack of money; from dishonest or gente decente attitudes of agents from the towns, etc. Both are limited by market and weather phenomena. Both have undergone marked population increase since the reform, with a growing shortage of land. Neither hacienda is one whit closer than the other—nor than the whole region—to a breakthrough into the neotechnic.

The implications of it all are obvious. There is a sense in which the values and motivations of individuals are minor. The piecemeal, Peace Corps, «community development» approach to modernization—build a latrine here, a water fountain there, teach people to cooperate—contains all the limits Erasmus (1968) noted in it. Neither the peasants of Palca nor of Pucara—despite the greater openness and even rather heroic efforts of the latter—are likely to make serious innovation by a local bootstrap operation. At most, the microvariation between the haciendas might be significant in making decisions as to where one might introduce a particular innovation—for example, a pilot operation in the intensive raising of sheep or wheat or recruitment for pioneer farming in the Chapáre. The greater openness and cooperativeness at Pucara might be significant in that it would be easier to persuade the smaller hacienda to accept the innovation. On the other hand, the greater wealth and prestige of Palca, its prominence in the region, might make it worth the effort it would require to begin a project there. In any case, what matters is not the small improvement of the type of backwaters I have studied but their transformation.

CHAPTER X

CONCLUSIONS

IF LOCAL PIECEMEAL change is ineffective, one might justifiably ask what would really make a difference in these people's lives? Before attempting to answer this question, I shall review my aims and propositions as set forth at the start of this work.

I aimed, first of all, in the broadest and most human sense, to discover what hacienda peasants in Bolivia are like. What motivates them? What do they want? What effects has the agrarian reform of 1953, which abolished centuries of serfdom, had on their lives? Intense, qualitative study of haciendas is rare; I felt that such a study, in the tradition of a Durkheimian «well-studied case,» might expose dimensions which work on agrarian reform of a broader survey type had overlooked.

On another level, I had hoped to relate my findings to the theoretical literature on revolution and modernization in general. The Bolivian revolution was a «restrained» or «simple» revolution in many ways (Patch, 1961; Johnson, 1966: 139). There was little chiliasm, little striving for transcendence in the sense of a radical mobilization for a total transformation of society, including values and the entire division of labor. At all points I strove—from my point of view at the local level in the countryside—to find out what happens when a truly «backward» nation of Latin America attempts a relatively humanistic revolution which is, also, relatively autocthonous in the sense of being detached from Maoist, Soviet, or Castroite influence. Specifically, I was concerned with the problem of subinstitutional continuity beneath the surface of institutional change; with the quality of the peasants' everyday interaction in work, the market, politics—the face of the «little man» behind the façade of history. I posited that a simple *gemeinschaft-gesellschaft,* Spencerian or Durkheimian model[183] is inadequate to describe or explain modernization in Latin America, where differentiated institutions have existed for a long time which do not function according to their avowed aims. I believed that much interactional continuity would persist, however altered or disguised; hence the structures introduced during the revolution articulating down to the peasants would hardly be revolutionary in their function. On the other hand the peasants—with the hacienda bred in their bones—would be

---

[183] That such more or less simplistic equation of social differentiation with modernization is not dead is shown from the recent writings of Smelser (1967).

too encogido to make demands on the system from the «grass-roots» up. The mere granting of land to create family farms in structure would not mean that family farmers had been formed on anything like the model of Western Europe or the United States; further, hacienda-type interaction patterns would survive most strongly where prereform conditions has been most severe.

In general, these propositions were supported. The peasants of the haciendas of Palca and Pucara in central Bolivia were found to share an extremely rudimentary (and in the case of Palca a somewhat confused and disorganized) culture consisting of a complex blend of traditional and modern traits, which represent a stripped version of the rural culture present in the upper Cochabamba valley. The peasants live on a kind of plateau technologically, economically, politically. They want all they can get in a material sense consistent with not having to risk too much to get it—risk, that is, not only of one's individual wealth on any given occasion, but the web of socioeconomic and attitudinal orientations they have built up which offer security in their environment, granted their technological situation. It seems the peasants cannot maximize at one and the same time resources in people and resources in cash. In analogy to biology, it is possible to argue that those very mechanisms which aid the peasants' adaptation to the environment at the level they are living on make it hard to break out of that level, and the better adapted they are, the harder it is to change. I have interpreted many of the campesinos' customs, technological (in regard to innovation), economic, social, ceremonial, in the light of this model.

Politically, the peasants seem to have sunk into a certain apathy after receiving their land; preeminently, the campesino movement in this area is, as Bernard (1969:1017) wrote, «limited by the aspirations of the peasants.» The nominally reform-oriented bureaucracies sponsored by the larger society, for their part, which articulate with the countryside, are largely self-serving. They bear out Tuma's (1965) conclusion that agrarian reform usually helps the reformers more than the people they aim to reform. Teachers seldom teach; doctors overcharge; extension agents fear or despise the peasants in typical creole *(criollo)*, manual-work-despising fashion and are reluctant to go into marginal areas. The peasants' own political leaders are more concerned with advancing their small careers than aiding the rank-and-file. The bones of a modernizing structure are all present, so to speak, but paralyzed or broken. Between the peasants' own institutions which work against innovation and the nominally modernizing but ineffective national bureaucracies, the campo stagnates despite minor sparks of change such as an influx of consumer goods and better roofs on the houses.

Yet anyone considering simply ways of helping the peasants break through into what Erasmus (1967) has termed the «neotechnic» must consider what this might mean in the long run for the peasants in the particular area. It might not be worthwhile to persuade the peasants of the Tiraque region to risk large expenditure on tractors and trucks only to find, within a few years, they cannot compete with other areas in Bolivia better suited for potato-raising, that they must go into sheep. Events in any one region, such as here, must be coordinated with events taking place elsewhere.

This raises my final, basic point. Serious change within this region is not likely to occur solely or even mainly as a result of internal factors but as a by-product of the history of the nation. Thus the values or motivations of the different haciendas, relative to prereform conditions, are minor; I am tempted to say the whole problem of individual values or motivations is secondary to the need to get people out of such back-waters as I have described and into national life. This means opening up large-scale employment opportunities, and in Bolivia these lie mainly in the east, in the lowlands of Santa Cruz, the Chapáre region of the Department of Cochabamba, the plains of the Beni, in regions potentially exploitable for commercial agriculture, cattle, oil. I believe that, in the long run, if opportunities are carved out here, people may move into them. Or at least discussion can be opened as to what incentives and initiatives are necessary to persuade people to take advantage of them, what are the spurs and hindrances to geographic mobility.

To take this position is to take sides in the implicit controversy between W. Arthur Lewis and Benjamin Higgins on one hand (Higgins, 1959; Lewis, 1955) and Everett Hagen and David McClelland on the other (Hagen, 1962; McClelland, 1961). Which are the most important blocks to modernization? Economic or institutional factors, or people's values and motivations? Without trying to single out one group of factors as essentially primary (since I see them as the result of different angles of vision on the same data, two sides of the same coin), I feel it is methodologically easier to attack economic and institutional factors than psychological since to change the latter would take very long (Higgins, 1959:312; McCord, 1965: 143). Further, there is no sense in (and small incentive for) formation of «achievement motivation» if you have no place to put it.

In short, I suspect it is more profitable to act as if «In the beginning was the deed»[184] and assume that, if opportunities are opened enough people over the long haul will move into them (or be organized or persuaded to move into them) to make a difference. If economic development occurs in Bolivia, it will happen mainly as a result of major innovations in various sectors and regions, which can then play with each other in a feedback process, provide employment for each other. Only such economic differentiation can hope to reclaim for the economy the ground, so to speak, it has lost to politics.

---

[184] There seems to be evidence that, once behavior is begun, values tend to fall into harmony with it. Cf. Festinger, 1957:260, 264; Kluckhohn, 1958:137; Kriesberg, 1963. Wallace (1961) has shown that consensus of values and motivations is not necessary for mutually predictable (cultural) behavior.

There are great problems. It is a moot point as to how far this process can proceed in Bolivia, and I do not for a second assume the Oriente is a panacea. In the first place, the failure of certain pioneer projects I visited [185] suggests the soil in the tropical parts of Bolivia may be poorer in some areas than at first supposed, that the east may not contain all the riches many Bolivians—with a kind of frontier mentality—want to believe. Marketing problems, lack of extension services and infrastructure plague the farmer there as elsewhere (Hickman, 1968). Furthermore, the forms of agriculture—soils, crops, the skills necessary for cultivation—are all vastly different in the tropics than in the highlands. Tropical farming is hard and full of risk from disease. A highland Andean farmer, particularly one from an ex-hacienda such as Palca, would suffer some of the same disabilities Salz (1955) envisioned for similar peasants in Ecuador confronted with industrialization:

1. The rudimentariness of their culture, while on the face of it making for flexibility [186] since they have, in some ways, so little to unlearn (Foster, 1967: 346), might well work against adaptability in a new environment since they have only rude skill on which to build (see p. 176). Ignorance, far from fostering a spirit of openness to new experience and willingness to experiment, can lead to rigidity (Moore and Tumin, 1949: 791). The poverty of his education and experience leaves the ex-hacienda peasant at something of a loss in the city, in the hospital, in any new context. He can see a pachamama in «far places» even on his own farm, and as Salz (1955: 191, 193) showed, such projections can become truly frightening to the peasant in a wholly new environment, which contains its own very real terrors such as wild animals and disease. Significantly, though the peasants of the Tiraque region are aware of the pioneering going on within less than 100 kilometers from where they live in the Chapáre province of their own department, none had yet left their homes for this,[187] and it is debatable—for the reasons above adumbrated—how long they would stick it out if they did embark on such a venture.

2. The peasants are deeply tied emotionally to their local communities and house-plots—witness the bitter struggle of those evicted

---

[185] At Carrasco near Caranavi in the Alto Beni northeast of La Paz. Here people settled from many parts of the nation in the hope of growing citrus fruit, which commands a fair price in the market. The trees grew to a certain height only, never flowered, and slowly died. At the time of my visit those colonists who remained were earning a poor living raising bananas and yucca.

[186] See p. 111. Palca youth at present are malleable; they can, I think, be taught. However it should also be pointed out that as they stand they tend to be somewhat dependent. A youth of twenty years can cry like a baby at being left overnight in the hospital. Of five youths drafted into the army, only two served their enlistment; three deserted. None stayed in the army as a career, and with the exception of Ricardo Rodríguez' son, none has traveled or stayed permanently away from the hacienda.

[187] Significantly, several individuals from the town of Tiraque had gone over the mountains to pioneer, but none from the local countryside.

from Palca by the patrón to return; to their kin and friendship groups, all the security-reinforcing mechanisms they have evolved in their precarious but familiar locale. The very mechanisms which are adaptive on the level at which they are living and which help keep them at that level (see Chapter V) might be expected to hinder geographic mobility also.

On the other hand, the practical, opportunistic orientation of many peasants has been noted, as well as their hunger for land. Pressure on the land at Palca, for example, may increase to such an extent that the prospect of new land in the east may lure some peasants down. On the other hand they may—as Ricardo Rodríguez has already done—acquire a bit of land in the towns and cities. Only future research can determine what will happen. For the present, it appears likely that nothing will happen,[188] that the peasants will continue to plant and reap their harvests of grain and potatoes and make what local shifts they can.

It is at this point, finally, it seems to me that the human element, the importance of human organizational factors, becomes apparent. While aware of the weight of economic and institutional factors in modernization, I do not necessarily follow McCord (1965:143) who writes of the developing nations that «Latent entrepreneurial[189] talent exists ... proper economic planning can bring it into action.» More than «economic planning» may be required to lure the growing peasant population of places like Palca and Pucara into farming in the east, not to mention transforming them into commercial farmers. A policy of planned change might be necessary, for example, which would involve moving peasants in groups (Salz, 1955:216), which allows them to maintain their familiar human solidarity ties. Attention to matters of education and health would be needed and perhaps, as Salz (1955:217) suggests, a measure of outright paternalism to sustain them under hardship, since hacienda peasants are very different from the individualistic farmers who pioneered North America. Thus «latent entrepreneurial talent»

---

[188] Political factors are of course an important variable here (see Chapter VI). News reports (e.g., the airmail dispatch *Latin America* dated August 14, 1970) tell of continued bitter infighting in the cabinet of General Ovando. «In» versus «out» politics continue; the numerous dissident political factions which this «restrained» revolution has allowed to survive always constitute a menace to the stability needed for a long-term program of development.

Anderson (1967:104) has perhaps put it best: politics in a country like Bolivia resembles a living museum where power contenders, even the most traditional, are hard to eliminate, and each exercises a veto power over the activities of others.

[189] It is of course crucial to specify what kind of entrepreneurs. As pointed out in Chapter V, the present middlemen entrepreneurs of the Punata area have a stake in preserving the status quo. The study of such middlemen, as well as examination of the pionneering projects of the east, is badly needed. Especially interesting to probe would be the links, if any, such middlemen have with politics.

cannot simply be assumed. While it is crucial to erect the necessary economic structures in which such talent can function, the structures must be adapted to the particular human and cultural needs of individuals.

APPENDIX

Pp. 109, 115, 140:

The incident of the jeep showed several things: It brought to my consciousnes, as an anthropologist, mistakes I made; it showed the degree to which haciendas in the area can, under certain conditions, envy one another; and it dramatized the dependent behavior among colonized peoples described for Madagascar by Mannoni (1964: 42). According to Mannoni,

A Malagasy receives from a European some favor which he badly needs, but would never have dreamed of asking for. Afterwards he comes of his own accord and asks for favors he could very well do without; he appears to feel he has some sort of claim upon the European who did him a kindness. Furthermore, he shows no gratitude—in our sense of the word— for the favors he has received.

Mannoni goes on to describe an incident involving his tennis coach, whom he cured of malaria and who subsequently importuned him for shoes, cigarette papers, etc., who attempted to secure him as his white man, his «patrón» (Mannoni, 1964: 43). Any effort on the part of the «patrón» to break the relationship would have led to hostility.

My relation to Don Dionisio followed this pattern closely. I thought it wise to do a favor for the community—eg., buy materials for the school—in order to gain entrance. The dirigente appeared fascinated by my jeep; I offered him a ride. Soon he demanded to be taken everywhere, always sitting in front where he could finger the gears. The fact that for humanitarian reasons I took peasants to the hospital frequently; the fact that I used my jeep to participate in political rallies, fiestas and marketing in the town, always taking peasants along and asking them questions—this gave more opportunity than ever for Don Dionisio to go along too. He got used to the jeep, feeling almost, at times, that it was his. The fact that, once in Tiraque another grumbled to us, saying «Why do you always stay in Palca? Why don't you stay with us too?» makes me think that we became something of a prestige symbol in the neighborhood, which the Palcans hated to lose.

We stayed in the old decayed hacienda house, which doubtless reinforced any tendency the peasants might have had to identify us with their ex-patrón. I don't regret this; I doubt whether we could have lived and worked as effectively in the lightless squalor of a peasant's hut, and to have moved in with one man might have stirred envy in others. But living in the house reinforced our identification with the patrón, which I reproach myself for not seeing clearly at the time. Further, we continued on in the house for a time after beginning to interview at Pucara—a definite error, though Pucara lies very close to Palca and intermarriage is not infrequent. I am certain from looks which Don Dionisio gave us as we walked to Pucara in the morning that he resented this.

Finally, in the case of Don Dionisio, the «reassuring relationship of dependence» which Mannoni sees as implicit in the colonial situation and which leads to hostility when broken, was tinged throughout with cynicism—«degraded,» in Mannoni's terms (1964:43). It was close to the attitude Katz (1967:99) noted in peasants: «In the end, only the family can be trusted, and everybody else is a fair target for exploitation (if one gets the chance).»

P. 19:

Heads of families who were evicted from the hacienda.

Agabito Linares	Zenon Rodríguez
Ignacio Claros	Víctor Lizzaraga
Sinforiano Valdez	Sinforiano Vargas
Agabo Claros	Cornelio Vargas
Jacinto Sánchez	Santos Lizzaraga
Leandro Najera	Emilio Ríos
Manuel Ochoa	Francisco Ríos
Eugenio Vargas	Julián Velardes
Miguel Lizzaraga	Cecilio Velardes
Luis Rodríguez	Nicanor Sánchez
Juan de Dios Flores	Manuel Claros
Mariano Alvarez	Nicolás Murillo
Ignacio Linares	Luciano Rojas
Quintín Mamani	Evaristo Marín
Cesario Zapata	Fortunato Ramallo

P. 115:

The life history of Casimiro García was very kindly gathered for me by Father Javier Albó, S.J., in Quechua, after I left Palca for good. I transcribe it almost literally from a letter:

Both his parents were from Arenpampa (Potosí), and they lived in the town, not outside. His father died when he was still a small child from «fever.» They were five:

José, the older brother, born from unwed mother, before she married his father. Much older than Casimiro. Supported the family when Dad died and while the family stayed together. He went to the Chaco War and died there.

Delfín, the second brother. About seven years older than Casimiro. Went also to the Chaco. Survived. About two years after this went to the mines, then to Capinota. That was a one-day walk then, no road. He bought a house there and lives there now.

Tiburcio, the third brother. Five years older than Casimiro. Went and died also in the Chaco War, in Boqueron Stroessner.

Casimiro—the fourth.

Last, came a girl whose name Father Javier did not remember. Died two years ago.

While he father lived, they were peasants with a small plot of land (piquería) of about 4 hectares. The father's name was Bernardino García and he died of «fiebre» when Casimiro was about two years old. After that, José worked the land to support the family. Casimiro speaks in a friendly way about the relatives of both his father and mother. He says that during childhood they (the children) were friendly and good, so that his mother did not have too much trouble with them. Then something happened that Father Javier tells me he did not understand, and Casimiro and his mother went alone to Sacaca while the rest of the family stayed behind in Arenpampa. Casimiro says he went through the fifth grade in both Arenpampa and Sacaca, which is a good education for a peasant at that time.

Meanwhile the Chaco War began (1932) and the three older brothers went immediately to the war. The mother and Casimiro returned to Arenpampa and stayed there three or four years with the small sister. Casimiro supported the home during this time and began to sleep with Braulia Negrete, his future wife. Hilde was born then, but Casimiro and Braulia did not marry yet.

Five months before the end of the Chaco War (1935), Casimiro was then seventeen, he went to the war. His mother did not want him to go, and she even got a document of exemption for her son. Casimiro interprets this maternal gesture as a special proof of the love of his mother. But it would seem that material reasons (he was the supporter of mother and sister) were also important. In spite of his mother's desires and of the exemption document, Casimiro went to the war. He points out as the reason that he did not want to be called a coward by all the other people in town: all the youth were going to the war and he was the only one left. When he was in Villamontes, at the edge of the battlefield, his mother went all the way there with the exemption document to dissuade him and the authorities. But he stayed in the war for the final five months. He says that he was awfully scared the first time that he went to a real battle.

After the war he married Braulia and they had the other sons and daughter: Adel, Roman, and Delma. I tried several times to get details about his married life then, unsuccessfully. He usually jumps to the time of the Agrarian Reform, his glorious era. However, it seems there was some kind of external pressure for his marriage. Indeed, he says that Braulia went to him and to the others saying that the little baby Hilde resembled him, that therefore he was the father, so Casimiro married her. He always stresses that they were never married in church, but only by civil law.

During the Villarroel presidency (1942-1945)—the first MNR era—several peasant sindicatos were organized in the Bolivian countryside. One of them was the «sindicato campesino (or, probably, indigena) provincia Bilbao.» Casimiro enrolled himself in it, not as a leader, but as a member, and went to some of the «*concentraciones*» and «*congreso indigenal*» in the departamentos of Oruro and La Paz, organized by Villarroel towards the end of his presidency. Casimiro says that he felt very strongly the political fever at that time. At that time he was twenty-seven years old (he mentions that age, and this certainly agrees with the age he said he had when he went to the Chaco war, ten years before). The sindicato disappeared when Villarroel died.

Some years before the second MNR era and the Agrarian Reform, Casimiro became a private miner. He discovered lead in his own lands and began to exploit it. This mining enterprise was improved during the first years of the MNR era, when he became peasant and municipal boss in Arenpampa. At that time he used to go to Santibáñez (Cochabamba) to hire up to fifty beasts to transport the mineral from the roadless Arenpampa up to Buen Retiro (the railroad station near Capinota) where he delivered it to the trains of the Banco Minero de Bolivia. Since he left Arenpampa this mining business has been left too, though he has been told that his ownership of the mine is being respected.

Shortly after the MNR came to power (1952) and certainly before the Agrarian Reform was signed in Ucureña (1953) the peasant sindicato of Arenpampa was structured. It was structured originally from the top, by order from the central government. He was among the founders, but originally there was another leader. I tried to find out why he emerged as the leader after a short time. He only says that this was a «petición de los mismos campesinos.» Apparently he was first «alcalde municipal» and only afterwards «secretario general de la central campesina» (with more than fifty sectional syndicates). I cannot get more details about his emergence, in spite of my frequent questions on that. He recognizes that at that time he used to keep a pistol in his pocket and sometimes used it without shooting to keep the respect of his men. But he repeats (and even makes oath) that he never killed anyone. At the beginning he didn't seem to have as much contact with Rojas as with Narciso Torrico. This was a famous peasant leader in the area of San Pedro de Buenavista, also in Northern Potosí. He was originally a miner. He was never a peasant before becoming their leader. His «central campesina» was in Charoma, almost one day walk from San Pedro. This Narciso was very influential in fostering the leadership of Casimiro in Arenpampa. But I cannot be sure whether he was already influential in Casimiro's emergence in the early days. In 1956-1957 there were a series of peasant uprisings in the whole area of San Pedro, Arenpampa, Acacio, etc. (you can see this in the newspapers), and this was probably also the climax of Casimiro's leadership. Once he heard this his friend and leader Narciso Torrico was threatened by the «pueblo»—dwellers of San Pedro. And he went there to help him, heading a peasant army of 5,000. This is probably true, since I have a paper clipping of April 26, 1957 (paper *El Pueblo* of Cochabamba), in which San Pedro, Arenpampa, Acacio, Tocorari are mentioned. This paper clipping adds that Torrico was put in prison but the next day a mass of 20,000 peasants from the whole region liberated him. Casimiro is exultant talking about this event: He led the whole crowd from provincia Bilbao. After two days they arrived at the place of Torrico. «Who are these?»—«García and his men.» And then Torrico and himself had a very strong embrace and abundant chicha libations.

There are several gaps at this point. It seems that it was around 1954 that he and his wife were separated. At least he told me once that around that time his boys and his daughters, together with his wife went to Catavi to live. If this is so, he was already alone during his climax of peasant leadership and alcaldeship. Whenever I ask him about the reasons why he left Arenpampa, he says they wanted to kill him. He mentions as his worst enemies two of his wife's cousins named Fernández—lawyers. I cannot get too much about that. Once he told me he spent only about eight years with his wife. But from other data it seems they were married from the early 40s if not the late 30s, and at least up to 1954.

Whatever happened, he came to Cochabamba around 1957. José Rojas named him to the Central Campesina de Tiraque («secretario de justicia,» while el Macho Méndez, from Sak-abambilla, was the «secretario general»), where he remained three years. He lived in Palca ever since. During his three years of leadership in Tiraque, he accompanied Rojas in several of his travels: they went together with five truckloads of campesinos to San Pedro de Buenavista on the occasion of new troubles of the «pueblo» with Narciso Torrico. About that time Narciso was killed and hanged by the pueblo (Casimiro says that Rojas and himself and all the Ucureños went to save Torrico; there are other versions that put Rojas against Torrico). He also went with Rojas and the Ucureños to Santa Cruz. I think at that time many Tiraqueño peasants went to Santa Cruz. As a matter of fact Casimiro and Donato Claros, also from Palca, remained in Santa Cruz and provinces about one month. Since 1960 he has not been a dirigente any more. And he says that he is more and more disappointed in politics.

I am not clear either about the time his sons and daughters came here. He says that his older son Adel (the one who first went to Catavi) came seeking him. The other son, Roman, has certainly been here for many years, since it is already about five years since he married (concubinato) a girl named Barrientos in Tiraque (he put a barbership there that lasted only a few weeks, and then he went with many Barrientos to the Vandiola Yunga of San Jorge, where they usually live). Casimiro told me the girls came to Palca only a couple of years ago. The wife also came after many years of being separated, and—always according to his own story—he sent her to hell (*a la mierda*) because she didn't look for him in his sad exodus from Arenpampa. Braulia presently lives in Capinota too. Perhaps some day I will be able to meet her and tell you the same story from another angle.

And now, let's come to the more recent chapter. Hilda and Delma do not live in Palca any more. One day I met Delma in Tiraque. She told me «Dad is a very bad man; you have to convert him.» And Casimiro told me, «My daughters are very bad. They are against me.» This morning I met Casimiro's padrino (Francisco Ayala) in Cochabamba. He told me that about one month ago, Casimiro was beaten, apparently by or in agreement with his daughters, and very badly. He also told me that Casimiro goes to him very seldom, because Casimiro knows that his padrino will scold him. Delma—according to Casimiro—went now to study in the Normal of Paracaya and put a judicial suit against her father because he does not want to defray for her school expenses. She demands 300 pesos a month. He only wants to pay 150. From the padrino, I heard that Delma is not in Paracaya yet, since all her belongings are still at his home in Cochabamba. The padrino deduces she didn't pass the admission exam, and that she went to her mother's home in Capinota.

The other recent trouble comes from his other son Roman. A couple of days ago Casimiro learned from his daughter-in-law (Barrientos) that Roman disappeared from San Jorge in Yunga twenty-five days ago. Nobody knows where he is. The first thing that came to Casimiro's mind, as he told me, was that probably something happened in the Yunga between Roman and his in-laws while drunk. But now he has come to Cochabamba to find out by phone or one way or another whether Roman went to any relative anywhere. Last night, when I was talking with him about that at Francisca's home, he seemed really sad and worried.

Some other details in nice disorder:

His mother died in Arenpampa a couple years ago. According to Casimiro, because of sadness of being away from her son (Casimiro) and of his troubles. He always talks very charmingly about his mother *(mamita)*.

Once, while both Francisca and Casimiro were drunk, Francisca mentioned a lady named Ch'ila, from Millumayu, near Tiraque, as a mistress of Casimiro's probably during his dirigente days.

About his relations with Francisca—my feeling is that the whole thing at least now is more than a mere affair. Casimiro is completely alone, and emotionally broken (Elidoro believes that presently he does not have any influence as a leader in Palca.) A solution is his almost constant drunkenness. He also becomes practically a member of the Ignacio-Francisca complex, being constantly with both of them, and friendly with both of them. Sometimes, while both were drunk, I heard Francisca scolding Casimiro with angry words. But usually Casimiro brings money to the complex and receives some emotional support from them. While I have been in Palca (living in the same room of Esteban Avelli) he is not there anymore, Francisca came to the old hacienda house very rarely. But Casimiro was almost constantly at Ignacio and Francisca's home. Francisca is really a rare woman. Very strong and harsh in her language when drunk (very often these days), especially against her husband. She constantly says to him (at least when drunk) «*bruto animal, chay mierda carajo* who cannot understand anything.» And Ignacio remains shy and silent doing whatever she says. Other people said to me that Francisca is a *demonio*.

Casimiro has been really friendly with me. He invited me to come back to Palca and has been my host. An excellent host within his possibilities. And willing to talk long with me, even when I didn't want to.

Presently he feels that all his relatives (wife, daughters and son—with the exception of his far away son, Adel) are against him. But he speaks well of his Capinota brother (Delfín) and of his cousins Luis (militar pilot) and Victor.»

P. 172:

Elidoro said he is 33 years old, born in Punata. His father was a *comerciante,* then worked in Siglo XX six years and then returned to work in the *municipalidad* in Punata. His mother was a small comerciante who used to go to Cochabamba to obtain vegetables to sell in the mines and then she returned with clothes to sell in Cochabamba. She traveled a great deal. Both parents were from Punata. His mother was *de pollera,* father *vestido* (typical), though actually his father was darker, more like an Indian racially than this mother, he said. His mother lives, his father died twelve years ago. He has seven living siblings, five boys, two girls. Victor is the oldest; then a woman; then two dead before himself. He said at first his family was a happy one, but as we shall see this is an ambiguous statement.

He said that when he was a child in school the family was well off because his father made money supplying meat for the workers on the Cochabamba highway; they had two houses, one in Punata, the other in the campo in the valley not far away. But his father was a *picaro,* and although he made good money, spent it on women everywhere and when the father died there was not much money left. «Economic matters decayed,» as he put it; and yet Elidoro said his father had much *cariño* for his family, «thought a lot about his family,» «was concerned»; but when he had money in his hands he would «lose control» and go with women and finally lost money. But his mother had land left to her by her parents and a house in Punata, which she has to this day. Today she buys a little papa and sells it in Cochabamba—is still a comerciante on a small scale. Elidoro said that when he was a small child he often traveled with his mother to the mines on her trading expeditions and at first he enjoyed going everywhere on the train, but as time passed he grew aware that it was a hard life for his mother: her bundles were sometimes stolen by workers on the train; she had to bribe train officials, conductors, etc., to get her bundles through, and all in all it was a hard life for not much money.

(Eusebio informs me that he has traveled much to and from the mines with his parents—his father is a piquero in Sacaba, who was a miner—tells me he had seen much abuse of the poor on the trains. The conductor and train workers often literally rob women of their bundles; he suspects sometimes sexual abuse: they have to submit to sexual intercourse in order to get their bundles back, or hand out bribes for this, especially on late night trains.)

Elidoro said he was about six years old when he went with his mother to the mines. Later he went to school in Punata and later he went to study in Cochabamba to be a priest in the colegio de Las Corazonistas in Quillacollo. He stayed there until the fifth year of secundaria. Just before leaving for Peru for the noviciado at age sixteen or seventeen, he left the priesthood «of my own free will» because he was «thinking of girls» *(piensos traviesos).* «I was curious,» he said. He met the sister of a co-student and wanted to go with her; and the school was very strict; and he was so enamored of her he couldn't think, study, etc. And he said he feels badly about this because he says he had a «vocation» and if he had kept going he would have been a priest. And they were very strict in that school, he said: If they found that you went with a girl, they would boot you out. It was a sin not to be always over your books; you couldn't day-dream or look distracted in class. If you did this and they caught you it was a sin you had to confess. They had to be humble and submissive—all obeyed the Superior—and if you weren't «they thought you were talking with Lucifer or the devils and kicked you out.» Elidoro thinks it was a poor education because there was no freedom and «without freedom you can't develop your mind.»

After leaving this school he didn't study for a year, did nothing for a year. He says that he had begun to study hard and very early, and the padres told him to take a year off to rest and then return to the same school. He was then twenty years old. During this time he says he engaged in sports (he is not a bad soccer player), went with girls and to club socials: «The world ate me up.» After a year he didn't go back to the priests' school but went to the normal school in La Villa (it is now in Paracaya) where he studied two years. (The course is four years but he said that since he had studied much before in the colegio they entered him right away in the third year; he went through faster for this reason.)

At this time, he claims that with muñeca you can get into the normal school easily, «the worst student can get in with this,» but before it was really hard to get in. Of 300 candidates he went in with, he says only 103 got through. Still, there were abuses: this was in 1956 and sons of MNR politicos could get certificates without training, he said. He feels, moreover, that the curriculum and teaching in the normal school was better then than now.

Elidoro said that when he went to the normal school in Villa, the director was Pastor Argote, brother of his wife's mother. He was a padrino of Isidoro, and Isidoro got through without examination, Elidoro said. In 1957, Elidoro came out as maestro und worked in Ucureña; in 1958, Punata; 1959, Camacho Rancho. In 1959 also he married Florencia Montaño, daughter of another teacher and student in the third year of colegio, fifteen or sixteen years old. At first he got along well with her, but later he went with other *chicas,* and his wife didn't like it. They had two kids, one who died, the other is now eight years old. They were civilly married only.

Then, Elidoro said, he came to Cochabamba for a fiesta on his aunt's birthday; returned to Punata and his wife had left him—just like that—gone to Argentina leaving nothing for him («*me ha pelado*»), taking the child with her and giving his property to her *familiares.* Elidoro said he «never thought of this,» never expected it—was working hard. But this knocked the pins out from under him. «I didn't care about work, anything. I was drinking, I never expected this, lost total interest in my work. I felt guilty that for chicas I lost my wife and child.»

But, he said, she returned with her child after a year and they renewed relations and lived a week together in Cochabamba. But the girl's mother told her: «Why did you come back to live with this man? He'll think you did bad things while you were in Argentina and get jealous and kill you.» And the girl listened to her mother, «all finally was mistrust,» and the girl returned to Argentina after about a week. His present wife (he calls her «*mujer*») was a friend of this girl and when they were single she used to help them get together, meet, etc.

The girl returned again after two years. He said he had «a lot of women» during this time, and he said his wife wrote him: «Why don't you stop drinking and going with women and change your life?» He says that all this time he was thinking of her and loved her—but some friends of his returned from Argentina and told him she was the worst *puta* in Jujuy, to forget her.

But she returned and they had another week together in Cochabamba. Her mother didn't know this, and he loved her all over again. But a Punateño arrived from Argentina and her mother told her: «Why don't you divorce him (Elidoro) and marry this man who has a lot of money, etc.?» And the girl believed her, believed the man had a lot of money (he was 39) and she divorced Elidoro and married the man. They lived together about a year in Punata and meanwhile Elidoro began living in concubinato with his present wife. At first, Elidoro said, his first wife lived well with her new man. But she found that he had no money or any real profession; was *cargador* (stevedore) and couldn't get work, so they began to fight.... The girl fought also with her mother, feeling betrayed, and beat her mother; and they owed money in Punata, so the girl took off for Argentina (where she has kin), again with her child, and Elidoro says he has no more interest in her because she had gone with another man (who also turned out to have another wife in Argentina). He says they escaped to Argentina where she found he was already married and had lied about having a house there, and now they're separated, and her relations have kicked her out because they say she has given herself over to a «*vida mala*» and now (Elidoro hears) she is living a life of prostitution in Jujuy. Elidoro says the Bolivian government takes 100 pesos per month from his salary for the support of his child by this girl. (He has two little ones and one on the way with his present wife.) He says his first wife comes from time to time to Punata to pick up the money from his salary; he sees her and says her face is «ruined»—the face of a young girl, once beautiful, is now ugly.

He says he is getting along all right with Doña Marta, his present wife, but she has a violent temper. «I'm old now and can't think about other women.» But he admits they have fought and have problems. I asked—later I thought this was rash of me—whether it was true what Hilde García told us in gossip, that one time he found his wife in bed in Punata with another man; and he said «Could be, but I don't remember.» I felt I ought not pursue this any more. (I have in my notes other indirect evidence about this marriage.)

We relaxed at this point and smoked and talked about Casimiro García. Elidoro said that Doña Rosa of Cochabamba, madrina of García and Doña Prima of Cochabamba (kin of García) visited him during the papa harvest and said that Casimiro was once alcalde of Arenpampa. And Casimiro had disputes with his wife: he was interested in political matters (this was in the time of Paz shortly after the agrarian reform) and Doña Braulia, his wife, was plenty corrupt—went crazy when she drank and would grab any man at hand and go to bed. And García drank and had other women too. So there was «incomprehension» between them. And one time García and his wife fought and the wife hit him on the head with an axe, split his head open and left him for dead. And one time García beat his wife and all but broke her leg. They fought a lot.

Elidoro said that García, in the name of the MNR as alcalde, ordered the death of a schoolteacher and others. The community reacted against García— wanted to kill him and he had to escape to Ucureña where he stayed a year and José Rojas helped him and sent him to Palca where he got lands. (And plenty of these, according to the map.) García had to escape at night with only the clothes on his back, the women told Elidoro.

GLOSSARY OF SPANISH AND QUECHUA TERMS

abarcas sandals made of leather and scraps of rubber tires worn by Bolivian peasants.

arroba measure of potatoes used by the peasants; about 25 pounds.

ayni reciprocal labor.

cántaro (or jarra) small pitcher of chicha sold in town chicherías or on the haciendas.

chacras plots of land.

charki sun-dried meat.

chicha common maize or maize and barley beer of the Andes.

chichería tavern where chicha is sold and consumed.

chicharrón chopped fried pork.

chuñu dry potatoes stripped of their skin. The tubers are moistened, trodden by the peasants with bare feet on wet grass and left in the sun to dry. Chuñu may be stored indefinitely.

c'oa green herb of the highlands· ground and used for a variety of ritual and curative purposes.

cueca popular dance of the Andes.

curaca foreman.

fachada smooth mud and straw used in housing.

huayños traditional popular song for dancing.

karasiri one believed to cause illness by extracting fat from the belly of another. The concept is deeply rooted in the Andes—see Chapter IV.

lampa half mattock dating from Inca times. Used in clearing irrigation ditches.

llajwa hot sauce made from ground peppers.

lliklla peasant woman's shawl.

locotos green peppers.

mechero small kerosene lamp used by the peasants, prereform.

minka festive labor.

muqu ground maize or maize and barley used in making chicha.

oca sweet starchy tuber grown in the highlands.

pachamama literally «earth mother.» Deity of Inca times crucial to the crops. Some of this meaning survives vestigially on the haciendas, but the word is applied mainly to vaguely conceptualized disease-causing agents believed to reside in remote or frightening places. See Chapter VI.

paja brava tough grass found on the high plains. Used as roofing material for the peasants' huts, prereform.

papalisa variety of small, red, starchy tuber.

pegujal plot of land.

perol great iron basin used in making chicha.

pollera gathered, full-length and often colorful skirt worn by peasant women.

pongo house-servant under the prereform system of pongueaje.

pongueaje prereform household service by Andean peons in the house of the patrón.

p'uñu medium-sized clay vessel used to carry chicha. The jug is usually carried strapped to a man's back by a leather thong, the waska.

pututu traditional trumpet made of an ox's horn. Used now by the peasants to call community meetings.

qena traditional Andean reed flute consisting of a single tube.

sara mut'i corn grains ripped from the cob and boiled.

suwas thieves.

tupu potato bag holding about 100 pounds.

urpu   homemade brown bread formed
in the shape of dolls for the fiesta
of Todos Santos.

waska   leather thong used by the peasants for many purposes such as
threshing and carrying chicha.

wawa   baby.

wirque   large clay vessel used in boiling ground maize and water in the
making of chicha.

yatiri   native curer who, in this region,
alone is believed capable of coping
with the effects of witchcraft.

zampoñas   type of reed flute ancient
in the Bolivian Andes; consists of
several reeds tied together.

BIBLIOGRAPHY

ALEXANDER, R. A.
  1958. The Bolivian National Revolution. New Brunswick, N. J.
ALMOND, G. A., and G. B. POWELL
  1966. Comparative Politics. Boston, Mass.
ANDERSON, C. W.
  1967. Politics and Economic Change in Latin America. Princeton, N. J.
ANTEZANA, L.
  1955. Resultados de la Reforma Agraria en Bolivia. Cochabamba.
BANFIELD, E.
  1958. The Moral Basis of A Backward Society. Glencoe, Ill.
BARNETT, H.
  1953. Innovation: The Basis of Culutral Change. New York.
BEQUIRAJ, M.
  1966. Peasantry and Revolution. Ithaca, N. Y.
BERNARD, J. P.
  1969. «Mouvements Paysans et Reform Agraire.» Revue Française de Science
    Politique, 19 (5): 982-1017.
BLASIER, C.
  1966. «Studies of Social Revolution: Origins in Mexico, Bolivia, Cuba.»
    Latin American Research Review, 2 (3): 28-64.
BREWSTER, J. M.
  1967. «Traditional Social Structures as Barriers to Change.» In Agricultural
    Development and Economic Growth, H. M. Southworth and B. F.
    Johnston, eds. Ithaca, N. Y. Pp. 66-68.
BRINTON, C.
  1965. The Anatomy of Revolution. New York.
BUNZEL, R.
  1940. «The Role of Alcoholism in Two Central American Cultures.» Psychi-
    atry, 3: 361-387.
BURKE, M.
  1967. An Analysis of the Bolivian Land Reform by Means of a Comparison
    Between Peruvian Haciendas and Bolivian Ex-Haciendas. Unpublished
    Ph. D. dissertation in Agricultural Economics, University of Pittsburgh.
CARROLL, T. F.
  1965. «The Land Reform Issue in Latin America.» In The Dynamics of Change
    in Latin American Politics, John Martz, ed. New York. Pp. 171-181.
CARTER, W. E.
  1963. The Ambiguity of Reform: Highland Bolivian Peasants and Their Land.
    Unpublished Ph. D. dissertation in Anthropology, Columbia University.
  1964. Aymara Communities and the Bolivian Agrarian Reform. University of
    Florida Monographs in Social Sciences, No. 24.
CHAYANOV, A.
  1966. A Theory of Peasant Economy. Homewood, Ill.

CHEVALIER, F.
  1969. «Decolonisation et Reforme Agraire en Amerique Latine.» Revue Française de Science Politique, 19 (5):973-981.
CHONCHOL, J.
  1965. «Land Tenure and Development in Latin America.» *In* Obstacles to Change in Latin America, C. Velíz, ed. London, Pp. 75-90.
CLARK, R. J.
  1968. «Land Reform and Peasant Market Participation in the North Highlands of Bolivia.» Land Economics, 44:153-172.
COMITAS, L.
  1968. «Educación y estratificación en Bolivia.» América Indígena, 28 (3): 631-651.
COTLER, J.
  1970*a*. «The Mechanics of Internal Domination and Social Change in Peru.» *In* Masses in Latin America, I. L. Horowitz, ed. New York. Pp. 407-444.
  1970*b*. «Traditional Haciendas and Communities in a Context of Political Mobilization in Peru.» *In* Agrarian Problems and Peasant. Movements in Latin America, R. Stavenhagen, ed. New York. Pp. 533-558.
DANDLER-HANHART, J.
  1967. Local Group, Community and Nation: A Study of Changing Structure in Ucureña, Bolivia. Unpublished M. A. thesis in Anthropology, University of Wisconsin, Madison.
  1968. «The Development, Structure, and Leadership of the Campesino Movement in Cochabamba, Bolivia (1945-69): Some Preliminary Considerations Prior to 1952.» Paper presented at the 68th Annual Meeting of the American Anthropological Association, New Orleans, La. November 20, 1969.
DÍAZ, M. N., FOSTER, G. and POTTER, J., eds.
  1967. Peasant Society: A Reader. Boston, Mass.
DÍAZ, M. N. and J. POTTER
  1967. «The Social Life of Peasants.» *In* Peasant Society: A Reader, M. N. Díaz, G. Foster and J. Potter, eds. Boston, Mass. Pp. 154-168.
EASTON, D.
  1953. The Political System. New York.
ERASMUS, C. J.
  1950. The Compadre System in Latin America. MS on file, Anthropology Library, University of California, Berkeley.
  1955. Reciprocal Labor: A Study of Its Occurrence and Disappearance Among Farming Peoples in Latin America. Unpublished Ph. D. dissertation in Anthropology, University of California, Berkeley.
  1961. Man Takes Control. Minneapolis, Minn.
  1964. «A Comparison of Agrarian Reform in Bolivia, Mexico and Venezuela.» *In* Land Reform and Social Revolution in Bolivia, D. B. Heath, C. J. Erasmus and H. Buechler. Unpublished MS.
  1965. «The Occurrence and Disappearance of Reciprocal Farm Labor in Latin America.» *In* Contemporary Cultures and Societies of Latin America, D. B. Heath and R. N. Adams, eds. New York. P.p. 173-199.
  1967. «Upper Limits of Peasantry and Agrarian Reform: Bolivia, Venezuela and Mexico Compared.» Ethnology, 6 (4):349-380.
  1968. «Community Development and the Encogido Syndrome.» Human Organization 27 (1):65-91.
ERASMUS, C. J., D. B. HEATH, and BUECHLER, H.

1964. Land Reform and Social Revolution in Bolivia, MS.

FERRAGUT, C.
1963. «La Reforma Agraria Boliviana: Sus Antecedentes, Fundamentos, Aplicaciones y Resultados.» Revista Interamericana de Ciencias Sociales 2 (1): 78-151.

FESTINGER, L.
1957. A. Theory of Cognitive Dissonance. Stanford, Calif.

FISHER, S. and S. E. CLEVELAND
1958. Body Image and Personality. New York.

FLORES MONCAYO, J.
1956. Derecho Agrario Boliviano. La Paz.

FORTÚN, J. E.
1968. «Indigenismo en Bolivia.» América Indígena, 28 (4): 1059-1075.

FOSTER, G. M.
1952. «Relations Between Theoretical and Applied Anthropology.» Human Organization, 11 (3): 5-16.
1960. Culture and Conquest: America's Spanish Heritage. New York.
1961. «The Dyadic Contract: A Model for the Social Structure of A Mexican Peasant Village.» American Anthropologist, 63 (6): 1173-1192.
1965: «Peasant Society and The Image of Limited Good.» American Anthropologist, 67 (2): 293-315.
1967. Applied Anthropology. Boston, Mass.

FRIED, J.
1962. «Social Organization and Personal Security in a Peruvian Hacienda Indian Community.» American Anthropologist, 64 (4): 771-780.

FRIED, M.
1967. The Evolution of Political Society. New York.

FRIEDRICH, C. J.
1961. «Political Leadership and The Problem of the Charismatic Power.» Journal of Politics, 23 (1): 3-23.

FREUD, S.
1949. Collected Papers. London.

GARCÍA, A.
1964. «La Reforma Agraria y el Desarrollo Social de Bolivia.» In Reformas Agrarias en América Latina: Procesos y Perspectivas, O. Delgado, ed. Mexico, D.F. Pp. 408-44.

GIBSON, C.
1963. «Colonial Institutions and Contemporary Latin America: Social and Cultural Life.» Hispanic American Historical Review, 43 (3): 380-389.

GOINS, J. F.
1954. Huayculi: The Quechua of the Cochabamba Valley, Bolivia. Unpublished Ph. D. dissertation in Anthropology, University of California, Berkeley.

GONZÁLEZ CASANOVA, P.
1965. Internal Colonialism and National Development. Washington University Monograph Series «Studies in Comparative International Development.» I, No. 4. St. Louis, Mo.

GOODE, W. J.
1951. Religion Among The Primitives. Glencoe, Ill.

HAGEN, E. E.
1962. On the Theory of Social Change: How Economic Growth Begins. Homewood, Ill.

HEATH, D. B.
1959. «Land Reform in Bolivia.» Inter-American Economic Affairs, 13 (2): 35-45.
1965. «Comments on David Mandelbaum's 'Alcohol and Culture'.» Current Anthropology, 6 (3): 289-290.
1969. «Peasant Syndicates Among the Aymara of the Yungas: A View from the Grass Roots.» *In* Latin American Peasant Movements, H. Landsberger, ed. Ithaca, N. Y. Pp. 170-209.
HEILBRONER, R.
1963. The Great Ascent. New York.
HENNESSEY, C. A. M.
1964. «Shifting Forces in the Bolivian Revolution.» World Today (May): 197-207.
HICKMAN, J.
1968. «Colonización y movilidad social en Bolivia.» América Indígena, 28 (2): 339-388.
HIGGINS, B.
1959. Economic Development. London.
HOLMBERG, A.
1960. «Changing Community Attitudes and Values in Peru: A Case Study in Guided Change.» *In* Social Change in Latin America Today, Philip Mosely, ed. New York. Pp. 63-107.
INTERNATIONAL LABOR ORGANIZATION (ILO)
1957. The Landless Farmer in Latin America. Geneva.
JOHNSON, C.
1966. Revolutionary Change. Boston, Mass.
JOHNSON, D.
1969. «On Oppressed Classes.» MS.
KATZ, E.
1967. «Comment on J. M. Brewster 'Traditional Social Structures as Barriers to Change'.» *In* Agricultural Development and Economic Growth, H. M. Southworth and B. F. Johnston, eds. Ithaca, N. Y. Pp. 99-106.
KLEIN, H.
1965. «David Toro and The Establishment of Military Socialism in Bolivia.» Hispanic-American Historical Review, 45 (1): 25-52.
1969. Parties and Political Change in Bolivia, 1880-1952. London.
KLING, M.
1956. «Toward A Theory of Power and Political Instability in Latin America.» Western Political Quarterly, 9 (1). Also *in* The Dynamics of Change in Latin American Politics, J. Martz, ed. New York, 1965. Pp. 130-139.
KLUCKHOHN, C.
1958. «Myths and Rituals: A General Theory.» *In* Reader in Comparative Religion, W. A. Lessa and E. Z. Vogt, eds. Evanston, Ill. Pp. 135-151.
KRIESBERG, L.
1963. «Los Impresarios en América Latina y El Papel de Los Procesos Culturales y Circonstancias.» América Latina, 6 (4): 27-42.
LAMBERT, J.
1967. Latin America. Berkeley and Los Angeles.
LEONARD, O.
1948. Canton Chullpas: A Socioeconomic Study in the Cochabamba Valley of Bolivia. Foreign Agricultural Report No. 27. Office of Foreign Agricultural Relations, U.S. Department of Agriculture, Washington, D. C.

1952. Bolivia: Land, People, and Institutions. Washington, D. C.
196. El Cambio Económico y Social en Cuatro Comunidades del Altiplano de Bolivia. Mexico, D. F.

LERNER, D.
1958. The Passing of Traditional Society: Modernizing the Middle East. Glencoe, Ill.

LEWIS, W. A.
1955. The Theory of Economic Growth. Homewood, Ill.

LORD, P.
1965. The Peasantry as an Emerging Factor in Mexico, Bolivia and Venezuela. Land Tenure Center Paper No. 35. University of Wisconsin, Madison.

MACCOBY, M.
1964. «Love and Authority: A Study of Mexican Villagers.» *In* Contemporary Latin American Culture: An Anthropological Sourcebook, G. Foster, ed. New York.

MALINOWSKI, B.
1935. Coral Gardens and Their Magic. 2 vols. New York.

MALLOY, J.
1968. Bolivia: A Study in Revolution. Unpublished Ph. D. dissertation, Political Science, University of Pittsburgh.

MANGIN, W.
1961. «Fiestas Among Andean Indians.» *In* Patterns of Land Utilization and Other Papers, V. E. Garfield, ed. Seattle, Wash.

MANNONI, O.
1964. Prospero and Caliban. New York.

MARX, K.
1968. The 18th Brumaire of Louis Bonaparte. New York.

McCLELLAND, D.
1961. The Achieving Society. New York.

McCORD, W.
1965. The Springtime of Freedom. New York.

MEAD, G. H.
1934. Mind, Self and Society. Chicago.

MERTON, R.
1957. Social Theory and Social Structure. Glencoe, Ill.

MINTZ, S. W., and E. R. WOLF
1957. Haciendas and Plantations in Middle America and the Antilles. Mona, Jamaica.
1967. «An Analysis of Ritual Co-Parenthood (Compadragzo).» *In* Peasant Society: A Reader, M. Díaz, G. Foster, and J. Potter, eds. Boston, Mass. Pp. 174-99.

MISHKIN, B.
1963. «The Contemporary Quechua.» Handbook of South American Indians, vol. 2. BAE Bulletin, 1943:411-470. Smithsonian Institution, Washington, D. C.

MOORE, BARRINGTON, Jr.
1966. Social Origins of Dictatorship and Democracy. Boston, Mass.

MOORE, W., and M. TUMIN
1949. «Some Sociological Functions of Ignorance.» American Sociological Review, 14:787-795.

MÖRNER, M.
1973. «The Spanish American Hacienda: A Survey of Recent Research and

Debate.» Hispanic American Historical Review 53, No. 2:183-216.

MORALES, R.
1966. Zarate, El «Temible» Willka: Historia de la Rebelión Indígena de 1899. La Paz.

MORSE, R. M.
1964. «The Heritage of Latin America.» *In* The Founding of New Societies, L. Hartz, ed. New York. Pp. 123-177.

MURDOCK, G.
1948. Social Structure. New York.

NASH, M.
1965. The Golden Road to Modernity: Village Life in Contemporary Burma. New York.
1966. Primitive and Peasant Economic Systems. Chicago, Ill.

NELSON, L.
1964. Some Social Aspects of Agrarian Reform in Mexico, Bolivia and Venezuela. (Mimeographed.) Pan American Union, Washington, D. C.

PAREDES, R. M.
1963. Mitos, Supersticiones y Supervivencias Populares de Bolivia. La Paz.

PARSONS, E. C.
1936. Mitla, Town of the Souls. Chicago.

PARSONS, K., P. M. RAUP, and R. J. PENN., ed.s
1951. Land Tenure: Proceedings of the International Conference on Land Tenure and Related Problems in World Agriculture. Madison, Wisc.

PARSONS, T., and R. F. BALES
1955. Family Socialization and Interaction Process. Glencoe, Ill.

PATCH, R. W.
1956. Social Implications of the Bolivian Agrarian Reform. Unpublished Ph. D. dissertation in Anthropology, Cornell University.
1960. «Bolivia: U.S. Assistance in A Revolutionary Setting.» *In* Social Change in Latin America Today, P. Mosely, ed. New York. Pp. 108-176.
1961. «Bolivia: The Restrained Revolution.» The Annals of the American Academy of Political and Social Sciences, 334:123-132.
1963. «Peasantry and National Revolution: Bolivia.» *In* Expectant Peoples: Nationalism and Development, K. Silvert, ed. New York. Pp. 95-126.

PEARSE, A.
1970. «Agrarian Change Trends in Latin America.» *In* Agrarian Problems and Peasant Movements in Latin America, R. Stavenhagen, ed. New York. Pp. 11-40.

PEINADO, M.
1969. Land Reform in Three Communities of Cochabamba, Bolivia. Unpublished Ph. D. dissertation in Agricultural Economics, University of Wisconsin, Madison.

PIERSON, D.
1948. Cruz das Almas: A Brazilian Village. Washington, D. C.

PIRENNE, H.
1967. «Aspects of Medieval Economy.» *In* Tribal and Peasant Economies, G. Dalton, ed. New York. Pp. 418-437.

POLANYI, K.
1957. The Great Transformation. Boston, Mass.

POTASH, R. A.
1963. «Colonial Institutions and Contemporary Latin America.» Hispanic-American Historical Review, 43 (3):390-394.

POWELL, J. D.
1964. Preliminary Report on the Federación Campesino de Venezuela: Origins, Organization, Leadership and Role in the Agrarian Reform Program. Land Tenure Research Paper No. 9, University of Wisconsin, Madison.
1969. «Venezuela: The Peasant Union Movement.» *In* Latin American Peasant Movements, H. Landsberger, ed. Ithaca, N. Y. Pp. 62-100.

POWELSON, J. P.
1964. Latin America: Today's Economic and Social Revolution. New York.

REINA, R.
1960. Chinautla: A Guatemalan Indian Community. Tulane University Middle American Research Institute, 24:55-130.

REYEROS, R.
1949. El Pongueaje. La Paz.

RICKABAUGH, C. G.
1966. The Politicization Function of Agrarian Interest Groups: A Case Study of the Bolivian Campesino Sindicatos. Unpublished Ph. D. dissertation in Political Science, University of Maryland.

ROGERS, E. M.
1969. Modernization Among Peasants: The Impact of Communication. New York.

ROWE, J. H.
1963. «Inca Culture at The Time of the Spanish Conquest.» *In* Handbook of South American Indians, vol. 2. BAE Bulletin, 143:183-330. Smithsonian Institution, Washington, D. C.

SALZ, B. R.
1955. The Human Element in Industrialization. American Anthropological Association Memoir, No. 85.

SAYRES, W. C.
1965. «Ritual Kinship and Negative Affect.» *In* Contemporary Latin American Culture: A Sourcebook, G. Foster, ed. New York.

SCHILDER, P.
1935. The Image and Appearance of the Human Body. London.

SCHULTZ, T. W.
1964. Transforming Traditional Agriculture. New Haven, Conn.

SCHWENG, L.
1966. «An Indian Community Development Project in Bolivia.» *In* A Casebook of Social Change, A. Niehoff, ed. Chicago, Ill. Pp. 44-57.

SIMMONS, O. G.
1965. «Popular and Modern Medicine in Mestizo Communities of Coastal Peru and Chile.» *In* Contemporary Latin American Culture: A Sourcebook, G. Foster, ed. New York.

SINGER, C. J., E. J. HOLMYARD, and A. R. HALL, eds.
1956. A History of Technology. Oxford.

SMELSER, N.
1967. «Toward A Theory of Modernization.» *In* Tribal and Peasant Economies, G. Dalton, ed. New York. Pp. 29-48.

SMITH, T. L., ed.
1965. Agrarian Reform in Latin America. New York.

STALEY, E.
1961. The Future of Underdeveloped Areas. New York.

STAVENHAGEN, R.
1965. Classes, Colonialism and Acculturation in Mesoamerica. Washington University Monograph Series «Studies in Comparative International Development I, No. 6. St. Louis, Mo.

STEIN, W.
1961. Hualcan: Life in the Highlands of Peru. Ithaca, N. Y.

STEWARD, J., and L. FARON
1959. Native Peoples of South America. New York.

TANNENBAUM, F.
1962. Ten Keys to Latin America. New York.

TSCHOPIK, H., Jr.
1963. «The Aymara.» *In* Handbook of South American Indians, vol. 2. BAE Bulletin, 143: 501-573. Smithsonian Institution, Washington, D. C.

TUMA, E. H.
1965. Twenty-Six Centuries of Agrarian Reform. Berkeley and Los Angeles.

URQUIDI, A.
1953. Plan General para El Estudio de la Reforma Agraria. Cochabamba.
1966. El Feudalismo en América y la Reforma Agraria Boliviana. Cochabamba.
1969. Bolivia y Su Reforma Agraria. Cochabamba.

VELÍZ, C., ed.
1965. Obstacles to Change in Latin America. London.
1967. The Politics of Conformity in Latin America. London.

VELLARD, J.
1963. Civilisations des Andes; évolution des populations du hautplateau Bolivien. Paris.

VIQUEIRA, C., and A. PALERM
1954. «Alcoholismo, Brujería y Homicidio en Dos Comunidades Rurales de Mexico.» América Indígena, 14 (1): 7-36.

WAGLEY, C.
1968. The Latin American Tradition. New York and London.

VALLACE, A. F. C.
1961. Culture and Personality. New York.

WEEKS, D.
1947. «Land Tenure in Bolivia.» Journal of Land and Public Utility Economics, 23 (3): 321-336.

WOLF, E. R.
1955. «Types of Latin American Peasantry.» American Anthropologist, 57 (3): 452-471.
1959. Sons of the Shaking Earth. Chicago, Ill.
1965. «Aspects of Group Relations in A Complex Society.» *In* Contemporary Cultures and Societies of Latin America, D. B. Heath and R. N. Adams, eds. New York. Pp. 85-101.
1966. Peasants. Englewood Cliffs, N. J.
1969. Peasant Wars of the Twentieth Century. New York.